The China Challenge

The China Challenge

Standing Strong against the Military, Economic, and Political Threats That Imperil America

Dana R. Dillon

ROWMAN & LITTLEFIELD PUBLISHERS, INC.
Lanham • Boulder • New York • Toronto • Plymouth, UK

ROWMAN & LITTLEFIELD PUBLISHERS, INC.

Published in the United States of America
by Rowman & Littlefield Publishers, Inc.
A wholly owned subsidiary of The Rowman & Littlefield Publishing Group, Inc.
4501 Forbes Boulevard, Suite 200, Lanham, Maryland 20706
www.rowmanlittlefield.com

Estover Road
Plymouth PL6 7PY
United Kingdom

Distributed by National Book Network

British Library Cataloguing in Publication Information Available

Library of Congress Cataloging-in-Publication Data

Dillon, Dana R.
The China challenge : standing strong against the military, economic, and political threats that imperil America / Dana R. Dillon.
p. cm.
Includes bibliographical references and index.
ISBN-13: 978-0-7425-5133-6 (cloth : alk. paper)
ISBN-10: 0-7425-5133-4 (cloth : alk. paper)
1. United States—Foreign relations—China. 2. China—Foreign relations—United States. 3. United States—Foreign relations—2001– I. Title.
E183.8.C6D56 2007
327.7305109'0511—dc22 2006034663

Printed in the United States of America

∞™ The paper used in this publication meets the minimum requirements of American National Standard for Information Sciences—Permanence of Paper for Printed Library Materials, ANSI/NISO Z39.48-1992.

This book is dedicated to my parents,
Dana and Frances Dillon,
whose fifty years of marriage, love, support, and patience
are the foundation of my life.

Contents

Acknowledgments

It is with the utmost gratitude that I acknowledge the family, friends, and colleagues who contributed to the writing of this book.

My friend and colleague John Tkacik wrote chapter 8 and contributed ideas and notes to other portions of the book. Long discussion with John heavily influenced my ideas on Taiwan and China.

The chapter on nuclear Asia was adapted from a paper I wrote with Baker Spring. Baker contributed much to my thoughts and ideas on the subject; in particular, it was Baker's idea to insist on a criterion-based exception for nonweapon states like India.

The chapter on maritime territorial disputes owes an intellectual debt to Mark J. Valencia for his extensive academic research on this subject. His ADELPHI Paper 298, "China and the South China Sea Disputes" (Oxford University Press, October 1995), was invaluable, as were his many other books and articles on the subject.

In researching material for this book I was generously assisted by my friend and colleague Ji Hye Shin and a small horde of interns. All of the interns deserve awards for their generous efforts, but two merit special mention, Chang Yu-Lan, who translated many Chinese language Web sites, and May Yin Chan, who continued to assist in research after the conclusion of her internship.

Lastly, I gratefully acknowledge the love, patience, and support of my extended family. My best friend and wife, Kelly S. Dillon, contributed her expertise to the trade chapter and selflessly reviewed and commented on many portions of the book. My father, Colonel (retired) Dana B. Dillon, refined my thoughts in the chapter on the war against terrorism. My children,

Nathalie and Samuel, have both supported my efforts and endured dinner table talk about my research. My sister-in-law Megan Sullivan pitched in to help around the house when my writing interrupted my contribution to household chores, and my niece Anne Dillon volunteered her ideas on names for the chapters.

Introduction

> All human situations have their inconveniences. We feel those of the present but neither see nor feel those of the future; and hence we often make troublesome changes without amendment, and frequently for the worse.
>
> —Benjamin Franklin

The purpose of this book is to take a new look at America's foreign policy in Asia and to provide American policymakers with a guide to the myriad and densely interwoven issues that will confront the United States in the twenty-first century. The book will also offer some prescriptions to certain policy issues.

Many commentators on the future of American foreign policy focus on single country assessments, Japan was the bogeyman of the 1980s and 1990s while China is the threat today, but that kind of analysis is too narrow to understand the strategic environment in which American foreign policy will be shaped. For example, although China will undoubtedly absorb a considerable amount of American security interest during the twenty-first century, China's neighborhood includes many countries hostile to China and suspicious of Beijing's objectives, but each of them have their own peculiar issues.

Some of the countries hostile to China are already allied with the United States, such as Japan and Korea, but they are equally distrustful of each other. Southeast Asia and India mark softer boundaries to China's ambitions and their struggle to retain sovereignty, independence, and territorial integrity against China's ambitions will affect American foreign policy. So how those countries develop during the twenty-first century will influence American foreign policy.

Also, focusing exclusively on the security challenge of a rising China or the economic problem of Japan's closed economy ignores the potential problems of emerging India, developing Indonesia, or unification of the Korean Peninsula. All of these issues may be affected by China or Japan, but they will develop and mature with or without them and thus must be examined on the basis of their own internal logic.

Some issues in Asia will affect American foreign policy, but there is no clearly defined American solution. Maritime piracy, for example, is threatening to slowly strangle maritime trade to and from Asia, but no amount of American might will stop the problem. Instead, the United States must convince the countries where maritime piracy is worst that fighting it is in their best interests as well as the interests of the world.

For most of this book, Asia will not be discussed country by country, but instead the discussion will focus on the issues that will confront the United States during this century. Countries will appear as issues are discussed and how each of them influences that particular issue. Some countries—such as China, Japan, India, and Indonesia—will appear more often than others.

Topics will include the global war on terrorism, nuclear proliferation, maritime piracy and maritime border disputes in the South China Sea, unification of the Korean peninsula, Taiwan, trade, and the Asian space race. By focusing on such issues, I hope to draw the reader's attention to the interaction of many players and provide a guide for future American policymakers to manage these issues.

The phrase "rise of China" is used so often that it has become a cliché; nevertheless, China will be a problem in the future. In the short term, China's worldview clashes with the Bush administration's unipolar paradigm, but long after George W. Bush is relegated to the history books, Washington and Beijing will still occupy opposing positions on a host of issues. China is a hegemonic power in Asia, and its newfound wealth propels the ambitions of China's leaders. Managing the relationship will occupy a considerable amount of American diplomatic and security resources.

China's neighbors in Southeast Asia recognize the threat posed by China, but they do not want to see their region become a cockpit of a superpower struggle, and neither do they want to choose between neighboring China and the United States. The United States must craft a strategy of regional resilience for Southeast Asia that encourages economic growth, military reform, and democratic transformation that will enable the countries of Southeast Asia to resist Chinese pressures.

But China will not be America's only challenge in Asia, as India, too, will become a great power in this century. Many commentators point out that India and the United States share democratic values and many national interests, including the rise of China as a potential problem, but India sees itself as a great power in its own right and will not sit in America's shadow. This problem is particularly evident in the arena of nuclear arms, where India developed and tested nuclear weapons in defiance of American objections and the international community.

Japan and Korea present their own set of problems for American statecraft. They are both democratic with developed open market economies, but they have small and aging populations compared to the other Asian giants. Despite the apparent benefits of a Korea-Japan entente, deep historical enmities slow substantive cooperation between the two countries. During the twenty-first century, the how and when of Korea's reunification, a reunified Korea's vision of its place in the world, and Tokyo's defiance of Beijing's presumptions of regional hegemony will be the major hazards to America's ship of state in Northeast Asia.

In order for the United States to survive and prosper in the pending supercompetitive environment in the Asia-Pacific, America must pursue a threefold strategy. First, it must support the internal resiliency of Asia's developing countries to resist being dominated by their elephantine neighbors, particularly along the great Asian power peripheries. Second, it must enforce rules-based international systems, such as the World Trade Organization (WTO) and the nonproliferation regime (NPT), and the United Nations Convention on the Law of the Sea (UNCLOS) that will embed Asia's great and small countries in a rules-based international system. These policies and agreements must protect the sovereignty, economies, and political independence of all the countries in the Asia-Pacific in order for them to protect the United States.

Lastly, policymakers in the White House and on Capitol Hill must prepare the country for a century of intense competition from Asia. On every front—economically, militarily, and politically—the United States will be challenged, and America must be nimble enough to beat its competitors. In order to have the financial resources to meet unexpected changes in the international situation, the government must be fiscally responsible by balancing the federal budget and controlling entitlement spending. The military must be strong enough to defeat all of America's enemies without being a burden to the economy, and the American people must be appropriately educated to exploit the global economy. Education standards should include the hard sciences, and second language education must move from focusing on European languages, such as French or German, to more useful Asian languages, such as Chinese Mandarin, Korean, Japanese, Urdu, or Indonesian.

Lastly, I cannot write a book on a topic as broad as American foreign policy in Asia and still manage to adequately address every important issue on that continent. Readers will notice great historical leaps, gaps in detail, and important countries overlooked as I explain my vision of the sweep of future events. Also, I will only collaterally address important issues such as human rights, panregional epidemics, and environmental degradation.

With that disclaimer, we can begin our grand march into the undiscovered future by briefly examining how we got where we are. The first chapter will set the stage by reviewing the history of Asia and placing the issues of the twenty-first century in the context in which they developed.

1

Rising Asia

> Though the Indian Union is an infant state, India is no newcomer to history, no offshoot or colony newly risen to nationhood. She is a mother country, venerable in her own right; and her past, which is ancient as civilization, belongs to the essence of man's achievement on this planet. Nor has India lain broken and buried under the tides of history for so long that, in her reemergence, she is a mere vestige of her former self. Measured against the millennia that went before, the two centuries of British rule formed only a brief, if critical, interlude. Now that is over, and India steps once more with unimpaired vigor into the mainstream of human affairs.
>
> —an Indian official[1]

China's military modernization since 1996 has been incredibly rapid, outpacing the wildest estimates of the U.S. intelligence community.[2] It is estimated that China is the third-largest military budget in the world and now the largest in Asia.

What does China intend to do with its new military might? Certainly, it intends to subdue democratic Taiwan with relentless threats of war—designed as much to cow the United States as to intimidate Taiwan's people. Some analysts see China's forced "unification" with Taiwan not as an end in itself but as key to developing a military power-projection capability in the western Pacific.[3] They cite a senior Chinese military theorist who sees Taiwan as of "far reaching significance to breaking international forces' blockade against China's maritime security. . . . Only when we break this blockade shall we be able to talk about China's rise. . . . [T]o rise suddenly, China must pass through oceans and go out of the oceans in its future development."[4]

There is no question that today the United States faces a new great power competitor. Secretary of State Condoleezza Rice admits that China is becoming a "military superpower" and that "it is crucial for the U.S. to help integrate China into an international, rules-based economy" before that happens.[5] Former deputy secretary of state Robert Zoellick says that "the focus now" is to make China a "stakeholder" in these systems, as if to say China has not been up to now.[6] In a September 2005 speech, Zoellick asked, "For the United States and the world, the essential question is—how will China use its influence?" To answer that question, he said, "We need to urge China to become a responsible stakeholder in that system."[7]

American disappointment in China's trade, financial, diplomatic, proliferation, human rights, and Taiwan policies are reflected in the poignant question mark in the title of Zoellick's speech, "Whither China—From Membership to Responsibility?" Indeed, China hasn't been, and there is little likelihood that China wants to be, a "stakeholder" in a status quo that it is intent on changing.

From an Asian point of view, the overriding characteristic of American foreign policy is its single-faceted focus on one issue. For example, for decades, the U.S. policy toward Indonesia focused almost exclusively on East Timor to the detriment of a host of other U.S.-Indonesian issues. Since 9/11, the war on terrorism has been practically the only issue the Bush administration addressed when engaging Asians. But, during the next hundred years, the rise of China will be the most important factor in American foreign policy, and ignoring the rest of Asia will alienate the very countries and peoples America needs to form an effective barrier to Chinese expansion.

The opening quote was about post-independence India, but it applies equally to all of twenty-first-century Asia. Consulting the statistics on Asia, one is staggered by its immensity. Three of the top ten economies in the world are in Asia: Japan, China, and South Korea. India is eleventh and rising rapidly. Of the top four-most populous countries in the world, three of them are in Asia: China, India, the United States, and Indonesia. The world's three largest democracies are India, the United States, and Indonesia. Indonesia is the world's largest Muslim country, and India is the world's largest Hindu country as well as the second largest Muslim country. The Malacca Straits, with fifty thousand ships a year passing between Indonesia and Malaysia, is the busiest waterway in the world. Singapore, which sits on the eastern mouth of the Malacca Straits, is one of the world's busiest ports. The Asia-Pacific Economic Cooperation forum (APEC) economies account for 47 percent of the world's trade and more than half of the world's gross domestic product at $20 trillion.

Asia is as diverse as it is big. Despite attempts by persons as accomplished as Maximilian Weber, a famous twentieth century political economist, and Lee Kwan Yew, former prime minister of Singapore, to construct a homogenous Asian identity, the peoples of Asia are far more heterogeneous than in Europe. For example, an estimated 236 languages are spoken in China, India has 428, and Indonesians speak an astonishing 742 languages. In comparison, the United Kingdom has 18 languages, while Russia has the most in Europe with 102. Religious affiliation is equally diverse with adherents to all the world's major religions, plus a plethora of native religions that are negligently understudied and frequently oppressed. Economically, Hong Kong and Singapore are two of the world's freest economies, while two other Asian countries, Burma and North Korea, are the most repressed.

Despite all of Asia's size and potential, Asian countries are underrepresented in many important international bodies. For example, the United Nations Security Council has five permanent members with veto power, but only one, China, is from Asia. Another important international body, the Group of 8 or G-8, was formed to facilitate economic cooperation among the world's largest economies, but Japan is Asia's only representative. China and Korea both have economies bigger than the G-8's eighth member, Russia. This lack of representation has important implications for gaining Asian ownership of rules-based international organizations. For international institutions to work effectively Pacific countries must feel that rules work for them as well as for the countries of the Atlantic.

Despite all my remonstrations in the introduction about focusing on issues over country assessments, this chapter will briefly examine the histories of each of the major powers in Asia. Placing the larger countries in the context of their history provides a guide to permanent national interests and decision tendencies among each country's policymakers. It is not the point of these histories to break any new ground on historical research, but to demonstrate the interrelations between Asia's countries and thus set the stage to examine the issues of the twenty-first century. We will begin, of course, with China.

CHINA

The foreign policy of China's emperors was characterized by the tributary system. The logic of the system was that China was the center or middle kingdom, and China's emperor was the son of heaven and thus all other countries and rulers were subordinate. Historians frequently depict the tributary system as a sort of peculiar, but benign trade relationship. Vassal states offered tribute and kowtowed to the emperor, he in turn provided gifts to his vassals that either equaled or exceeded in value the tribute, and both sides profited. There may have been an economic benefit to the tributary system, but ultimately it was a foreign policy, not a trade relationship. The Chinese Empire was no more benign than was the Roman Empire. Once a foreign leader kowtowed to the emperor, voluntarily or not, after that if he disagreed with China's policies he risked arrest, execution, and his country occupied by Chinese troops. The countries that fell under the tributary system included Japan, Korea, Vietnam, and many of the ancient kingdoms of Southeast and South Asia as well. It was the rise of Europe that shook loose China's grip on its vassal states.

From 1405 to 1433, China's Ming Dynasty sent out seven great maritime expeditions to explore the world and expand the tribute system. Although the tribute system did generate some trade for China, unlike the European voyages of exploration, the expeditions were not commercial in nature and represented a significant government expense. The emperors were forced to stop the expeditions and afterward the Chinese bureaucracy tried to cover them up. Although the Ming Dynasty, 1368 to 1644, was one of the most stable periods of Chinese history, the decision to end the expeditions marked a prolonged period of self-imposed isolation and stagnation.

The modern world caught up to China in the form of the Opium war. Europe was suffering a substantial trade deficit with China because China was willing to sell its porcelain, but the emperor had no interest in purchasing Europe's manufactured goods. The British, however, had a monopoly on the production and distribution of Indian opium and China was a huge market for the product. Because of the debilitating effects of opium on Chinese society China banned the use and import of the drug. But through the end of the eighteenth century and beginning of the nineteenth century, the British continued to bring the drug into the country. Finally, in 1839, the Chinese seized British opium, destroyed it, and banned trade with Great Britain. In response British troops from India landed in China in 1840, defeated the Chinese army, and forced the emperor to sign the Treaty of Nanjing, which ceded Hong Kong to the British and opened China to the global marketplace including, of course, opium.

The Treaty of Nanjing was the first of the many so-called unequal treaties forced on the emperor by the European powers, the United States, and

Japan. Many of China's vassals had stopped sending tribute decades before because of the expansion of Europe's colonies in Bengal, Ceylon, and Sumatra, but after the Treaty of Nanjing, vassals bordering China were pulled away, too. In deference to the British, Nepal sent its last tribute in 1852. In 1885, the Sino-French war forced China to recognize Vietnam's independence and turn over the Emperor's tributary rights in upper Burma to the British; China lost Korea to Japan in 1895; in 1911, Mongolia, with Russian assistance, gained independence; and Tibet declared independence in 1912, but for a number of geopolitical reasons, the European empires and the United States continued to recognize China's suzerainty, but not its sovereignty, over Tibet.[8]

The Chinese considered the treaties as unequal because they were forced on the emperor against his will, but that opinion is little more than self-pitying sanctimony. The European powers were no more avaricious than Beijing's sordid intentions when it brought the tributary states under Chinese hegemony in the first place. For the peoples of tributary states, despite the published rhetoric of "independence" from China, the transfers were nothing more than exchanging one foreign occupation for another.

Revolution came to China in 1911 in the form of a nationalist uprising, with a doctrine modeled on Japan and led by Sun Yat-sen (who was in America when the uprising spontaneously erupted), who seized power and forced the abdication of China's last emperor in favor of the Republic of China in 1912. Despite the democratic aspects in Sun's doctrine the revolution was hijacked and Sun Yat-sen died of cancer in 1925 without realizing his dream of a democratic China. The nationalist movement eventually split into two parts (there was so much political upheaval in China during this period that there were actually three capitols at one point): the right-wing Kuomintang led by Chiang Kai-shek and the left-wing Communist Party of China eventually led by Mao Zedung.

When the second Sino-Japanese war started China was a country at the brink of civil war. The Kuomintang (KMT) and the Communist Party of China (CPC) did attempt to ally to fight the Japanese invasion. In fact, there were at least two KMT-CPC alliances; the second was formed in 1937, and it permitted the Nationalists to commit their best troops to the fight against the Japanese. In a three-month battle for Shanghai, the Chinese nationalist army inflicted severe casualties on the Japanese, but at the loss of its own best formations. The Japanese army, smarting from the tough battle for Shanghai, chased the remnants of the Chinese army to Nanjing, defeated it again, and then embarked on the infamous Nanjing massacre in retribution for the tough Chinese resistance.

Following the battle of Shanghai, Chiang Kai-shek was reluctant to commit his forces to a pitched battle with the Japanese and conserved his forces for the eventual showdown with the communist armies. During World War II, the United States provided significant military assistance to the KMT, but relations were rocky because the Chinese could not be lured into battle. The CPC, although nominally allied with the KMT, took advantage of the weakened nationalist forces to spread its influence. There is very little evidence that the CPC engaged in any major battles with the Japanese and instead focused on building up its strength for the civil war that was sure to follow the Sino-Japanese war.

At the conclusion of World War II, Nationalist China was made one of the founding members of the United Nations—the only Asian country so honored. Nevertheless, the civil war resumed in earnest. Although the United States' principal interest was in a republican China, American diplomats and soldiers alike quickly realized that Chiang Kai-shek's government was too corrupt to win and withdrew all military support in 1947. Mao's early emphasis on the peasants over the urban proletariat paid off, and the communist armies simply overwhelmed the nationalist forces, which withdrew to Taiwan in 1949 declaring Taipei to be the temporary capital of the Republic of China.

From a historical perspective, the establishment of the People's Republic of China in Beijing in October 1949 only changed the actors, but the stage and China's national interests remained the same. Despite the fact that Japan was a destroyed and occupied country, Beijing's first act was to negotiate an anti-Japanese friendship pact with Moscow. In little more than a year after the communists came to power, China was reasserting its self-entitled prerogatives on its former tributary states. In 1950, China invaded Korea; "liberated" Tibet from itself in 1951; and invaded India in 1962, seizing more than one hundred thousand square miles of disputed territory. Chinese and Russian troops reportedly clashed over Mongolia during the 1960s. In 1979, China briefly attacked Vietnam to "teach Hanoi a lesson" for defying China's interests in Cambodia and Laos. Through the end of the twentieth century, Beijing seized a number of islands, atolls, and reefs in order to assert sovereignty over vast reaches of the South China Sea also claimed by Vietnam, Malaysia, Brunei, and the Philippines. The lesson here is that the People's Republic of China is no less acquisitive than was the Celestial Empire in its day, but modern China is developing the economic clout to back up its ambitions.

The emperor was uninterested in trade largely because his tax revenues came from land and increasing trade had no benefit for him. China's communist leaders, however, are very dependent on trade for economic development. In the beginning, the Chinese communists experimented with a variety of socialist economic policies, all of which failed, sometimes with catastrophic impact, such as the Great Leap Forward, that resulted in the deaths of millions. After Mao's death, however, the Chinese government, under the leadership of Deng Xiaoping, began to permit grassroots policy changes that let farmers make money selling surplus crops. "Once farmers began to make some money on their own, they looked for ways to make money with their money."[9] These tiny beginnings spawned cascading reforms, and now China's economy is the sixth largest in the world and expected to pass the United States in gross size before the end of the century. This rapid economic growth has permitted vastly increased military spending and the world anxiously watches and wonders about the intentions of rising China.

During the Cold War, the United States and China enjoyed a brief period of cooperation. The grand organizing principle that cemented the U.S.-China relationship from 1972 to 1992 was the "Soviet Threat."[10] But the Soviet threat has been dead and buried for fifteen years, and so too has been the entire raison d'être of a U.S.-China "strategic partnership." Indeed, the Chinese Communist Party believed its very legitimacy was shaken with the disintegration of the communist world in Europe, because the party could no longer claim the dogmatic orthodoxy of "Marxism-Leninism" to justify its governance of China without the consent of the governed. China's communist party, like all good bureaucracies facing obsolescence, chose to redefine its legitimacy by substituting a nationalism-based doctrine that posits as its ultimate goal the reclamation of China's ancient place as the preeminent power in Asia—and in the process, the displacement of the United States as superpower in the Asia-Pacific region.

Beijing's neocommunist mandarins are using China's newfound economic muscle to expand its interests far beyond those of the imperial China. From southern Africa to South America, China is providing political, diplomatic, and security support to dictatorships. Beijing is not allying with these governments for ideological reasons, but to expand China's influence.

Zimbabwe, for example, is a resource-rich southern African nation, suffering a major economic crisis, with inflation at 400 percent and unemployment at about 70 percent. Zimbabwe's per capita income has nosedived over the past eight years, from $682 in 1998 to $521 in 2002. President Robert Mugabe abused his office to suppress opposition parties and maintain his grip on power. His ruling party won an overwhelming victory in March 2005 in elections not believed to be free or fair by most Western countries.

Amid sanctions imposed by the European Union and the United States, China delivered $240 million in military goods to Zimbabwe, including thousands of AK-47 assault rifles, riot gear, and mobile water cannons. Mugabe's security forces used the weapons to break up opposition political rallies and demonstrations. Beijing also provided radio-jamming equipment to Harare, thwarting prodemocracy broadcasts during the last "election" campaign.

In return for China's military equipment, President Mugabe is said to have promised China land and access to mineral resources. In November 2004, Wu Bangguo, chairman of the standing committee of China's National People's Congress, paid a visit to Zimbabwe and signed six economic agreements. Emmerson Mnangagwa, speaker of the Zimbabwean national assembly, said the national assembly would lay down laws to ensure that high priority be given to Chinese enterprises.

In return for China's uncritical political support, Mugabe does his best to please his new master by helping to isolate Taiwan. The ministry of foreign affairs of Zimbabwe said in March 2005 that Zimbabwe firmly supports China's antisecession law, which authorizes the use of military force to prevent Taiwanese independence.

In 2006, China increased its defense spending for the eighteenth straight year giving China the largest defense budget in Asia and the third largest in the world. China's defense spending is rising faster than its economic growth, but no country is making claims to Chinese territory or threatening China's interests. One can only assume that it is China that intends to upset the current world order.

JAPAN

When Commodore Matthew Perry sailed into Tokyo Bay in 1854, Japan had been a military dictatorship, known as the Tokugawa Shogunate, closed to the outside world for 250 years. President Fillmore sent Perry to Japan to protect the rights of American whalers, set up navy coaling stations, and open the country for trade. Perry managed to gain the first two objectives in the Treaty of Kanagawa of 1854, and in 1858, the U.S. Consul to Tokyo completed negotiations of the commercial treaty.

These treaties with the United States were the catalyst to a chain of events that ten years later led to the Meiji Restoration, 1866–1869, when the Japanese emperor retook power and began the industrial revolution, which was to transform Japan to a world-class industrial and military power by the end of that century. Nevertheless, these changes did not break the military's strong control of the government, and the military was to be a key decision maker until Japan's defeat in World War II.

In 1876, Japan forced the hermit Kingdom of Korea, over which China's emperor claimed suzerainty for the previous two hundred years, to open trade with Japan and to declare independence from China in its foreign relations. Although the treaty was forced on the king, it was Korea's first modern treaty and the first time that Korea was treated as an equal in international negotiations.

Despite the Japanese characterization of its maneuvers on the peninsula as seeking Korean independence, China and Japan were intensely competitive over who would rule Korea. Both countries frequently interfered with Korean political development, including arresting and executing Korean leaders, and seeking to undermine any government that Tokyo or Beijing believed conflicted with their national interests. Both countries stationed ever-larger numbers of troops in the country. Finally, war broke out in 1894, and Japan's modern military easily beat China's antiquated forces. In the 1895 Treaty of Shimonoseki that ended what was to be only the first Sino-Japanese war, Korea was transferred from Chinese suzerainty to become a protectorate of Japan. China also ceded Formosa (Taiwan) and Port Arthur to Japan.

Diplomatic pressures from the French, German, and the Russian Empires prevented Japan's emperor from taking Port Arthur. Two years later the Russians forced Beijing to lease Port Arthur to Moscow setting the stage for the Russo-Japanese war of 1904. Russia wanted to extend its sphere of influence in Manchuria and Korea, at the expense of China and the new acquisitions of the Japanese Empire. Following months of fruitless negotiations, Japan declared war on Russia and in a very short campaign defeated the Russian army and navy. In the Treaty of Portsmouth (signed in Portsmouth, New Hampshire), Russia acknowledged Japanese control of Korea, transferred the lease of Port Arthur to the Japanese, and both countries evacuated Manchuria.

The second Sino-Japanese war began when Japan, which still coveted Chinese territory, created a series of incidents that gave the Japanese army an excuse to seize Manchuria in 1931. In 1937, the Japanese army manufactured another incident, attacked Chinese forces, and greatly expanded its control over northern China, including the infamous occupation of Nanjing.

In the city of Nanjing, the Japanese army embarked on a systematic program of butchery in which an estimated three hundred thousand unarmed

Chinese civilians died. Despite overwhelming evidence, including eyewitness accounts from Japanese soldiers confirming the size and brutality of the massacre, Japanese historians and politicians alike continue to deny or excuse the massacre.[11]

Although Japan's ally, Germany, also committed horrendous acts of barbarism during the war, the Germans have fully admitted to the crimes and tried to atone for the behavior. But the Japanese seem unable to comprehend the anger in many Asian countries generated by the behavior of the Japanese army in World War II—and worse, the continued Japanese denial, despite the overwhelming evidence, increases the anger in many countries, especially potential friends such as Korea, Singapore, and Philippines. Consequently, although the Chinese communists' policies are responsible for the deaths of millions, the Japanese are constantly blindsided by China's sanctimonious rehashing of the massacres, and Tokyo is unable to generate sympathy from its friends and neighbors to defend Japan's postwar behavior.

The massacres also had a debilitating effect on Japan's prosecution of the war. Accounts of the Nanjing massacre from Western journalists helped turn American public opinion against the Japanese. The American government began a not so covert program of military assistance to the Chinese nationalists fighting the Japanese and imposed broad embargoes of raw materials, including oil. Tokyo was unwilling to curb its imperial ambitions in the face of these sanctions and instead decided to seize what it needed and drive America out of the Pacific with a surprise attack at its naval base at Pearl Harbor on December 7, 1941, bringing the United States into World War II.

Japan's armed forces were initially successful. Japan seized all of Southeast Asia and was marching on British India before the end of 1942. Although most of the countries occupied by Japan were still European colonies, only Indians and Indonesians initially welcomed the Japanese as liberators.

The Philippines was already transitioning from colony to independent country, and Japan's invasion was viewed as an unwelcome setback. Filipinos fought the Japanese tooth-and-nail, inviting harsh retribution from Japanese occupation forces. In the British colonies of Malaysia and Singapore, the minority Chinese that the British had brought to those colonies as laborers volunteered for service with the British in large numbers, and the Japanese took terrible vengeance, massacring thousands of Chinese during the occupation.

On the other hand, Sukarno, an Indonesian independence activist, collaborated with the Japanese, raising millions of volunteer laborers. Near the end of the war, Japan actually formed an Indonesian army to defend against a Western invasion. Japan also formed the Indian National Army (INA) of Indian deserters from the British army to help them fight the British in the China-Burma-India theater.

Nevertheless, Japan was defeated, surrendering unconditionally on August 15, 1945. The home islands were devastated by the war, and Japan was forced to surrender all of its colonies. Russia still occupies four small islands in the north that were never disputed territory. American occupiers demilitarized the country and forced a democratic pacifist constitution on the government. Japan was not permitted to possess a military, only a self-defense force.

The war had finally broken the military's hold on the Japanese government, and postwar Japan's energy was focused on economic development. Japan's economic model was characterized by high household savings rates, with banks playing a leading role in financing; long-term contracting among closely associated firms, a system known as *keiretsu*; and strong government influence through industrial policy.[12] This system worked well for forty years, raising Japan to become the world's second-largest economy. With this new status, Japan began to look for a role for itself on the world stage equivalent to its economic clout.

Japan became philanthropic, becoming Asia's biggest aid donor. Japan also sought a permanent seat on the United Nations Security Council, but even the United States frustrated Tokyo's ambitions. Japan is also seeking to create a normal military with a Ministry of Defense and to participate with the United Nations in a variety of peacekeeping missions and with the United States in the global war on terrorism and ballistic missile defense, but these ambitions are frustrated by Japan's postwar constitution and the vocal complaints of its neighbors. Adding to these frustrations, beginning in the 1990s, Japan experienced a prolonged period of economic stagnation and even recession, largely due to inherent weaknesses in Japan's development model and the inability of the government, business, and society to adjust to the new economic realities.

INDIA

Like China, India is both a modern state and the home of an ancient culture. In ancient times, Indian culture spread throughout the subcontinent and crossed the Himalayan Mountains to the Tibetan plateau. At sea, the Indian culture spread to most of mainland and insular Southeast Asia, including ancient Cambodia and the Malay-Indonesian archipelago.

Indian cultural influence can be seen from Angkor Wat in Cambodia to the island of Bali, Indonesia, the last remaining remnant of India's Hindu influence. The most aggressive Indian empire was the Buddhist Mauryas (321 to 181 B.C.). As a record of the Mauryas' influence, on the Indonesian island of Java is the spectacular Borbadour, the largest Buddhist temple in the world, in what is now predominantly Muslim Indonesia. However, even the Mauryas did not colonize militarily but developed more of a cultural capital, spreading its influence, but not its armies.[13]

Also like China, India paid the price of ignoring its maritime interests by eventually becoming a colony of countries that controlled the seas. In 1857, the British Empire, the supreme naval power of its day, formally made India a colony and remained the colonial power until the close of World War II.

After Japan's defeat in World War II, the British captured members of the Japanese sponsored Indian National Army (INA), brought them under arrest to New Delhi, and put three of them, including their leader Subhas Chandra Bose, on trial for treason. Bose's lawyers included Jawarhal Nehru, who would become India's first prime minister. Nehru argued that the INA members were freedom fighters against the British occupation and thus could not be tried for treason. The highly publicized trial inspired mutinies among Britain's colonial forces and was a leading factor in forcing the British to give up India.[14]

Significantly, Nehru marginalized Bose and the INA. Although the British were forced to release Bose and his companions, in a deal with Lord Mountbatten, the British negotiator for India's independence, members of the INA were not permitted to join the postindependence army. Thus, India's early political leadership was dominated by Nehru and Gandhi, proponents of nonviolent resistance and socialism.

When discussing history with Indians or Pakistanis, every discussion eventually turns to Partition, the British plan to leave India, as the source of all troubles. Both Pakistan and India are ethnically Indian. In fact, the Indus Valley, from whence the name *India* comes, is in modern-day Pakistan. Pakistan is not a former kingdom but the creation of Muslim Indians. The name *Pakistan* is an acronym from Punjab, Afghanistan, Kashmir, and Baluchistan and means "land of the pure" in Persian. Muslim Indians wanted to create a Muslim homeland so that they would not be a permanent minority in a Hindu state.[15]

The British plan to partition India was announced in June 1947, Pakistan declared its independence on August 14, 1947, and India became independent the next day. Partition was accompanied by bloody rioting and eventually three wars and the creation of a third state, Bangladesh, in 1971. The India-Pakistan relationship continues to bedevil the foreign policy of both countries to this day.

In foreign policy outside its relationship with Pakistan, like their imperial antecedents, India's new democratic leaders were reluctant to use force to defend New Delhi's national interests. India nominally refused to take sides in the Cold War. Instead, India, along with Indonesia, was one of the founders and leaders of the Non-Aligned Movement (NAM).

The NAM was formed at the Bandung Conference in 1955, where the founding countries declared their determination not to be drawn into the Cold War superpower contest. The NAM eventually gained one hundred member countries. The original impetus for the NAM was to use its numbers and the United Nations to protect the sovereignty of the many new, post-colonial countries. Unfortunately, dictators in member countries were soon using NAM principles as a convenient shield against international criticism of their regime's "internal affairs." Additionally, despite its nonaligned rhetoric, many member countries, including India, were sympathetic with the Soviet Union and became largely dependent on Soviet subsidies, industrial technology, and weapons.

Besides becoming a defender of dictators, New Delhi's passive foreign policy was exploited by China in Tibet. India's cultural affinity with the Tibetan people and its geostrategic location as a buffer between India and China made Tibet a particular concern of independent New Delhi's early foreign policy. New Delhi felt it had inherited Britain's policy toward Tibet, simultaneously recognizing China's suzerainty over Tibet while defending its autonomy.

India allowed Britain and the United States to provide military assistance to the Tibetan army so it could resist People's Liberation Army (PLA) encroachment and sought to raise Tibet's profile as a discrete sovereign nation. China had other plans. Beijing insisted that Tibet was sovereign Chinese territory and that Tibetans were actually Chinese. In 1951, the PLA invaded Tibet and embarked on a campaign to wipe out the Tibetan culture by "reforming" Tibetans to be more like China's dominant Han culture. Prime Minister Nehru's response was to encourage the Tibetans in nonviolent resistance.[16]

When China discovered that it would be more convenient to control Tibet if it possessed part of India, too, the PLA invaded India and took two large swaths of "disputed" Indian territory in 1962. New Delhi's meek response was to break off diplomatic relations with Beijing. Fifteen years later, with no territorial concessions from China, India restored diplomatic relations. India and

China began an annual dialogue in 1980, and in 1988, Prime Minister Rajiv Gandhi visited China, the first such meeting in twenty-eight years. At the end of the twentieth century, it appeared that trade and mutual political support were improving between New Delhi and Beijing.

Throughout the second half of the twentieth century, New Delhi's politicians appeared to operate under an assumption that its socialist economy, pacifist foreign policy, and championship of third world causes provided India with a cloak of moral authority that gave India a special rank in the world, but like the emperor's new clothes, that cloak was invisible to everyone else. For the rest of the world, India was an inconsequential participant in the world economy, Russia's patsy, China's doormat, and the advocate for the prerogatives for third world dictators. Although India remained democratic, it was distrusted by the "first world" democracies and was marginalized during the first fifty years of independence.

The Soviet Union disappeared in 1990, and New Delhi leaders faced the reality that India was part of a new world order where it occupied the bottom rung. India became determined to reassert its rightful place in the world and embarked on a comprehensive campaign to reform its economic and foreign policies. The government began a process of economic reform that resulted in the fastest economic growth in Indian history. New Delhi also sought to develop a new relationship with Washington, gain a seat on the United Nations Security Council, and elbow its way into the ranks of the nuclear powers by testing a nuclear weapon in 1998.

I was assigned to the Army Staff at the Pentagon in April 1998 when the U.S. Army Chief of Staff, General Dennis Reimer, visited India and Pakistan. I provided policy guidance on South Asia for the Chief of Staff and helped prepare Reimer for his trip. When General Reimer was in South Asia, senior Indian military and civilian officials bombarded him with alarming descriptions of the Chinese threat to India.

When the Chief of Staff returned, those of us who covered India and China greeted Reimer's comments with surprise, there had been few prior indications of a sour Chinese-Indian relationship. Reimer ordered an intelligence investigation into India-China relations. I helped with the investigation (although my contribution consisted mostly of shoulder shrugs and sympathetic nods), while the intelligence officers did most of the data review and analysis.

Despite a thorough investigation, the Army staff was unable to uncover any new troop movements or change in China's military posture that would provoke such concern in India. There were a few rationalizations, such as the

1962 Sino-Indo border dispute, and China's support to Pakistan's nuclear program, but until then India had passively accepted those situations.

On May 11, the mystery deepened when India tested three nuclear devices and then two more on May 13. Prime Minister Atal Bihari Vajpayee sent a letter to President Bill Clinton explaining why India needed nuclear weapons. The threat from China figured prominently in Vajpayee's explanation.

The surprise at the Pentagon was complete, but no one was more surprised than the Chinese. Up to 1998, China believed that its relations with India were good and steadily improving, so it was a huge shock in Beijing when it suddenly found itself the target of India's nuclear weapons program. After Vajpayee's letter to President Clinton, Beijing immediately retaliated, canceling boundary talks and pushing through United Nations Security Council Resolution 1172 calling for a rollback of India and Pakistan's nuclear programs.

In retrospect, it is obvious that the nationalist government under Prime Minister Vajpayee was determined to make India a nuclear power, and China provided the excuse. Vajpayee authorized the test on April 8, 1998, just before General Reimer's arrival in India. Senior Indian military and civilian officials complained to Reimer about China as part of a campaign to prepare the United States for a nuclear-armed India.

Examining India's Chinese threat from a purely military standpoint, as we did, would never provide the answer of why India tested its nuclear weapons. India developed nuclear weapons not because of a military disadvantage but because of its view of itself as a great power.

From India's point of view, it is no coincidence that the five weapon states of the nonproliferation treaty (NPT) are also the same five countries that hold permanent seats and veto power in the United Nations Security Council. Furthermore, there was no surprise in the Pentagon that India and Pakistan had nuclear weapons. In fact, I recall joking during one Pentagon meeting that the nuclear tests in India and Pakistan had temporarily reduced the number of nuclear devices in South Asia. The real surprise in Washington and Beijing was that India would dare to challenge the comfortably superior positions of the established powers.

In its drive for great power status, India is also trying to rid itself of the dispute with Pakistan. Despite protests to the contrary in New Delhi, most observers view India's foreign policy as centered on Pakistan. As a great power, India needs a global foreign policy and not have its every action interpreted in the context of its relations with Pakistan. Furthermore, India cannot be taken seriously as a broker of international disputes if it cannot resolve disputes with its neighbors. To rid itself of the historical albatross of its relationship with Pakistan, in 2003, New Delhi negotiated a cease-fire with Islamabad and opened talks to resolve their sixty-year-old feud.

The India-Pakistan cease-fire has held since November 2003, but the talks to move from a cease-fire to a peace agreement seem little closer to resolution than when they began. The obstacle is that neither side has the political will to compromise on Kashmir. The official position on Kashmir has not changed in either country. India wants to establish the Line of Control (LOC)—the military line that divides Kashmir—as the permanent international border between Pakistan and India. Pakistan, on the other hand, refuses to accept the LOC as the permanent border.

Despite this seeming conundrum, since November 2003, diplomatic success has been steady. In January 2004, then Prime Minister Vajpayee spent an hour in talks with President Pervez Musharraf. In February, India and Pakistan began formal talks. In June, they established a hotline and both countries renewed their ban on nuclear testing. A year after the cease-fire, India began withdrawing troops from the border. In February 2005, New Delhi and Islamabad launched bus service across cease-fire lines and in January 2006, the two countries renewed direct railroad access. In April 2005, Musharraf and Singh signed a declaration that the peace process was irreversible. In October 2005, India and Pakistan signed two security cooperation accords. The agreements include a deal promising advance warning of ballistic missile tests and another setting up a hotline between coastguards. Both sides are also working toward greater economic integration. Although final resolution to the question of Kashmir seems distant, there appears to be little desire for a return to military confrontation.

Although India is demonstrating farsighted diplomacy in its relationship with Pakistan, the world's largest democracy can still be very shortsighted, too. There are few democracies in India's neighborhood and fewer signs that India is acting as a beacon for democracy movements. With Burma for example, rather than looking to Burma's future under a democratic government, New Delhi competes with Beijing for influence over the bloody-minded junta that has ruled that unfortunate country since 1962.

As a new century begins India is carving out a new role for itself as a great power. In a few years, India's economy may rival the world's largest economies, its navy is venturing into Southeast Asia as far as Vietnam. India has a long-range missile program that will soon be capable of threatening Beijing and a space program that will most likely include manned launches in this century. After sixty years of independence, India is finally stepping onto the world stage, and New Delhi's performance as a regional and global leader is a keen interest of the United States.

SOUTHEAST ASIA

There are great differences among the countries of Southeast Asia, but they are also bound together by their shared history and national interests. How these disparate countries ended up together forming the most important multilateral organization in Asia is written in their history. In order to stay within the bounds of a single book, we will briefly examine the modern histories of only Vietnam and Indonesia, the region's largest and most disparate members.

For millennia, Southeast Asia has been a crossroads of Asia. Some of the world's oldest prehistoric remains, such as the famous Java man,[17] were discovered there. As noted earlier, the region's early history was strongly influenced by India, but Chinese merchants operated throughout Southeast Asia, and the emperor claimed suzerainty over a number of Southeast Asian kingdoms long before European colonizers arrived. All the countries of Southeast Asia, with the exception of Thailand, eventually became European colonies.

Vietnam was a colony of China for almost a thousand years and then spent the next thousand years in and out of tributary status until the French seized the country in the nineteenth century. Unlike the Japanese presence in the rest of Southeast Asia, Japan occupied Vietnam without a fight. When World War II began for Southeast Asia, France had already lost the war to Japan's allies in Europe. Japan occupied French Indo-China with an agreement with the Vichy government, which was governing France during the German occupation. The agreement permitted the French colonial forces to continue governing Indo-China while Japan looked after its external security.

Although there were communist insurgencies throughout Southeast Asia during this period, Vietnam's communists were ardent nationalists more than they were ideologues. The Viet Minh were led by Ho Chi Minh, who became a communist while studying in Paris and was one of the founding members of France's communist party. Unlike his French colleagues, however, Ho saw communism as a world revolution that promised independence from the foreign oppressors.[18]

During the Japanese occupation, the French colonial forces continued to fight the communist Viet Minh to maintain French control of Indo-China. Although there were many noncommunist independence groups in Vietnam, the Viet Minh success against the French verified their credentials as a nationalist movement and drew Vietnamese recruits to its ranks from across the political spectrum.

In March 1945, the Japanese seized direct control of Indo-China from the French and in August set up a puppet government under the Vietnamese emperor Bao Dai. Most Vietnamese considered the new "independent" government a transparent Japanese trick to maintain control of Vietnam. Furthermore, the Japanese tactic made the Vietnamese suspicious of future attempts by other foreign powers to set up governments in Vietnam.

When the Japanese lost World War II, the French returned and attempted to reestablish their colonial rule. Until the French could arrive, the British governed the southern half of the country while nationalist Chinese forces acted as representatives of the allied forces in northern Vietnam. The Viet Minh began attacking the French as soon as they arrived and continued to escalate the war until they beat them militarily in 1954.

In the context of the Cold War, the United States saw the war in Vietnam in starkly different terms than did the Vietnamese. Washington policymakers viewed the Viet Minh "communists" as Soviet proxies and did not fully grasp the import of the nationalist element until America was deeply committed to a war it could not win. The war ended in the withdrawal of American forces in 1972 and the reunification of the country in 1975.

In 1979, the newly united Socialist Republic of Vietnam invaded Cambodia and Laos. The army became bogged down fighting Cambodian insurgents who were inspired by the same sense of nationalism that had served Vietnam so well. Unable to achieve victory there, Vietnam withdrew from Cambodia in 1989.

Following its defeat in Cambodia and the collapse of the Soviet Union, Hanoi set out to reform Vietnam's economy and foreign policy. The country signed a peace agreement with Cambodia in 1991 and shortly thereafter restored diplomatic relations with China. The peace agreement forged the way for Vietnam to join the Association of Southeast Asian Nations (ASEAN). In 1995, the United States and Vietnam reestablished diplomatic relations. In 2006, Vietnam joined the World Trade Organization, and President George Bush attended the Asia-Pacific Economic Cooperation forum (APEC) hosted by Vietnam in Hanoi.

The region's biggest country is Indonesia. Although Indonesia is the world's fourth-most populous country, third largest democracy, the world's largest Muslim country, and it lies across sea lanes vital to world trade, few Americans could find Indonesia on a well-marked map. Nevertheless, the

United States and Japan were pivotal to Indonesian independence, and Indonesia will be crucial to American interests in the twenty-first century.

When World War II began, Indonesia had been a Dutch colony for more than two hundred years. The Dutch forces in Indonesia were quickly defeated by the invading Japanese and by the end of 1942 all of the Dutch East Indies was under Japanese occupation. Although the Japanese army committed the usual abuses in Indonesia, such as drafting comfort women, and requisitioning food and other goods without fair compensation, overall the Japanese occupation in Indonesia was without the harsh measures taken elsewhere in Asia.

Many Indonesians collaborated with the Japanese in the hope of permanently ridding Indonesia of the Dutch and of gaining eventual independence. Surprisingly, the Japanese occupation authorities were accommodating of Indonesian nationalists. The Japanese army established a puppet Indonesian government with Sukarno[19] as its head. By the end of the war, Sukarno had recruited almost two million Indonesians for service with the Japanese as either laborers or military auxiliaries.

As Japan's military fortunes waned, more of its soldiers were reassigned from Indonesia to other theaters. In an effort to maintain its military strength, Japan moved from individual Indonesian auxiliaries serving in Japanese units, to recruiting an Indonesian army to operate under Japanese control. The new force was called *Pembela Tanah Air* ("defenders of the motherland"), or PETA. PETA was the genesis of the modern Indonesian army. Among the many luminaries that served in PETA was General, later President, Suharto.

Near the end of the war, the Japanese and Indonesian collaborators began working on a formula for postwar Indonesia. In March 1945, the Japanese announced the formation of a committee to prepare for Indonesian independence. On August 6, the United States dropped its first atomic bomb on Japan. On August 9, the same day the Americans dropped the second atomic bomb, the Japanese flew Sukarno to Vietnam, where the Japanese informed him that they would grant Indonesia independence on August 24.

Sukarno returned to Jakarta on August 14 realizing that the Japanese were no longer in control of Indonesia's future. Japan surrendered on August 15, and Sukarno declared Indonesia's independence on August 17, 1945. Sukarno's goal was to secure Indonesian independence before the Dutch could return to claim their former colonies.

The Dutch reached an accord with the British, and Australian and British troops landed in Indonesia by the beginning of September, but the

British were using many Indian troops. Nehru strongly protested the use of Indian soldiers to suppress an independence movement and forced the British to speed up their withdrawal from Indonesia. The Dutch began to arrive before the end of the year, but they faced widespread revolution.

Although the Indonesians in August 1945 were no closer to independence than was the United States in July 1776, there were already three elements in Indonesia's polity that would affect the region to the present day. The first was the Indonesian Communist Party (PKI). The second was a group of greater Malay irredentists that wanted Indonesia not only to free Indonesia from the Dutch but also to absorb the British colonies of Malaysia, Brunei, Singapore, and the Portuguese colony of East Timor. The last was a group of Islamic radicals known as Darul Islam that wanted to form Indonesia as an Islamic state. In the twenty-first century, Darul Islam would become infamous for its association with terrorist group Jemaah Islamiyah.

Unlike in Vietnam, the communists were not the dominant force in the revolution. Once Sukarno declared independence, PETA and other groups rallied around him. The communists tried to wrest the revolution from Sukarno by an attempted coup in Madiun, Indonesia, in September 1948. Several Indonesian government officials were killed, but then the Indonesian army recaptured Madiun and wiped out any collaborators, and PKI leaders fled to China.

The effect of the Madiun coup was to reassure the American public that the Indonesian revolution was not a communist proxy but a true independence movement. The United States began to assist the Indonesians in the United Nations and pressure the Dutch to surrender Indonesia, including a threat to cut off Marshall Plan aid to Holland. By December 1949, the Dutch transferred sovereignty to the Indonesians.

Following independence, Sukarno talents continued to be oriented toward revolution rather than nation building. His most disruptive policy was *Konfrontasi*, in which Sukarno claimed that the formation of an independent Malaysia was British neoimperialism and that Indonesia would crush Malaysia. Konfrontasi soon extended to Singapore and Brunei. Although there was military activity all along Indonesia's borders with Malaysia in Borneo, paratroops landing on the Malaysian peninsula, and terrorist attacks in Singapore, Konfrontasi was never a coherent military campaign and failed to achieve any of its goals.

President Sukarno was overthrown in a coup in 1965 that the military blamed on the communists and Chinese. General Suharto became president in 1966. Suharto signed a peace treaty with Malaysia in 1966, and Indonesia,

Malaysia, Philippines, Singapore, and Thailand formed the Association of Southeast Asian Nations in 1967.

The Association of Southeast Asian Nations (ASEAN) is the oldest, largest, and most important Asian organization. Originally formed to smooth over the legacy of Konfrontasi, it soon became the megaphone through which the countries of Southeast Asia spoke to the world. Although the organization never became a regional alliance, security was always at the top of its agenda. The ASEAN countries were anticommunist during the Cold War largely because of Indonesia's influence, but that tendency was reinforced after Vietnam's invasion of Cambodia. Nevertheless, ASEAN practiced nonalignment and avoided becoming pawns to the big powers.

The ASEAN countries, led by Indonesia, preferred instead to focus on "national resiliency," meaning economic development and internal security. By the end of the 1980s, most domestic insurgencies had been neutralized, and the ASEAN countries were experiencing remarkable economic growth, inspiring many observers to venerate the seeming "Asian Miracle."

Emboldened by their success, in the 1990s, the original five members of ASEAN expanded the membership and the role of the organization. Brunei joined in 1984, Vietnam joined in 1995, Laos and Burma joined in 1997, and Cambodia was welcomed into the organization in 1999. The ASEAN states also created the ASEAN Free Trade Area (AFTA) to integrate their economies and the ASEAN Regional Forum (ARF) to manage regional security issues.

Unfortunately, these new measures had uneven success. When asking new countries to join, ASEAN failed to set any preconditions for membership other than race and geography. Among the new members, only Vietnam has exceeded expectations to become a valuable asset to the organization. Burma, on the other hand, has dissolved into a security, economic, and political nightmare, dragging ASEAN through crisis after crisis and threatening to make ASEAN an international pariah.

There is an active movement among member countries to suspend Burma's membership. This is particularly true among ASEAN's democratic countries—Thailand, Philippines, and Indonesia—but even less democratic countries such as Malaysia, Singapore, and Vietnam express deep misgivings about Burma's continued participation in ASEAN.

AFTA is equally unsuccessful. ASEAN economies range from Singapore, the second most open economy in the world,[20] to Burma, whose economy exists largely in the black market, making economic integration problematic at best. Additionally, many countries that signed AFTA strongly resist exposing protected industries to even regional competition. Finally, in 1997, many of the weaknesses in the ASEAN economic model coalesced and Asia experienced a major financial crisis, which for years weakened the political will in ASEAN to comply with AFTA. The result is that ASEAN's economies are only marginally better integrated than they were at the beginning of the process and they continue to grow at rates slower than their pre-1997 growth rates.

Another casualty of the 1997 Asian financial crisis was President Suharto. He resigned in 1998 after thirty-two years of authoritarian rule backed by the military. Although Suharto did preside over remarkable economic development, the unrestrained corruption that marked his regime contributed to the financial crisis that brought him down. Over the next six years Indonesia would transition to a mature and dynamic democracy by 2004, when a new national legislature was elected and Indonesia carried out its first direct presidential election.

Each country in Southeast Asia found its way to the twenty-first century along a different path, but ultimately they arrived together. ASEAN now has a population of six hundred million people and a gross domestic product (GDP) exceeding two trillion U.S. dollars. It is a vital American interest that the countries of Southeast Asia continue to work together to protect their sovereignty, complete their transition to democracy, and develop their economies. ASEAN is the principal existing tool for achieving those goals, and U.S. policy should work to strengthen the integration of the region.

CONCLUSION

If history is any guide at all, Americans can expect to see Asian countries dominating the headlines throughout the next century. In pure size the Chinese economy will most likely pass the United States sometime midcentury. India's economy may catch up to our own by the end of the century, and all Asian countries will experience rapid economic development.

This newfound wealth will translate directly into military and political power that will allow them to pursue their national interests with a capability relative to the United States and Europe that Asia has not possessed for centuries. In particular, history shows us that the Chinese consider themselves to be the world's natural leader and that when given the opportunity, Beijing will reassert itself on the world stage.

China will challenge America's current position as the world's only superpower. Nevertheless, the United States and the People's Republic of China will not face off in a superpower death match. Instead, China is geographically enclosed in a ring of countries with long histories and deep memories of China. The evolution of American and Chinese relations will be decisively influenced by these other countries.

There are two important lessons in outlining the rise of Asia. The first is to demonstrate how the roots of each of the countries are deeply intertwined with the others. The second is to use history as a guide on how each of these countries may choose when faced with a geopolitical decision that will affect the United States.

India, for example, is not seeking to become a world power to further American interests. To the contrary, India seeks a leading role because Indians do not believe that the current world order benefits India, and they want a seat in the decision-making bodies to advance India's interests.

In the twenty-first century, the United States cannot have a China policy without an Asia policy. As China asserts its traditional role, Washington policymakers must consider the host of issues that interest the United States and the available policy tools, and then construct an integrated Asia policy that best serves those interests. America will ignore the rest of Asia at its own peril.

• 2 •

South China Sea Maritime Territorial Disputes

Good fences make good neighbors.

—Robert Frost

In July 2006, three U.S. aircraft carrier strike groups—USS *Kitty Hawk*, USS *Lincoln*, and the USS *Ronald Reagan*—with 22,000 military personnel, 27 other warships, and 280 aircraft conducted the largest carrier naval exercise since the Vietnam War. Navy spokesmen denied that the exercise was intended to send a message to China, but Chinese observers were present, and it was in the right location to do just that. In fact, Washington needs to do a lot more of the same as a first step toward protecting American interests in the South China Sea.

The United States is the world's largest trading nation; 90 percent of the world's trade moves via ship, and 45 percent of all shipping moves through the lawless waters of the South China Sea. America's continued prosperity requires free access to the markets and producers of Asia, and the United States Navy is the only reliable guarantor of freedom of navigation in Asia's seas.

But China's sweeping territorial claims in the South China Sea and distorted interpretation of the law of the sea are an explicit threat to the freedom of navigation. Six countries claim maritime borders in the South China Sea, but Beijing claims virtually the entire waterway as Chinese territory and declares that foreign warships traversing its maritime territory must first gain China's permission. Beijing's penchant for unilateral military action against the territorial claims of other countries in the region, such as establishing a naval outpost on Mischief Reef less than two hundred miles from the Philippines, further militarizes the dispute and forces the countries of Southeast Asia to choose between confronting or submitting to Beijing's threats.

Thus far, the U.S. has failed to meet China's challenge. America's milquetoast diplomatic response to Beijing's blatant territorial grab has been to remain neutral on the competing maritime border claims and to avoid criticism of China. Other countries in the region have made attempts to defuse the problem, such as Indonesia's informal conferences in the 1990s, but Beijing has refused multilateral solutions that do not recognize Chinese sovereignty. If Washington continues to allow Beijing's willful misinterpretation of the United Nations Convention on the Law of the Sea (UNCLOS) to remain unchallenged, the South China Sea will become a de facto Chinese lake, the countries of Southeast Asia will be subject to Beijing's interpretations of international law and sovereignty, and the U.S. Navy will have to ask permission from China to transit this vital international waterway.

To avoid this outcome, the United States must make it clear to China and other claimants that America opposes extreme claims that interfere with or threaten freedom of navigation. Washington also must unequivocally oppose the use of force to resolve territorial disputes and insist on demilitarization of the islands and reefs in, the South China Sea. Finally, Washington should insist that the competing claimants formulate a process to resolve the dispute. If these measures fail to produce an equitable solution that protects freedom of navigation, then the United States must abandon neutrality and side with its friends and allies in the region by supporting their claims against China's maritime empire building.

PRICELESS REAL ESTATE

The South China Sea comprises one of the most valuable maritime territories in the world. The Sea encompasses a portion of the Pacific Ocean from Singapore and the Straits of Malacca in the Southwest to the Strait of Taiwan in the northeast. The sea stretches across an area of 1,351,358 square miles and is the largest sea body after the five oceans.

The sea is bordered by densely populated archipelagos and peninsulas and contains more than two hundred small islands, rocks, and coral reefs, with the majority of them located in the Spratly and Paracel Islands. Most of these islands are partially submerged islets, rocks, and reefs that are little more than shipping hazards, none are suitable for permanent habitation, but the seas around teem with fish and the seabed underneath is thought to have substantial reserves of oil and gas.[1]

GEOLOGY

The Sea has striking geologic and tectonic settings. It contains a broad shallow shelf on the south, extending along the Vietnamese-Chinese coast to the Taiwan Strait on the north, a deep-sea basin in the center, and a dangerous ground near Spratly Islands with numerous reef islands over the southeast.[2] The sea has a wide variation of sea floors, ranging from one hundred meters deep on the continental Sunda shelf and over five thousand meters in the Philippine basin.[3]

Extensive continental shelves (less than one hundred meters deep) are found on the western and southern parts, while steep slopes with almost no shelves are found in the eastern part of SCS.[4] While the continental shelf is flat, the continental slope of the South China Sea has a complicated terrain.[5]

It has a bottom topography that makes it a unique semienclosed ocean basin overlaid by a pronounced monsoon surface wind. The South China Sea region's unusual reversing monsoon seasons play an important role in determining upper-sea water circulation with incredible regularity.

ENERGY RESERVES

The lower seabed temperature-pressure regimes in the South China Sea are low. When combined with its rich organic layers of sedimentary deposits, the region becomes an ideal geologic environment for the generation and accumulation of hydrocarbon minerals like natural gas.[6] In addition to the discovery and drilling of vast reserves of oil and natural gas, Chinese scientists have recently found an alternative energy supply on the South China Sea floor they call the *wide fuel ice band*. Fuel ice is a transparent crystal of methane-kind natural gas formed under low temperature and pressure of the seabed. (One stere[7] of fuel ice contains an energy amount equaling 164-stere natural gas.[8])

Traditional natural energy resources in the South China Sea region are abundant, especially oil and natural gas (see table 2.1). The region has proven oil reserves of approximately seven billion barrels, and oil production

Table 2.1. Oil and Gas Reserves and Production

	Proven Oil Reserves (Billion Barrels)	*Proven Gas Reserves (Trillion Cubic Feet)*	*Oil Production (Barrels/Day)*	*Gas Production (Billion Cubic Feet)*
Brunei	1.4	13.8	189,000	366
Cambodia	0	0	0	0
China	1 (est.)	5.0 (est.)	350,000 (est.)	200 (est.)
Indonesia	0.1 (est.)	32.0 (est.)	323,000 (est.)	50 (est.)
Malaysia	3.0	75.0	751,973	1,895
Philippines	0.2	3.8	24,512	<1
Singapore	0	0	0	0
Taiwan	<0.01	2.7	3,300	26
Thailand	0.6	13.3	193,162	661
Vietnam	0.6	6.8	339,595	46
Total	7.0 (est.)	150.3 (est.)	2,174,542	3,244

Source: U.S. Energy Information Administration, http://www.eia.doe.gov/emeu/cabs/schinatab.html.

is currently at 2.17 million barrels a day. Malaysia currently dominates oil production in Southeast Asia, producing almost half of the total oil output.

Because of the ongoing territorial disputes that prohibit thorough exploration, oil reserve estimates do not include the seabed under the Spratly and Paracel Islands. Significantly, there is tremendous optimism among Chinese oil analysts about the potential for oil reserves under the Spratly Islands. Oil resource estimates among Chinese oil analysts vary greatly. The estimates range from a moderate 105 billion barrels to approximately 200 billion barrels.[9] Outside of Chinese claims, there is little evidence to support the view that the region is what Beijing believes to be the "second Persian Gulf"[10] (see table 2.2). Few, if any, commercial oil companies have expressed interest in oil exploration and drilling in the Spratly Islands, and so far no oil or gas has been discovered there.

Table 2.2. Oil and Gas in the South China Sea: Comparison with Other Regions

	Proven Oil Reserves (Billion Barrels)	*Proven Gas Reserves (Trillion Cubic Feet)*	*Oil Production (Barrels/Day)*	*Gas Production (Billion Cubic Feet)*
Caspian Sea Region	17.2–32.8	232	1.6	4.5
North Sea Region	16.8	178.7	6.4	9.4
Persian Gulf	674.0	1,923.0	19.3	8.0
South China Sea	7.0 (est.)	150.3 (est.)	2.2	3.2

Source: U.S. Energy Information Administration, http://www.eia.doe.gov/emeu/cabs/schinatab.html.

The more abundant hydrocarbon mineral in the region is natural gas, which can be found in almost all countries surrounding the South China Sea. The U.S. Geological Survey estimates that 60–70 percent of the South China Sea region's hydrocarbon resources are natural gas, not oil. The most updated proven gas reserves estimate is 150 trillion cubit feet, and gas production is currently at over 3.2 trillion cubit feet. As with oil production, Malaysia is also the biggest producer of natural gas though the lack of infrastructure has held back further exploration of this vast reserve of natural gas.

COMMERCIAL FISHING

The South China Sea's unusual geology and climate characteristics explain the presence of a tremendous amount of biodiversity and genetic resources. Because of this wealth of biological assets, the fishery industry is a vital source of food and exports for the region.

At least 270 million people now live along the coastlines of the seven nations, and the coastal population is expected to double over the next thirty years. Many Southeast Asians are economically dependent on the sea and the coral reefs. About 60 percent of the region's animal protein comes from the sea. Fisheries extend from near shore to far off reefs.[11]

The fishing zone around the South China Sea ranks fourth among the world's nineteen fishing zones in terms of total annual marine production.[12] The importance of the fishing zone around the South China Sea will increase in the near future. Fishing exports from the South China Sea zone have risen in response to increasing demand for seafood in nearby markets. The region is close to the world's top consumers of fish and seafood, Japan, South Korea, and China. Because of overfishing in the northern seas, the South China Sea is seen as becoming the region's alternative source for large-scale commercial fishing.

SEA LINES OF COMMUNICATIONS

The importance of the South China Sea is most evident as the world's second-busiest international sea lanes. Every year, more than half of the world's supertanker traffic passes through the South China Sea via the Straits of Malacca, Lumbok, or Sunda. Oil tanker traffic in the Strait of Malacca is three times that of the Suez Canal and more than five times the tanker traffic of the Panama Canal. Almost all shipments passing through the Malacca and Sunda straits must pass near the disputed Spratly Islands.[13]

The sea's strategic location makes it a particularly important passageway between the oil-exporting states in the Middle East and the oil-hungry economies in Northeast Asia. The tremendous growth of these Northeast Asian markets like China and Taiwan has resulted in an increasing demand for energy resources.

Hence, shipments passing through the South China Sea/Strait of Malacca are dominated by raw materials such as crude oil and liquefied natural gas (LNG) en route to Northeast Asian countries.

Nearly two-thirds of shipping (by tonnage) passes through the Malacca Straits, and half of the volume passing through the Spratly Islands is crude oil from the Persian Gulf.[14]

Two-thirds of the world's LNG trade passes through the South China Sea, and over half of these LNG shipments through the Sea head to Northeast Asian states. Japan is by far the world's largest consumer of LNG, followed by South Korea (second largest) and Taiwan (fifth largest),[15] and 80 percent of crude oil shipments for Japan, South Korea, and Taiwan pass through the Sea from the Middle East, Africa, and Southeast Asia.

The expected increase in consumption of energy resources among Northeast Asian markets has important implications for the increased reliance on the South China Sea passageways. In the next twenty years, oil consumption among the Asian markets is expected to rise 3 percent annually on average, with one-third of this increase coming from China alone.[16] At the same time, natural gas usage is expected to rise 4.5 percent annually on average through 2025—faster than any other fuel—with almost half of this increase coming from China.[17]

MARITIME PIRACY

Pirates seem to understand the lack of maritime policing and the absence of clear international maritime law. Given the large volume of shipping in the South China Sea and Strait of Malacca, piracy and armed robbery against shipping vessels have become a growing concern for the shipping industry, especially oil carriers. According to the International Maritime Bureau (IMB), the Indonesian/Malaysian waters around the Strait of Malacca are considered the world's most dangerous, accounting for a quarter of reported piracy cases worldwide.[18] So much piracy is based in this region that the IMB, the maritime crime prevention division of the International Chamber of Commerce, bases its Piracy Reporting Center in Kuala Lumpur, Malaysia.[19]

IMB reports that piracy attacks in the region are not only more frequent but becoming more violent. The Malaysian and Indonesian pirates are highly trained, well armed, and closely linked with the organized crime groups with an extensive network through which they sell stolen cargo.[20] Pirates now do not only steal cargo; they sometimes hijack or kill crewmembers and take the whole ship. For example, in November 1998, several pirates boarded the Panama-flagged MV *Cheung Son* and took over the ship, which carried a cargo of furnaces. They gathered the crew members together on the deck, shot the twenty-three Chinese crewmen and threw their bodies overboard.[21] Stolen vessels "disappear" when the vessel is painted with a new name and then reflagged with a different country flag.

In 2004 alone, 330 piracy cases were recorded worldwide—a notable decline from the previous year's 452 cases, but still a substantially higher figure than any year of the twentieth century. Over half of the attacks worldwide, 169 cases in 2004, occurred in Southeast Asia.[22]

ENVIRONMENTAL POLLUTION

Oil transit tankers have also been responsible for oil spills and waste dumping. Spills occur mostly by collisions or grounding. Ships also deliberately dump oil waste into the water. It is likely that they do this after cleaning the tanks to avoid having to pay to have them cleaned. These problems of environmental pollution only exacerbated transnational pollution concerns related to industrial and agricultural runoff and discharges from the South China Sea's coastal cities.

OVERFISHING

Overfishing is feared to threaten the extensive fishing industry around the South China Sea. Because of a decline in overall average fish catch, fishermen are resorting to more efficient and aggressive fishing techniques. There have also been reports of the use of illegal methods of commercial fishing like blast fishing and cyanide poisoning.[23] Overfishing not only depletes fish stocks of target species, but also changes the dynamics of the entire reef.

Over 30 percent of the world's coral reefs are found in Southeast Asia, especially around the Indonesian and Philippine islands. The destruction of the coral reefs is caused by a number of sources: overfishing, oil spills, land sedimentation from construction and land reclamation, and industrial disposal of organic and inorganic wastes like sewage and chemicals.

EAST OF EDEN

The littoral states have experienced rapid industrialization and growth over the past three decades. They exploited the natural resources of the South China Sea and its importance as one of the world's busiest shipping lanes. Unfortunately, while economic growth of these littoral countries increased the value of the South China Sea, it has also increased the military capability of the same nations. This problem is aggravated by the competing border disputes and the unwillingness of the participants, especially China, to enter into treaties that might compromise their territorial claims. The more important concern is that the slowly percolating dispute or the unrestrained maritime piracy could interrupt traffic on the sea lanes. Other problems caused by the unresolved territorial disputes are underexploitation of oil and gas reserves and overexploitation of the sea's biological wealth.

The failure to resolve the numerous and overlapping disputes has turned the South China Sea into a zone of anarchy. The various claimants not only have failed to negotiate boundaries but also have failed to regulate fishing and exploitation of seabed resources or to control maritime piracy. The result is underexploited oil and gas reserves, overfishing, rapid environmental degradation, and the worst maritime piracy anywhere in the world. The South China Sea's rapid decline will progress unchallenged until countries in the region agree to resolve their disputes.[24]

TERRITORIAL DISPUTES

The most important obstacle to conflict resolution in the South China Sea is the unresolved, overlapping territorial claims. The South China Sea issue appears complicated because of the competing claims of six different governments, the arcane nature of the various historical claims, and the impotence caused by voluntary enforcement of the United Nations Convention on the Law of the Sea. In reality, the dispute is relatively easy to understand. Starting a process to resolve or neutralize the problem, however, requires American leadership and resolve.

Six countries claim the islands of the South China Sea: the People's Republic of China, the Republic of China (Taiwan), Vietnam, Malaysia, the Philippines, and Brunei.[25] China, Taiwan, and Vietnam claim all of the islands in the South China Sea based largely on historical documents. The Philippines, Malaysia, and Brunei claim all or parts of the Spratly Islands based largely on their respective Exclusive Economic Zones (EEZs) and continental shelf. According to UNCLOS, an EEZ extends two hundred nautical miles from the low-water line on a country's coast.[26]

All the claimant countries use legal arguments, often based on exaggerated interpretations of UNCLOS articles, to justify their territorial claims. Only China, however, exhibits the combination of broad territorial claims; economic, political, and military strength; an uncompromising diplomatic stance; and demonstrated aggressiveness in pursuing its objectives. This unique combination of traits makes Beijing at once the most important player in resolving the territorial disputes and the biggest obstacle to doing so.

China's Claim

Although Beijing persists in reminding all other claimant countries that the South China Sea is Chinese sovereign territory, China has been very careful about not demarcating its specific maritime claims through international arbitration, and thus the claims are not definitively adjudicated. Other countries can only infer China's specific claims from Beijing's statements and actions, and China retains the power to define its maritime border according to its ability to intimidate smaller countries with competing claims. The following analysis, therefore, is drawn from the large body of information published about the dispute but should not be considered the final word on China's position.[27]

The Standing Committee of the National People's Congress adopted the Law on the Territorial Waters and Their Contiguous Areas (Territorial Sea Law) on February 25, 1992.

In support of that law, China's State Bureau of Surveying and Mapping (SBSM) maintains a website with a "standard" map showing the entire South China Sea from Taiwan to Indonesia's Natuna Island in an enclosed loop as territorial waters. Moreover, the SBSM website also contains regulations that govern how the standard map is used; making any version that does not include the South China Sea as Chinese territory illegal in China.[28]

Beijing uses a combination of tactics to justify its claims to the entire South China Sea. One tactic is China's interpretation of certain articles in the UNCLOS. The impracticality of drawing coastal boundaries for countries with complex and deeply indented coastlines, such as Norway, or for archipelagic states, such as the Philippines or Indonesia, was recognized in such UNCLOS provisions as Article 7, "Straight Baselines," and Article 47, "Archipelagic Baselines." These articles permit countries to draw straight boundary lines across complex or closely spaced coastal features and islands as long as they do not interfere with customary freedom of navigation. Beijing, however, uses overstated definitions of these articles and its claimed islands and coastal features to draw its territorial borders more than a thousand miles from the Chinese mainland.[29]

Additionally, although most countries involved in the dispute use the same fuzzy or exaggerated definitions of UNCLOS provisions to justify their maritime borders, Beijing does them one better by also proffering a different definition of "territorial" waters than the one proscribed in UNCLOS. For most countries, "territorial waters" extend twelve nautical miles from the low-water line along a country's coast. When Beijing signed UNCLOS, however, it included a declaration that postulated definitions of territorial waters and rights of coastal states different from those written in UNCLOS.[30] Among other things, China declared:

1. In accordance with the provisions of the United Nations Convention on the Law of the Sea, The People's Republic of China shall enjoy sovereign rights and jurisdiction over an exclusive economic zone of 200 nautical miles and the continental shelf.
2. The People's Republic of China will effect, through consultations, the delimitation of boundary of maritime jurisdiction with the states with coasts opposite or adjacent to China respectively on the basis of international law and in accordance with the equitable principle.
3. The People's Republic of China reaffirms the sovereignty over all its archipelagoes and islands as listed in Article 2 of the Law of the People's Republic of China on the Territorial Sea and Contiguous Zone which was promulgated on 25 February 1992.
4. The People's Republic of China reaffirms that the provisions of the United Nations Convention on the Law of the Sea concerning inno-

> cent passage through the territorial sea shall not prejudice the right of a coastal state to request, in accordance with its laws and regulations, a foreign state to obtain advance approval from or give prior notification to the coastal state for the passage of its warships through the territorial sea of the coastal state.

By making this declaration, China is defining how it will interpret certain sections of UNCLOS and how they apply to China's existing territorial claims. China is saying that its sovereign maritime border is two hundred nautical miles, not the traditional twelve miles. Beijing is also claiming that the islands and reefs of the South China Sea are Chinese territory and thus also have EEZs extending an additional two hundred nautical miles from these points. Finally, it is redefining China's rights as a coastal state by insisting that warships making innocent passage must first obtain Chinese permission, again a violation of both UNCLOS and the traditional laws of the sea.

The position of the Chinese government has direct implications for the freedom of navigation of all vessels traversing the South China Sea, but most importantly for America's navy and air force vessels. China's insistence that any warship traversing the South China Sea must first gain permission nullifies the rights of foreign warships to conduct innocent passage. Furthermore, warships that do traverse territorial waters have severe restrictions applied to their operations. The following are some examples as outlined by Article 19 of UNCLOS:

a) Any threat or use of force.
b) Any exercise or practice with weapons of any kind.
c) Any act aimed at collecting information.
d) Any act of propaganda.
e) The launching, landing or taking on board of any aircraft.
f) The launching, landing or taking on board any military device.
g) The carrying out of research or survey activities.

These restrictions, if applied to the entire South China Sea, would severely restrict the operations of the United Sates Navy and hinder its ability to protect both American and international shipping. For example, under the territorial waters restrictions, American carriers would be prohibited from launching aircraft. In modern navies, aircraft operations are indispensable for air-sea reconnaissance, marine mine detection, and attacking hostile ships and aircraft. Therefore, if a hostile force were to assault American or allied shipping in the South China Sea, the U.S. Navy would be helpless to detect or prevent such an attack.

Furthermore, in light of China's stated position, the dispute between China and the United States in April 2001 over the collision between a Chinese F-7 fighter and an American EP-3 reconnaissance airplane that were flying in airspace that UNCLOS defines as international should not be seen as an isolated incident. Rather, the behavior of the Chinese fighter that caused the accident (it made repeated close passes of the American aircraft to force the crew to change course, until the last pass where the Chinese fighter collided with the U.S. plane) can only be interpreted as China trying to enforce its skewed interpretation of territorial waters. China's position on its territorial waters ensures that the brazen attack on American naval aircraft could well be the first round in an escalating confrontation between China and the United States over the navigation rights in the South China Sea.

CHINA COERCES OTHER CLAIMANTS

In addition to being an explicit threat to freedom of navigation, China's penchant for unilateral use of force has unnecessarily militarized the dispute. Vietnam and China dispute ownership of the Paracel Islands. The last time there was a clash of arms between claimants was in 1988 when Chinese and Vietnamese navies fired on one another. China defeated the Vietnamese navy and now occupies all of the Paracel Islands. As far as Beijing is concerned, the Paracel Islands are no longer an issue for discussion. After this success, China signed UNCLOS, which provides arbitration mechanisms in similar territorial disputes.

Before 1995, China participated in five Indonesia hosted unofficial conferences on the South China Sea designed to explore territorial disputes. China participated in each of these conferences and agreed to the unofficial statements, including the prohibition on the use of force. Then, in 1995, it was discovered that China had built a navy station on Mischief Reef, a reef that is almost one thousand miles from the Chinese mainland, completely under water even at low tide and well within the EEZ of the Philippines. Neither the reef's location adjacent to the Philippines or its lack of dry surface prevented Chinese officials from declaring the reef "historical" Chinese territory.

From 1995 until 2005, China refused to negotiate multilaterally over the Mischief Reef, and bilateral negotiations were fruitless for Manila. The

Philippine government frequently attempted to bring Mischief Reef to the table at the ASEAN Regional Forum (ARF) and other international meetings, but without effect.

ASEAN's only diplomatic "success" was the "Declaration on the Conduct of Parties in the South China Sea" signed on November 4, 2002,[31] and the protections of that document are completely illusory. In that agreement China and the ASEAN countries agreed to peaceful resolution of the disputes and to refrain from escalating the conflict—all provisions already articulated in UNCLOS, which was signed by all the claimant countries prior to negotiating the declaration.

But redundancy is not the worst feature of the declaration; it actually nullifies UNCLOS provisions that would have benefited the smaller claimant countries in negotiations with China. Although settlement of the disputes and the UNCLOS are mentioned several times in the declaration, the document fails to layout a timetable for settlement, provide for means to compel parties to settle, or even to specifically mention UNCLOS provisions for adjudicating maritime territorial disputes. Worse yet, the declaration does not require the parties to pull back their military garrisons from disputed territories. The result is that China still maintains a military presence inside disputed territories across the South China Sea.

Since the declaration was signed, Beijing has refrained from seizing more territory in South China Sea, but considering China's already enveloping military presence throughout the disputed waters, the provision for restraint benefits China and curbs the behavior of the other claimant states. For example, the 2002 declaration prevents claimants from evicting Chinese military installations from their EEZs because that activity would "escalate" the dispute. Furthermore, the declaration also limits negotiations to those states "directly concerned." This provision prevents multilateral solutions and excludes nonclaimant states, such as the United States, from participating.

Despite the outwardly multilateral nature of an ASEAN-China declaration, the reality is that the declarations strip away ASEAN's protection provided by UNCLOS exposing the smaller countries to Chinese intimidation. Since the declaration was signed country after country has signed treaties that advantage China. For example, in 2004, after decades of negotiations, Vietnam's National Assembly ratified an agreement on the Sino-Viet boundary in the Gulf of Tonkin. In the new treaty, Beijing forced Hanoi to discard the UNCLOS-specified straight baseline, abandon Vietnam's historical claims derived from the 1887 French-Chinese Border Treaty, and concede considerable marine territory to China.[32] A year later and less than three years after signing the "Declaration on the Conduct of Parties in the South China Sea," President Arroyo of the Philippines also capitulated to Beijing's demands and signed a confidential protocol that permitted China to explore for mineral resources inside the Philippine EEZ.

Hanoi's and Manila's concessions to Beijing are critical for two reasons. First, the concessions demonstrate the efficacy of China's policy of not negotiating multilaterally; second, they validate China's territorial claims. In short, China attends international fora and signs pleasant-sounding statements but steadfastly refuses multilateral negotiations, insisting that each dispute must be resolved bilaterally, while it acts unilaterally. By so doing, it nullifies the UNCLOS arbitration mechanisms and the ASEAN unofficial conferences. Meanwhile, China continues to build up its naval and air forces in the region.

HOW STRONG IS CHINA'S CLAIM?

As stated earlier, China's claims are based largely on Beijing's unique interpretations of various articles of UNCLOS. But even a cursory examination of the articles in question indicates that China's position is not sustainable. For example, China's entire ten thousand–mile coastline is not severely indented, as is Norway's coast, and its claim to a handful of uninhabited islands and reefs do not make China an archipelago.

To demonstrate the drastic impact of China's inflated claims, one need only to examine what America's territorial boundaries would be if Washington used the same interpretations of UNCLOS that Beijing uses. In that scenario, the United States could claim a maritime border from the coast of California west past the Hawaiian Islands all the way to Guam; from Alaska and the Aleutian Islands in the north; south to Howland, Baker, and Jarvis Islands on the equator. Virtually the entire northern Pacific would be American "internal waters."[33] Furthermore, American claims would actually be more substantive because many of America's islands actually fit the UNCLOS definition of islands. UNCLOS requires that islands be inhabited and support an economy.[34] The American islands mentioned are inhabited, in some cases with robust economies, while China's "islands" are uninhabited or, in some cases, submerged reefs.

For its part, Beijing cannot demonstrate that Chinese ever inhabited the Spratly or Paracel Islands, because they are uninhabitable. There are no sources of fresh water, and these low and in some cases submerged features are seasonally exposed to the monsoons of the region. Today, the only permanent populations of these islands and reefs are military garrisons maintained at immense expense to their respective governments and at great personal risk to the members of the garrisons.

Beijing also cites various vague, questionable, and off-point historical writings supposedly dating back more than two thousand years in its attempt to document its claimed sovereignty over the South China Sea.[35] Without doubt, Chinese explorers and fishermen sailed the South China Sea for thousands of years and in some cases recorded their exploits, as did all the littoral countries, but it is equally clear that the Chinese traditionally viewed Hainan Island as the southernmost outpost of their civilization, certainly until the end of the nineteenth century.[36]

Finally, ancient Chinese commentary does not nullify the territorial rights of the indigenous Vietnamese, Philippine, Malaysian, and Bruneian peoples. The ancestors of today's Filipinos, Malaysians, and Bruneians arrived on their archipelagos long before China's written history. They did not walk to those islands, so they must have sailed or paddled through the Spratly and Paracel Islands to arrive where they are living today. Although the Spratly and Paracel Islands are too small for habitation, these people settled on every habitable island close by, and it is reasonable to assume that prehistoric Filipinos and Malays fished and economically exploited the South China Sea and its tiny islands at least as much as the distant Chinese.

FEEBLE AMERICAN POLICY

In the beginning of this new century, China is swiftly becoming the dominant power in the South China Sea. China's spectacular double-digit economic growth, vigorous foreign investment, and a military rapidly expanding in size and capability have thoroughly intimidated countries in the region. Meanwhile American foreign policy has ignored Southeast Asia, focusing only on single-faceted issues such as human rights or terrorism, while ignoring America's broader interests in the region. The only American successes have been disaster relief, but waiting to act until the next tsunami or typhoon is not a foreign policy.

So far, Washington has steadfastly refused to take sides in territorial disputes even when China occupied a reef within the EEZ of an American ally, the Philippines, and continues to expand its ever-bigger naval outpost at that location. The United States has maintained strict neutrality, refusing to condemn China's actions and merely calling for all sides to refrain from the use of force. With the most powerful country on Earth appearing afraid to antagonize Beijing, it is little wonder that the countries of ASEAN have been unwilling to take a unified stand: They fear being exposed, unprotected, to China's anger. The result: Individual countries are forced into impotent diplomatic objections, and eventually, like Vietnam and the Philippines, they capitulate to Chinese bullying and make concessions unwarranted by reasonable interpretations of UNCLOS.

Finally, American diplomacy on this issue is crippled by the Senate's failure to ratify UNCLOS or the Law of the Sea Treaty. The United Nations has been negotiating UNCLOS since 1945 when President Truman asserted U.S. jurisdiction over America's continental shelf. The negotiations were largely complete in 1982, and President Reagan's administration supported the bulk of the treaty. However, the United States and many industrialized countries objected to certain provisions, such as the decision-making process of the International Seabed Authority (ISA) and deep-sea mining regulations that would have been contrary to American interests and free market principles.

In the early 1990s, after the fall of the Soviet Union, the objectionable portions of the treaty were renegotiated and most of the countries in the world, 149 in 2006, have become parties to the treaty, including major seagoing nations and important allies of the United States such as Australia in 1999 and the United Kingdom in 2003. For the United States, both Presidents Bill Clinton and George W. Bush declared that the fixes to the treaty were sufficient, and the Senate Foreign Relations committee reported favorably on the changes in 2004, but the treaty remains unratified.[37]

The costs to the United States of not ratifying the treaty are enormous. China's growing claims over high-seas areas, not only in the South China Sea but in other adjacent seas as well, if unchallenged will limit traditional navigation of these regions. Despite China's declarations, those claims are not supported by the treaty, but only the United States navy has the ability to enforce the provisions of the treaty. Without Senate ratification, it is awkward for Washington to insist on Beijing's adherence to a treaty to which America refuses to join.

Also, because the Senate did not ratify the treaty, the United States lost its seat on the International Seabed Authority, the body set up by UNCLOS to govern sea mining. Thus the United States has no formal say in the decision making. There is also a provision for dispute settlement that could alleviate many of the disputes in the South China Sea, but again Washington cannot drag China into UNCLOS courts without ratification.

What Washington Can Do

America cannot allow China's interpretation of international law to remain unchallenged and become dominant in the region. It is in America's national interest to uphold the principle of freedom of navigation, seek stability in a volatile region, and restore order to a commercially important waterway. Furthermore, freedom of navigation in the South China Sea is of major concern to Japan, Korea, Philippines, and Australia, stalwarts in America's alliance system in Asia.

Working closely with Tokyo and Canberra, Washington should construct a caucus of countries that are not party to the territorial dispute but are directly affected by it to insist on resolution in accordance with UNCLOS. Additional countries could be Indonesia, Thailand, Singapore, South Korea, India, and the European Union. This South China Sea caucus could express the concerns of the outside countries that there must be a resolution to the territorial disputes, and it must be made based on UNCLOS and traditional law of the sea, rather than Beijing's methodology—might makes right.

The caucus can acknowledge that each of the claimants has reasons to assert its maritime borders in the South China Sea and avoid taking sides as long as the claimants adhere to a timely arbitration process. The current state of anarchy is unacceptable to American and international interests, and a clear mechanism for dispute resolution needs to be established. UNCLOS provides for an arbitration process, and Indonesia's former multilateral efforts supply a venue.

If China does not submit to a timely arbitration process, then Washington and the South China Sea caucus must abandon its agnosticism in the territorial disputes and make it clear that they view the claims of the People's Republic of China, in particular, as wholly unreasonable and a threat to international peace.

China's passive-aggressive tactic of retaining military garrisons inside disputed territory must be challenged. The U.S. and SCS caucus should make known that demilitarization of the disputed territories is key to the equitable resolution of the dispute.

As a further demonstration of the importance of unrestricted access to international waters, the United States should continue to conduct regular multilateral freedom of navigation exercises in every corner of the South China Sea. These exercises would be even more effective if they were done in collaboration with American allies, such as the Philippines, Japan, South Korea, and Australia. Inviting friendly powers such as India would escalate the importance of the exercises.

CONCLUSION

Heightened U.S. participation in resolving the maritime border dispute would encourage the smaller countries with maritime borders in the South China Sea and at the same time discourage China from further attempts to impose its will unilaterally. Substantive solutions to the border dispute, however, will require all claimant countries to negotiate in good faith and accept compromises in their most controversial claims.

To protect freedom of navigation, the United States must convince the countries in the region that continued anarchy in the South China Sea is not in their interests either. All claimant countries must demonstrate their willingness to protect their own long-term interests by seeking equitable and legally consistent solutions to the border dispute.

Lastly, it is in the world's best interests that China be embedded in rules-based organizations and that Beijing adhere to those rules. The best way for Washington to set that example is for the United States to ratify the law of the sea treaty.

• 3 •

The War on Terrorism

> Never, never, never believe any war will be smooth and easy, or that anyone who embarks on the strange voyage can measure the tides and hurricanes he will encounter. The statesman that yields to war fever must realize that once the signal is given, he is no longer the master of policy but the slave of unforeseeable and uncontrollable events.
>
> —Winston Churchill

> Force is all-conquering, but its victories are short-lived.
>
> —Abraham Lincoln

The war on terrorism is an important American foreign policy goal in Asia, and the countries with the worst terrorist problems are the countries with weak rule of law. From Japan to Pakistan and south to Australia, almost every country in the Asia-Pacific region has a terrorist group or insurgency of some kind, but terrorism is strongest in countries where the rule of law is weak. For example, in the Philippines, a democracy and an American ally, the terrorists are gaining strength, while in Indonesia, which in 1998 was ruled by an oppressive authoritarian government and was a hotbed of terrorist activities, the threat of terrorism is declining; terrorist leaders have been killed or captured, and the once-thriving terrorist organizations are dissolving from lack of new recruits.

The evolution of the war on terrorism in Indonesia and the Philippines sheds some light on what is wrong with the American counterterrorism strategy and the gaps in American counterterrorism efforts. We will examine the differences between the evolving war on terrorism in two countries, the Philippines and Indonesia, and use the lessons there to draw conclusions about America's security strategy in the region.

These mixed results illustrate some blind spots, both in regional strategy and in the American policymaking apparatus. The first limitation is in the policymaking machinery that has demonstrated a preference for military solutions to the detriment of other proven policy prescriptions. One example of this misappropriation of emphasis is in the Philippines where the bulk of American security assistance is for the armed forces when it is the Philippines' law enforcement agencies that are doing the most to combat terrorism in the country.

This problem can be traced to the Bush administration's insistence that the war on terrorism is a military effort similar to wars like World War II. President Bush has placed the Department of Defense in the lead of the global war on terrorism (GWOT) and in the absence of a regional interagency headquarters, other U.S. departments and even Congress frequently default to the military's geographic combatant commands (GCCs) to prioritize policies.

The other problem is the lack of tangible metrics to measure the success or failure of the U.S. counterterrorist strategy. Although the war against terrorism is now in its sixth year, the administration has not developed any means to measure its policies and falls back on rhetoric of a "long war" to explain the continued presence of terrorists in Asia. Not only does this oversight fail to explain the presence of terrorists, but it also overlooks the successes against the terrorist menace.

The theme of this book is that the countries of Asia should become stakeholders in the international rules-based systems, but this applies equally to the rule of law inside Asian countries. This chapter will examine the differences between the evolving war on terrorism in the Philippines and Indonesia and draw conclusions about America's security strategy in the region.

INDONESIA

After the fall of the authoritarian cleptocrat President Haji Mohammad Suharto in 1998, Indonesia was host to a number of terrorist groups and insurgencies, of which the most prominent was Jemaah Islamiyah (JI)—an Al Qaeda–linked group that had its theological genesis in Darul Islam but now spread across Southeast Asia. JI chapters were found in Indonesia, Singapore, Philippines, and Malaysia. Estimates of its size ranged into the tens of thousands.

Following the October 2002 bombing in Bali and the increasing evidence of the organization's responsibility for a series of devastating bomb attacks all across Southeast Asia, JI was considered to be the most dangerous terrorist group in Southeast Asia. Additional terrorist activity in Indonesia included the Free Aceh Movement and a number of other smaller Islamic and ethnic militant groups.

As thousands continued dying from terrorist attacks across the Indonesian archipelago, terrorism posed the most urgent security threat facing the weak Indonesian government. Because of the Indonesian military's association with the former dictatorship, its poor human rights record, and manifest corruption, American, Australian, and Japanese policy proscribed providing security assistance to the military. Instead, the United States and other countries focused on training and equipping law enforcement institutions such as the police, prosecutors, and the judicial system.

While the United States was a key player in providing training and assistance to the Indonesian police and in establishing an elite antiterrorist police unit, called Detachment 88, Australia was also aggressive in pursuing reform and training of Indonesia's police force. Most of the victims of the 2002 Bali bombing were Australian and Canberra made reform of Indonesia's police force a national priority. Australia contributed significantly to building Indonesia's counterterrorism capacity by training Indonesian law enforcement in counterterrorism and transnational crime, money laundering and the flow of funds to terrorists, and enhancing travel security by strengthening airport, immigration, and customs control capabilities.

The most remarkable changes in Indonesia, however, occurred among Indonesians and its government. In 1998, Indonesia was ruled by a corrupt and authoritarian dictatorship propped up by the military. While Indonesia's dictator, President Suharto, had already fallen by 9/11, Indonesia was still undergoing a painful transition to democracy. The country was also still recovering from the impact of the 1997 Asian economic crisis, and a series of post-Suharto presidents was too weak to overcome the instability left by the political vacuum in the once tightly controlled central government. A combination of these factors plus a lack of political will to confront militant Islam, evident by the Indonesian government's outright denial of the existence of terrorists in the country, hampered Indonesia's war against terrorism.

Then on October 12, 2002, several bombs detonated in a crowded tourist area of Bali, killing more than two hundred people. The Bali bombing was followed by a series of other bombings across the country including key landmarks in the capital Jakarta. Although the bombers claimed they were aiming to kill foreigners, most victims were Muslim Indonesians. These bombings marked a wakeup call for the Indonesians. Terrorism was no longer seen as a foreign or American problem but a dangerous domestic disease.

Moving parallel to Indonesians' realization that they were the targets of terrorists was a remarkable democratic transition. Few countries can claim to have moved from dictatorship to democracy, unaided, in only six years. By 2004, Indonesia had eliminated the military's appointed seats in the national legislature, separated its police from the military, held nationwide legislative elections, and for the first time directly elected its president.

The transformation of Indonesia's terrorist threat was equally remarkable. Today, JI is significantly weaker, divided and on the run. JI's membership and recruiting have steeply declined. The International Crisis Group characterizes the remaining JI membership as divided, split between a small fanatic core of about fifty people that still want to continue the terrorist campaign and a main body of around one thousand that cling to the dream of an Indonesian Islamic state but are reluctant to participate in indiscriminate terrorist attacks.

Almost all of JI's leadership is detained or killed, and two hundred of their adherents have been arrested. In the meantime, the Indonesian police keep a close watch on militant offshoots of what's left of the organization. In 2006, Indonesian police killed JI's top bomb maker, Azahari bin Husin, who was responsible for the second Bali bombing in November 2005. Husin's other chief tactical expert, Noordin Top, is now under intense police pressure and stays on the run.

In addition to defeating JI, President Susilo Bambang Yudhoyono also successfully negotiated a peace agreement with the Free Aceh Movement, ending one of Indonesia's oldest and bloodiest insurgencies and significantly improving security in the Malacca Straits. Most of the militant groups that operated in Indonesia have either disappeared or have substantially reduced capabilities.

THE PHILIPPINES

On the surface, the Philippines appeared to be Southeast Asia's most enthusiastic ally in the war on terrorism, but in reality, Manila has been a weak and troublesome partner. The Philippines is a treaty ally of the United States and suffers from its own terrorist problem. After 9/11, President Gloria Macapagal-Arroyo invoked the U.S.-Philippine security treaty and publicly declared that her country was firmly allied with the United States in the war on terrorism. In fact, Philippine politicians are fond of saying that on 9/11 America joined the Philippines in the war against terrorism.

In return, Washington provided about $100 million a year to the Philippines in various aid packages, mostly in the form of security assistance to the military. That figure does not include the cost to the Pentagon for American military training exercises in the Philippines. After the U.S.-Philippines Visiting Forces Agreement was signed in 1998,[1] the United States and the Philippines have conducted a number of joint military exercises, which accelerated in size and duration after 9/11. In comparison, over the same years, American assistance to Indonesia's counterterrorism programs totaled only $27 million.[2]

Despite this enormous commitment of American resources, the Philippine state was dissolving out from under American efforts. Lurching from crisis to crisis, the Philippine government appears incapable of undertaking a long-term counterterrorist strategy, and the Bush administration continues to pour in more and more money without any change to strategy or priorities.

The State Department's 2004 *Country Report on Terrorism* states, "The Philippines continues to cooperate on a range of bilateral and multilateral counterterrorism efforts," and "Philippine authorities had a number of successes against terrorists in 2004." The report goes on to describe the accomplishments of the Philippine antiterrorism efforts, but without presenting analysis on how these "successes" have diminished the terrorist threat. In fact, the terrorist threat is growing in the Philippines.

The 2005 *Country Report on Terrorism* is much better at recognizing the disintegrating security situation in the country. The Philippine section acknowledges, "The major and disturbing trend has been the growing cooperation among Islamic terrorist organizations operating in the country." But the report, which came out in May 2006, was too late to stop another budget increase for the Philippines in 2006. In that year, the level of assistance topped 130 million U.S. dollars.

There are three main terrorist groups in the Philippines: the communist New People's Army (NPA); the Moro Islamic Liberation Front (MILF), a Muslim/ethnic separatist organization; and the Abu Sayyaf Group (ASG), a true terrorist group with direct links to Al Qaeda. Despite the "successes" trumpeted in the 2004 *Country Report on Terrorism*, since 9/11, the Philippines has made no substantial progress against any of these terrorist groups. The State Department's successes are just meaningless lists of terrorists arrested and programs implemented, free of any content or analysis. Meanwhile, reports suggest that all three organizations are growing in size and capability.

The New People's Army, which had nearly dropped out of sight after the fall of President Ferdinand Marcos in 1986 and the fall of the Soviet Union in 1989, is growing again. The strength of the NPA fell dramatically from its Marcos-era peak of twenty-five thousand to approximately six thousand by 2000. Since 9/11, the NPA has gained new strength, and estimates of the number of active fighters ranged as high as ten thousand in 2006.

In 2001, the Philippine government was negotiating with the MILF with hopes of finding a political solution to the insurgency, similar to the political agreement made with the Moro National Liberation Front (MNLF) in 1996. The United States, however, was concerned that the MILF was harboring a number of international terrorists and operating terrorist training camps in its territory. Despite these misgivings, Washington supported Manila's negotiation efforts. Today, Manila and the MILF negotiations have made no substantive progress, and the MILF still harbors and trains terrorist groups in its territory.

In the beginning of the war on terrorism, President Arroyo repeatedly vowed to crush the Abu Sayyaf Group. American-Philippine military operations soon displaced Abu Sayyaf from its base on Basilan Island and reduced its number from an estimated 1,000 terrorists to less than 250. Despite this initial success, by 2006, the Abu Sayyaf has returned to its former prominence, claiming responsibility for a host of terrorist attacks across the Philippine archipelago.

The fault of the Philippine counterterrorism strategy appears to lie, at least in part, with the Filipinos' view of President Arroyo as corrupt and above the law. While the 2004 elections in Indonesia strengthened the legitimacy and authority of the state, the 2004 presidential election in the Philippines delegitimized the state and ignited a period of chronic crisis in Manila.

Many Filipinos believe that the 2004 elections were stolen by Arroyo. The release of a tape in 2005, mockingly called the "Hello Garcia" tape, in which Arroyo was caught in a telephone conversation with an election official in an apparent attempt to rig the 2004 election, pulverized her popularity. Soon street protests and calls for "People Power" paralyzed metro-Manila. To preempt yet another extraconstitutional change of president (the third including Marcos's ouster, and Arroyo came to power in the second people power demonstration), her political party, which held a majority in the Philippine Congress, prevented her impeachment.

Arroyo's diminished administration is unable to rule. Not only is terrorism on the rise, but lawlessness and extrajudicial murders are also proliferating. The Reporters without Borders website says that fifty-two reporters who covered the Philippines have been murdered between 1986 and 2006, and forty-two of those cases remain unsolved. The Committee for the Protection of Journalists says that twenty-two have been murdered since 2000, making the Philippines the most murderous country in the world for journalists over that period.

On April 5, 2006, the *New York Times* carried a story that alleges intimidation of the press by security forces in the Philippines. Members of the Philippines press corps whom I spoke with in Washington confirmed a campaign of oppression and at least one of them had been directly intimidated and had property confiscated by the Philippines military.[3] Elsewhere, Philippines troops surrounded a television station on the islands for more than a week recently to punish negative reporting.

No one claims that President Arroyo ordered or knew of any of the killings of reporters, but the government's inability to apprehend the killers is an indicator of how much the rule of law has deteriorated under President Arroyo. Meanwhile, the Bush administration continues to prop up the Arroyo regime with huge aid packages.

The differences between Indonesia and the Philippines are not black-and-white. There is still a considerable amount of gray in both countries. For example, Indonesia has yet to declare Jemaah Islamiyah as a terrorist group, the bloody intercommunal civil war in the Moluccas Islands continues unabated, and the Indonesian military operations in Papua continue to aggravate a chronic insurgency. Furthermore, although organized, centrally planned terrorist attacks are on the decline, there are still many microgroups, committing attacks on their own initiative.

In her defense, Arroyo is not the only president to experience trouble governing in the Philippines. She labors inside a constitutional structure that suppresses economic development and diffuses legislative accountability to a degree that practically guarantees demagoguery and corruption.

Fault lies in Washington as well. American counterterrorism assistance was way off target in Southeast Asia. Before 2006, American security assistance focused on the Indonesian police largely because the Indonesian military was disqualified by Congress, not because of a clever strategy. Proof is in the Philippines, where American strategy did focus on security assistance to the military. There are fewer Philippine police than soldiers, but the police are capturing the lion's share of terrorists.

When one compares results, Indonesia is clearly more successful than the Philippines in reducing the terrorist threat. The implications for American strategy are clear as well. The current approach of fighting the war on terrorism with the military and focusing on military assistance needs to change. The terrorist threat is not a military threat but a law-and-order issue. Furthermore, there is no effort (at least no public effort) in Washington to collect data on the war on terrorism and then to analyze that data to adjust the counterterrorism strategy.

SINS OF OMISSION

The problem of the American combating terrorism policy appears to stem from two omissions, first the lack of a multiagency regional headquarters to craft and execute a regional strategy and second, the lack of metrics to measure the success (or lack of it) of any given policy or strategy against the terrorists.

Almost every cabinet level department in the U.S. government have regional organizations—for example, the Department of States has a Bureau of East Asia and Pacific Affairs and an Office of the Coordinator for Counter terrorism—but these Asia-Pacific-focused organizations in each of the departments rarely, if ever, meet to discuss the war against terrorism in Asia. Instead, the Bush administration gave the Department of Defense the lead and the other departments support.

The Defense Department did form a Joint Interagency Coordination Group (JIACG) to "establish operational connections between civilian and military departments and agencies that will improve planning and coordination within the government."[4] But this organization faces two hurdles: one, it is not a command but a coordinating group; and second, it is a department of defense organization, and the war against terrorism in the Asia-Pacific has no military solution.

UNITED STATES PACIFIC COMMAND (USPACOM)

American policy acknowledges the need for a comprehensive approach including economic, political, law enforcement, and military dimensions, but the only regional organizations to execute such a policy are the Department of Defense's Geographic Combatant Commands (GCCs).

In the Asia-Pacific, the GCC is the Pacific Command, or PACOM. No other cabinet-level department maintains such high-level regionally based headquarters to coordinate its responsibilities in the national counterterrorism strategy. Nor is there a single regionally based headquarters that coordinates all of the various departmental slices of plans and resources. The consequence of this omission is that the terrorist strategy is invariably defined by the headquarters that is there. In Asia, it is PACOM.

PACOM's first priority is to "prosecute and win the global war on terrorism." That leaves little room to doubt that PACOM considers the GWOT a military fight. Because of the authority that regional perspective gives PACOM, and the lack of any other regionally based headquarters to provide alternative solutions, Congress and the administration invariably default to PACOM's recommendation, and military assistance gains the lion's share of the counterterrorism resources in Asia.

Despite PACOM's recognition of an interagency view of the region, seeing over the rim of the military box is clearly a problem for PACOM's commanders. For example, in the Philippines, one Philippine embassy official stationed in Washington said that the police apprehended 80 percent of the terrorists captured in that country. In numerous interviews with Filipino officials, of all political stripes, they emphasize the need for greater law enforcement in the country. One senior member of the Reform Army Movement suggested that to fight terrorism in the Philippines, it would be better to reduce the Philippine army to a single battalion and use the money saved to increase the size and capability of the police force.[5]

By 2006, the State Department had partially gotten the message. The department's 2005 *Country Reports on Terrorism* states, "Special counterterrorism units within the police still played the lead role in conducting counterterrorism investigations."[6] Additionally, the report identifies some of the many law enforcement shortcomings, including the absence of an antiterrorist law, restrictions on gathering evidence, and "rampant corruption, low morale, inadequate salaries, recruitment and retention difficulties, lack of information technology upgrades, and lack of cooperation between police and prosecutors."[7] These problems need to be addressed, and American counterterrorism assistance to the police could help Indonesia combat its terrorist problem.

A Congressional Research Service (CRS) report for Congress on trends in terrorism in 2006 noted that "terrorist acts are becoming more the product of localized micro-actors, it raises the question of whether United

States anti-terror strategy and tactics should reflect a more international law-enforcement approach."[8]

But law enforcement is not where the money is. Because of PACOM's unchallenged authority on regional issues in Congress and the administration, American aid to the Philippines continues to focus on military assistance. The U.S. fiscal year 2006 security assistance budget to the Philippine military was ten times the law enforcement assistance—$50.5 million for the military compared with $5 million for law enforcement projects, out of a total aid budget of $130 million for the Philippines.

The same military blinders can be seen in PACOM's policy toward Indonesia. In Indonesia, the military has almost no role in the war on terrorism. Instead, the government has delegated the job to the police. General Dai Bachtiar, Indonesia's national police chief, best expressed Indonesia's designation of authority in 2005 when he said, "Indonesia's police are in charge of the war on terror."[9]

Nevertheless, a succession of PACOM commanders misstate the nature of Indonesia's participation in the war on terrorism and assert a role for the Indonesian military (known by its Indonesian acronym TNI, for *Tentara Nasional Indonesia*) that is simply not correct.

In March 2002, Admiral Dennis Blair, then commander of Pacific Command, told journalists at the Council of Foreign Relations that "the TNI have counter-terrorism responsibilities."[10]

Again in June 2003, in front of the House International Relations Committee, PACOM's next commander, Admiral Thomas B. Fargo, said about the TNI, "Particularly important is influencing the younger generation of officers to support the struggle against terrorism."[11]

With another opportunity to get it right in March 2006, Admiral Fargo's replacement as PACOM commander, Admiral William J. Fallon, repeated Fargo's and Blair's mistaken assertions to the Senate. Fallon's testimony provides a clear window on the myopia of military leadership in Asia:

> To support and accelerate the Indonesian counter-terrorism actions, and to enhance maritime security, particularly in the strategically important Straits of Malacca, we endorse a rapid, concerted infusion of assistance. Aid to the Indonesian military (TNI) will help sustain ongoing reforms as well as increase capacity for actions against security threats and bolster their professionalism. Our assistance to the TNI will contribute to the long-term success of the Indonesian democracy—and ultimately—help remove conditions that breed terrorism.[12]

Like old-time elixir salesmen, PACOM commanders sell security cooperation as a cure to every ill of developing countries. Reviewing Fallon's statement, one can see that he attributes almost mystical properties to security assistance. Fallon proposes that it will not only cure terrorism but "bolster professionalism" and promote the "long term success of democracy," and later in his testimony he touts the TNI's "demonstrated support for human rights."

Not only is PACOM's position different from the Indonesian government's position, but it is also coming into conflict with American policy. For example, Congress is not as sanguine about the human rights record of the Indonesian military (the TNI's immolation of East Timor in 1999; its current operations in West Papua highlight the problem). Congress continues to express concerns about the TNI and to carefully observe how security assistance is used.

Additionally, although GCCs are required to synchronize their theater security cooperation strategies with ambassadors, there are many problems in execution. For example, PACOM's position interfered with the U.S. Embassy in Jakarta's ability to execute American policy. Robert Gelbard, ambassador to Indonesia from 1998 to 2002, had a running feud over PACOM's foreign policy versus the foreign policy of the United States.

The persistent emphasis on military solutions over other more effective programs is a reflection of the PACOM commanders' bureaucratic responsibility to promote military priorities. This is not to say that PACOM does not recognize the value of allowing other agencies to participate in the GWOT in the Pacific. PACOM formed a Joint Interagency Coordination Group for Counter Terrorism (JIACG-CT) in 2003. By 2006, the interagency group was called the Joint Interagency Task Force—West (JIATF-W) with the mission of fighting the war on terror by attacking transnational crime.[13] But GCC subordinate organizations, led by the military, still place military priorities over the considerations of other agencies.

To overcome military dominance of strategy,[14] the Asia-Pacific needs a regional interagency headquarters. The current U.S. embassy system provides a model on how a regional interagency headquarters would work. Each country ambassador has an interagency "country team" with representatives from most government agencies. But the ambassador's authority does not extend beyond the borders of the country to which he or she is accredited.

A regional assistant secretary should have a staff that includes PACOM as a subordinate headquarters and the equivalent regional headquarters from the Departments of Justice, State, Treasury, Labor, Commerce, and Homeland Security. This headquarters should be permanently stationed in the theater.

Planning and implementation must be done in the theater, in concert with the military and other agencies, where planners can gain firsthand knowledge of the success and failure of their strategies and the conditions that affect policies.

A similar idea was originally proposed by James Carafano and I when we wrote "Winning the Peace: Principles for Post Conflict Operations,"[15] but the proposal in that paper does not resolve the issue of a dominant military perspective because the proposed interagency staff was still under the GCC commander. This new proposal is to reverse that bureaucratic relationship and subordinate the GCCs to the regional assistant secretaries.

Because of the broad political perspective of an assistant secretary with an interagency staff and a regional strategy, the functions of the position could extend beyond the war on terrorism to other regional security issues, such as drug smuggling, disaster response, and even international trade. The Asia-Pacific assistant secretary would have the mission and resources to tailor the American policy according to national interests.

MEASURING SUCCESS

The other missing element in the regional strategy is the lack of metrics to measure whether or not the counterterrorism strategy is working.

The most prominent example of the lack of quantitative data or analysis is the Department of State's publication *Patterns of Global Terrorism*, which was discontinued in 2003 in a storm of controversy and replaced in 2004 by the far less analytical (and thus less controversial) *Country Reports on Terrorism*. The 2004 report provides a comprehensive list of countries with terrorist problems and another list of terrorist groups, but it is studiously lacking in data or analysis. The 2005 report was much better, but the numbers focused solely on terrorist incidents and did not provide data about the capture or neutralization of terrorists or terrorist groups. Without that information, it is difficult to measure the success of a policy or strategy.

Essentially, the State Department is measuring quantitative data or "outputs" and not analyzing the outcomes. For example, if one hundred terrorists are captured in country X, does that mean all the terrorists were captured in that country or that only 10 percent of the terrorists were captured?

The Department of State (DOS) is required by law to provide this report to Congress every year. It is not the best solution for DOS to meet Congress's minimum requirements and dumb down the report to avoid controversy. Instead, DOS should refine the report to make it a more useful tool for combating terrorism. Or, perhaps more appropriately, Congress could task the intelligence community—which is, after all, composed of research organizations—to research and publish an unclassified terrorist report with sufficient data and analysis to be a useful tool to Washington policymakers.

The controversy over *Patterns of Global Terrorism* had to do with a dispute over the number of reported terrorist attacks. Simply knowing the number of terrorist attacks alone is insufficient to judge the relative success of a particular policy or strategy. For example, even though terrorists and their organizations are on the decline in Indonesia, there are still a small number of active and dedicated terrorists who can and do launch attacks, so simply knowing the number of attacks does not clarify the fundamentals of success against terrorism. The following are some factors that should be captured in an improved *Global Report on Terrorism.*

How many terrorists have been captured? The data should include the total number of suspected terrorists captured by American and foreign governments. How many were subsequently released, prosecuted, or detained as enemy combatants? Provide information on where and under what circumstances they were captured.

Who captured the terrorists? The data should explain who captured them, whether by police or whether they were picked up on the battlefield by the military. Was American cooperation involved, and if so, which programs were the most helpful?

How many terrorist groups are there? Useful information would include how big the groups are. Provide data that shows whether they are getting bigger or smaller and whether or not a country is getting more or fewer terrorist groups.

One might wonder whether this kind of data is already being collected and analyzed by the intelligence community, such as the Central Intelligence Agency, the Defense Intelligence Agency, and others. We do not have access to classified reports so cannot say what is or is not available to policymakers, but it is evident that either the intelligence community is not conducting analysis in a form that policymakers find useful, or they are publishing a similar document, but the analysis is being ignored by policymakers. In either case, an annual unclassified report to Congress that contains that kind of information and is available to the public would be a powerful tool for citizen oversight of the war on terrorism.

Another metric that is overlooked is public opinion polling in terrorist source countries. The terrorist, like Mao's famous dictum about guerrillas, "moves among the people as a fish swims in the sea." Terrorists cannot function without popular support or at least acceptance.

There are a number of groups taking public opinion polls in Asia, and these polls, if used properly, could serve as barometers of terrorist support and for effectiveness of American policies. One example is the Pew Charitable Trusts, which is a nonprofit organization that publishes a host of reputable public opinion polls, some which touch on issues dealing with the war on terrorism. The most important polling organization for understanding the progress of American policies in the war on terrorism is Terror Free Tomorrow (TFT), a Washington-based nongovernmental organization (NGO) whose mission is to "understand and erode the popular support base that empowers global terrorism."

TFT has taken public opinion polls in Indonesia and Pakistan with remarkable results. Pakistanis were polled in November 2005, one month after a devastating earthquake shook the country. The poll found that American aid to earthquake victims sparked a surge in the favorable opinion of the United States and an equal downturn in support for Osama bin Laden. TFT found the same change in public opinion in Indonesia after the tsunami.[16]

I spoke with Ken Ballen, TFT president, about expanding his organization to take many more polls by contracting with the government. His concern was that accepting government money could stigmatize his efforts by associating his organization with the government's policies that he was measuring. He may be right, but there are a host of corporations, such as the Gallup Organization, that do public opinion polling as a business. Public opinion polling is an invaluable tool to forming counterterrorist strategies and measuring their success. Not only should American policymakers follow already-published polls, but they should also fund additional polling to measure the effect of specific policies and strategies.

CONCLUSION

In World War II, President Franklin Delano Roosevelt did not send J. Edgar Hoover, the director of the Federal Bureau of Investigation, to command an aircraft carrier task force against the Japanese in the Pacific. Analogous to that scenario, in the GWOT, the president should not expect admirals to fight terrorists in Philippine barrios or Indonesian kampongs, but that is exactly what has happened.

The war against terrorism in Asia is no more a military campaign than the "war on drugs" or the "war against poverty." Although there are some successes, they are made despite the military rather than because of it. Instead, what is needed in the Asia-Pacific theater is a civilian at the rank of ambassador or assistant secretary with an interagency headquarters, the political backing of the president and Congress, subordinate only to the secretary of state, with a portfolio to combat terrorism, transnational crimes, and other security threats.

Al Qaeda and its affiliate terrorist groups, such as Jemaah Islamiyah and Abu Sayyaf, are still at large and still dangerous. The world's governments have taken actions aimed at crippling the terrorist organizations, but much more needs to be done. No matter the title of the position, America needs one person in the Asia-Pacific region to see the big picture and to coordinate the myriad U.S. programs to win the war on terror. Lastly, that person needs good intelligence and the metrics by which he or she can judge the success of American policies.

• 4 •

Nuclear-Armed Asia

I know not with what weapons World War III will be fought,
but World War IV will be fought with sticks and stones.

—Albert Einstein

In the Asia-Pacific region, there are five nuclear-armed states: the United States, China, India, Pakistan, and North Korea. It is no coincidence that among these five countries, the worst proliferators of nuclear weapon technology, China, North Korea, and Pakistan, are also the least democratic.

Despite its continued violation of nonproliferation rules and standards, China continues to enjoy the same privileges as the United States and the other nuclear powers under the rules of international nuclear nonproliferation because China conducted nuclear tests before 1967. At the same time, North Korea, Pakistan, and India are treated equally as pariah states, because they developed nuclear programs after that arbitrary date.

Dealing with the complex and interrelated problems posed by these nuclear-armed states will challenge American foreign policy in Asia and globally. The trick will be to accommodate the undeniable fact of friendly, democratic India as a nuclear power while maintaining America's long-term nonproliferation goals.[1]

DEFINING TERMS AND INSTITUTIONS

As arms control amateurs, we have found that the language of arms control is too complex and technical for comprehending its challenges, especially in an international context. Proliferation jargon is filled with arcane language, unfamiliar acronyms, and bureaucratic definitions. To assist the reader, we will begin by defining some of the terms and institutions that make up the international nuclear nonproliferation regime and define the rest as we come to them in the narrative.

International Nuclear Nonproliferation Regime

This regime is defined as the collection of international treaties, agreements, and institutions that govern the production and transfer of nuclear weapons, related technologies, and their means of delivery. The means of delivery is usually defined as missiles.

The Nuclear Suppliers Group (NSG)

NSG was established in 1975 in response to India's 1974 nuclear test. The NSG is comprised of forty-four countries that produce and supply nuclear technologies. The institution sets guidelines on export controls to ensure that nuclear transfers do not get diverted to unsafeguarded nuclear fuel cycles or for nuclear weapons programs.

The Proliferation Security Initiative (PSI)

PSI was formed in 2003, as a response to 9/11 and the acknowledgment of the numerous loopholes in the current nonproliferation arrangements. It is a partnership of member states that seek to harmonize effective and coordinated security methods to prevent and stop shipments of weapons of mass destruction (WMD) and nuclear technology from getting into the hands of terrorists or rogue countries. Intervention can and does mean intercepting ships, planes, or land transfers of nuclear contraband.

International Atomic Energy Agency (IAEA)

The IAEA is the United Nations watchdog group tasked to assist in the expansion of the use of nuclear energy while ensuring that the reactors and technologies under its jurisdiction are not used for military purposes.

De Jure Nuclear Weapons States

This term refers to the five acknowledged nuclear weapons states at the time the Nuclear Nonproliferation Treaty was opened for signature.[2] These countries are the United States, United Kingdom, France, the Soviet Union (now Russia), and China.

De Facto Nuclear Weapons States

This refers to states that have never joined the Nuclear Nonproliferation Treaty or have withdrawn from the treaty to develop nuclear weapons capability.[3] These countries are Israel, India, Pakistan, and North Korea. At the time of this writing, Iran is believed to have an active nuclear weapons program.

SRBM, MRBM, LRBM, and ICBM

Respectively, these acronyms refer to short-range, medium-range, long-range, and intercontinental ballistic missiles.

THE INDISPENSABLE TREATY

The Treaty on the Non-Proliferation of Nuclear Weapons (NPT) is the world's most important diplomatic tool for controlling the spread of nuclear weapons and technology. All the other agreements and institutions of the nonproliferation regime are based on NPT principles and designed to support the goals set forth in the NPT.

The treaty was endorsed by the United Nations and opened for signing in 1968. The primary goal of the NPT bargain was to first slow down the speed of nuclear proliferation, which at that time was rapidly gaining momentum. The NPT does this by limiting the number of states with nuclear weapons. It designates countries that prior to January 1967 had detonated a nuclear device be declared Nuclear Weapon States. Those countries that did not possess nuclear weapons promised not to pursue them. In return for not developing nuclear weapon technology, the nonweapon states are guaranteed that peaceful nuclear technology would be available for their use. Eventually, however, the NPT aims to persuade all countries to nuclear disarmament altogether.

At its inception, the treaty preempted the nuclear weapon programs of a number of states, including Germany, Italy, Japan, Sweden, and Switzerland. The United States used this principle set out in the NPT to pressure countries that began nuclear weapon programs like South Africa, South Korea, Taiwan, Brazil, and Argentina to give them up. At the end of the Cold War, the international community pursued NPT goals in the former Soviet republics and managed to persuade all former Soviet states but Russia to give up the weapons they had inherited from the Soviet Union. These examples demonstrate that dismantling nuclear arsenals is possible and that the NPT is by far the most effective instrument to achieve this.

Lastly, there are a large and growing number of countries that possess the technological capability to build the bomb but have not done so because of their commitments to the NPT and because they trust in the efficacy of the treaty to prevent other states from gaining new nuclear weapons.

Without question, the NPT continues to be a valuable foreign policy tool in nonproliferation issues. Because the NPT is the foundation of almost all nonproliferation efforts, attempts to undermine the treaty will create a negative domino effect on the international nonproliferation regime and then create an extremely dangerous security problem for the United States and the rest of the world.

THE PROBLEM OF DE FACTO WEAPON STATES

During the Cold War, the five de jure weapon states formed two blocks, with the NATO countries of the United States, France, and the United Kingdom on one side and the Soviet Union on the opposing side. Although China was a weapon state, its limited capability gave Beijing little leverage or motivation to play a role in the arms control debates of the period.

The Cold War antagonists possessed sufficient nuclear weapons to wipe out all life on Earth several times over, but from the perspective of a proliferation regime, negotiations were eased by the mere fact that there were so few parties to negotiate with. The growing number of countries with nuclear weapons, countries with nuclear technology, or countries that do not possess either weapons or nuclear reactors but have sophisticated industries capable of producing dual-use items, has substantially multiplied the negotiating parties and increased the opportunity for intended or mistaken proliferation.

Another problem is that the Cold War motivations for possessing nuclear weapons no longer apply. The de facto weapon states develop nuclear capability for a variety of reasons, not all of them related to deterrence. For example, Israel is presumed to have the weapons for traditional, threat-based deterrence, but North Korea appears to possess nuclear weapons for use as a bargaining tool.

New Delhi, on the other hand, considers that its balance of power with China is lopsided, not only because of India's former lack of a nuclear deterrence but also because of China's place as a permanent member of the United Nations Security Council and an official NPT nuclear weapon state. So New Delhi is not ashamed to admit that one of the reasons for developing its weapons is to gain the trappings of a great power New Delhi believes is denied India by the NPT and the United Nations.

Lastly, the de facto weapon states differ from one another in their commitment to the broader principles of nonproliferation and norms of international behavior. Israel, for example, does not regularly threaten its neighbors with total destruction, as North Korea has. Neither does India proliferate nuclear technology as Pakistan has. Thus negotiators wishing to convince countries to reduce or eliminate their nuclear weapons must address concerns beyond the balance of power considerations of the Cold War.

ASIAN PROLIFERATION

For the purposes of this chapter, it is instructive to examine Asia's nuclear weapon technology proliferation networks in order to guide American policymakers. In the last few years the world's efforts to contain nuclear technology have benefited from the decision by Pakistan and Libya to be transparent about their proliferation activities. The full extent of these networks and the ease with which Asian countries can bypass the NPT regime is both revealing and frightening.

THE A. Q. KHAN NUCLEAR PROLIFERATION NETWORK

Dr. Abdul Qadeer Khan, the father of Pakistan's bomb, was born in Bhopal, India, in 1935 into a middle-class Muslim family. They migrated to Pakistan in 1952 following the partition of India. Khan graduated from Karachi University as an engineer and then moved to Europe to complete his studies, eventually earning his doctorate in 1972 from Catholic University of Leuven in Belgium.

Following his graduation, Khan found a position with the Physical Dynamics Research Laboratory in Amsterdam, Netherlands, which was a subcontractor for URENCO, an organization founded in 1970 to produce enriched uranium for Europe's nuclear reactors. By May 1974, the same time India tested its first nuclear weapons, Khan already had access to most of URENCO's secret technologies.

Khan immediately began stealing URENCO's nuclear technology secrets and passed them to Pakistani intelligence agents. Although Dutch authorities appeared completely oblivious to Khan's espionage activities, he departed suddenly for Pakistan in January 1976. Back in Pakistan he established the A. Q. Khan Research Laboratories (KRL) that, besides nuclear weapons, also carries out other high-tech weapon development, including Pakistan's missile program.

The Khan network began as an import operation to supply Pakistan's gas-centrifuge program in the 1970s, evolving slowly into a transnational network that traded gas centrifuges[4] and production capabilities, nuclear weapons designs and parts, and also provided technical consulting to assemble and operate sensitive facilities.

Although the key leaders and providers of the network were located in Pakistan, the Khan network had other associates spread across the world, including Switzerland, the United Kingdom, the United Arab Emirates, Turkey, South Africa, and Malaysia (see table 4.1).[5]

The network decentralized its operations across countries so that its support group of technicians, suppliers, and manufacturers remained ignorant of their role.[6] After a supplier/manufacturer produced an item, the Khan network created complicated transportation arrangements to confuse authorities on final destination and end-user details. Key workshops include the following:

- Scomi Precision Engineering (SCOPE), Malaysia, production of centrifuge components
- Tradefin Engineering,[7] South Africa, production of equipment to withdraw hexafluoride gas from uranium enriched in centrifuge
- Krisch Engineering, Germany, supplier
- Gulf Technical Industries, Dubai, front company—co-owned by Paul Griffin and BSA Tahir
- SMB Companies, Dubai/Malaysia, front company—used to cover orders and financial transactions

The key behind the Khan network's success in escaping nonproliferation mechanisms lay in its ability to exploit weaknesses in national export control systems. In fact, two of the network's suppliers were NSG members, Turkey

Table 4.1. The Global A. Q. Khan Network

Gerhard Wisser	German	Coordinated production of centrifuges in South Africa for delivery to Libya
Gotthard Lerch	German	Coordinated production of centrifuges in South Africa for delivery to Libya
Heinz Mebus	German	Involved in discussions between the nuclear arms expert and Iran to supply centrifuge designs about 1984–1985
Urs Tinner	Swiss	Oversaw production of centrifuges in Malaysia for delivery to Libya
Gunas Jireh	Turkish	Alleged to have supplied aluminum casting and dynamo to Libya at the request of the nuclear arms expert
Selim Alguadis	Turkish	Supplied electrical cabinets and power supplier-voltage regulator to Libya. Two weeks after action against the ship *BBC China* in Taranto, Italy, on October 4, 2003, Tahir arranged the transshipment of electrical cabinets and power supplier-voltage regulator to Libya through Dubai on behalf of Selim Alguadis.
Peter and Paul Griffin	British (currently in France)	Supplied the layout plan for the Machine Shop 1001 for Libya. Arranged for Libyan technicians to attend training in Spain. Supplies Libya with Italian technician.
B. S. A. Tahir	Sri Lankan	Based in Dubai; middleman for deliveries to Libya and Iran; money-laundering payments. Also oversaw the activities at SCOPE. (Tahir married a Malaysian and has PR status in Malaysia. His contacts with Khan go back to the 1980s when his company, SMB Group, supplied air conditioning to the Khan Research Laboratory.*)

*Source: Malaysian Investigation Report, http://www.rmp.gov.my/rmp03/040220scomi_eng.htm.

and South Africa.[8] Despite their commitments, these two NSG members did not implement NSG guidelines adequately, leading to their ignorance to how they were being exploited for the illegal production of centrifuge materials. This highlights the weaknesses in the nonproliferation institutions and demonstrates that nonproliferation efforts must go beyond simple membership and require the proper execution of pledged guidelines.

The Khan network was also masterful at identifying non-NSG countries that had advanced technology and infrastructure to manufacture direct-use nuclear items, but because they were not members of the nuclear supplier group, they had either little knowledge of nuclear technology or inadequate national export laws.[9]

Revelations following Libya's renouncement of nuclear weapons identified six key workshops across Asia, Africa, and the Middle East that were contracted to make centrifuge components for the Khan network, but none of them were members of the NSG.[10] The most public of these was a Malaysian company, Scomi Precision Engineering (SCOPE), which manufactured stationary aluminum and centrifuge components. Some of SCOPE's production destined for Libya was seized on the German-owned vessel *BBC China*.[11]

The Malaysian case highlights the risk posed by states outside the NSG that are ill equipped to deal with the nature of what seemed like standard manufacturing. According to the Malaysian investigation on SCOPE, its owners were unaware of the network's activities.[12]

The United Arab Emirates' port of Dubai was a critical logistical hub for the network's operations. Because of its international free zone, Dubai places few meaningful controls on incoming or outgoing shipments. In the case of Libya, nuclear components from the network's chain of suppliers are all transported via Dubai.[13]

The KRL sold two types of uranium enrichment technologies known as P1 and P2 centrifuges. The P1 centrifuge machine uses an aluminum rotor to enrich uranium. The P2 uses a steel rotor, which is stronger and spins faster, therefore enriching more uranium than the P1.

Khan's first major exporting operations began in 1987 in a deal to provide Iran with a Pakistani centrifuge design for Iran's uranium enrichment technology.[14] The deal was for assistance to build a cascade of fifty thousand P1 centrifuges.[15] The first transfer of nuclear technology began in 1989. Khan claims that these sales stopped in 1991, but the IAEA uncovered evidence that Pakistani assistance continued as late as 1996.[16] Initial exports of P1 centrifuges included five hundred machines retired from Pakistan's nuclear program. These centrifuges would only be able to produce a quarter of a bomb's worth of weapons-grade uranium in a year.[17] In March 2005, Pakistan acknowledged A. Q. Khan had provided centrifuges to Iran, though it denied having had any knowledge of the transactions.[18]

Libya became Khan's biggest customer. The network provided Libya with a large gas centrifuge plant with enough uranium enriching capability for ten nuclear weapons annually, including ongoing technical assistance to assemble and operate the plant.[19]

While Pakistani P1 machines were provided, the network focused on producing P2 components from outside Pakistan. The Libyans confirmed to the IAEA that it placed an order for a total of ten thousand P2 machines.[20]

Later, Libyans ordered a sophisticated manufacturing center, code-named Machine Shop 1001, to produce and repair their own centrifuge components.[21] Libya was also given the technical know-how to build a nuclear weapon. This included component designs, component fabrication information, and nuclear weapons assembly instructions.[22]

In 1992, Pakistan began missile cooperation with North Korea. Within Pakistan, Khan's laboratories were responsible for missile research to develop the Ghauri missile with North Korean assistance.[23] It is during this missile cooperation with Pyongyang that contacts were made for Khan's future nuclear proliferation trade with North Korea.

Throughout the 1990s, Khan visited North Korea thirteen times. Though this may have been part of the Pakistan-DPRK missile cooperation business, Khan is believed to have arranged nuclear weapons deals as well. From 1997 to 2001, Khan began transfers to North Korea with old and discarded centrifuge and enrichment machines together with sets of drawings, sketches, technical data, and depleted uranium hexafluoride.[24] In August 2005, President Pervez Musharraf confirmed that Khan had provided North Korea with centrifuges, both in parts and in complete forms.[25] The Khan network also offered assistance to Iraq, Egypt, and Syria, but it is believed that those parties declined the offer.

The government of Pakistan maintains that it did not proliferate and that the proliferation activities of Khan and his agents were entirely private. Belying that declaration, KRL has a unique position in Pakistan's industry, reporting directly to the prime minister's office, and KRL has an active and close relationship with the military.

Despite intense American pressure following the revelation of the full extent of the Khan network, Pakistan refused to detain Khan, who is seen as a national hero for making the country a nuclear state. In March 2001, Khan was promoted to the inner circle of the country's military leadership as special science and technology adviser to President Musharraf. But under intense pressure following the events of 9/11, Khan was quietly moved from that position and arrested in January 2004, and then pardoned in February 2004.[26]

It seems wildly improbable that Khan developed this highly sophisticated and wide-ranging network as a private enterprise. To some authors, it is far more believable that because of Pakistan's limited financial resources, Khan and his laboratories developed the proliferation network as a means to fund the development of Pakistan's nuclear weapons. Nevertheless, the United States supported Pakistan's pardon of Khan, saying that it was an internal matter.

CHINA AS A PROLIFERATOR

China's communist party has been a poor steward of China's security. Chinese politicians frequently decry American security policies as designed to contain China. Even if containment were a true American policy objective, Washington could not hope to succeed as well as Beijing has in creating a circle of nuclear armed countries around China. To China's east is nuclear-armed North Korea. In the south and west are Pakistan and India, and to the north is Russia.

Looking at China from the outside, Beijing seems an unlikely proliferator. As a de jure nuclear state, China's own nuclear weapons programs are unchallenged by the international community. Beijing acceded to the Nonproliferation Treaty in March 1992 and signed the Comprehensive Test Ban Treaty in September 1996.

By the standards of the Russian and American nuclear arsenals, which at one time contained thousands of nuclear weapons and missiles, China has a modest nuclear capability. The United States Defense Department Annual Report to Congress, "The Military Power of the PRC 2005," projects a nuclear arsenal of twenty CSS-4 ICBMs as its primary nuclear deterrent, and another twenty CSS-3 ICBMs for its regional nuclear deterrent. China's PLA is also believed to possess

- 50–100 DF-3 (CSS-2) and DF-21 (CSS-5) medium-range ballistic missiles;
- 1 ballistic-missile submarine, but its operational status is in question (this vessel carries 12 single-warhead Julang I SLBMs); and
- 100–120 Hong-6 strategic bombers—these bombers are based on the 1950s-era Soviet Tu-16 long-range bomber.

Although limited in number and capability, these weapons provided China with an affordable deterrent and a comfortable local superiority—*as long as there were no new nuclear powers in Asia*. Remarkably, it was China's own policies of selling nuclear and missile technology that has eroded China's military superiority and sparked an Asian arms race.

China's nuclear cooperation with North Korea began in 1959 when the two countries signed protocols on the peaceful uses of nuclear energy. However, in 1987, suspicious that North Korea was pursuing a nuclear weapons program at a nuclear waste site in Yongbyon, China halted all transfers of nuclear technology and withdrew its nuclear technicians from North Korea.

Since then, Beijing has officially refused to provide any nuclear-related assistance to Pyongyang. However, the nuclear weapons technology discovered in North Korea's nuclear program, including large numbers of centrifuge machines to produce weapons-grade uranium, has its origins in Chinese assistance to Pakistan's nuclear programs. It seems most unlikely that Islamabad would have passed on Chinese-origin nuclear technology in such quantities to North Korea without Beijing's knowledge and consent.[27]

China's missile assistance to North Korea began in the 1970s with Chinese missile technology of Soviet design. Throughout the 1980s and 1990s, China transferred short-range ballistic missiles and production technologies, assisted North Korea in a long-range ballistic missile project, and trained North Korean engineers in Beijing.[28] North Korea acquired "Scud-B" technology through collaboration with China and Iran, and the long-range Taepodong-2 reportedly replicated in large part the Chinese CSS-2 intermediate-range ballistic missile.

A November 2003 Central Intelligence Agency (CIA) report to Congress notes that in November 2000, China committed not to assist any country in the development of ballistic missiles that could be used to deliver nuclear weapons and in August 2002, as part of that commitment, promulgated a comprehensive missile-related export control system, similar in scope to the Missile Technology Control Regime (MTCR) Annex.[29] However, the same report also notes that Chinese firms continue to provide North Korea with dual-use missile-related items, raw materials, and assistance.[30]

For Pakistan, China sold M-11 missiles and related technology and also provided nuclear technology-related assistance to Pakistan all the way up to 1992 when Beijing joined the NPT. Afterward, in 1995, China exported five thousand specially designed ring magnets to an unsafeguarded nuclear laboratory in Pakistan that was allegedly involved in nuclear weapons work. Then in 2004, Chinese-language nuclear weapons design documents, originally addressed to Pakistan, were discovered in Libya. The documents suggest that China continued to provide training to Pakistani scientists over the course of several years after joining the NPT.

Until recently, China's southwestern border, Central Asia, was largely free of nuclear weapons and ballistic missiles, but Chinese assistance is helping create a nuclear Iran with intercontinental ballistic missiles. Chinese agencies have become an integral part of Iran's proliferation network. For example on December 23, 2005, the United States imposed sanctions on six Chinese companies for violating the Iran Nonproliferation Act of 2000. Three of these companies had already been sanctioned in the past.

Iran's missiles have sufficient range to hit Israel or China depending on the mood of the unstable Iranian regime. Furthermore, there is little reason to believe that the reactionary theocrats of Iran will suddenly show restraint and restrain from proliferating to other Central Asian countries. In fact, the logic of proliferation demands that Iran find buyers for its technologies in order to finance the continued development of its own arsenal.

Finally, Japan, India, and South Korea are participating in the American-sponsored ballistic missile defense system to protect against Chinese assisted missile threats from North Korea and Pakistan—incidentally protecting them from China's nuclear deterrent as well.

The motivations of the neocommunist mandarins in Beijing for provoking a regional arms race are difficult to discern. It could be that the communist party simply did not anticipate the results of its shortsighted policies. It is also not certain that all of China's companies that sell nuclear technology are sanctioned by the government. Official corruption and China's opaque bureaucracy limit the government's ability to regulate its nuclear industry.

There are some indications that Chinese policymakers have belatedly awakened to the danger it created. Beijing recently took positive steps toward nonproliferation by joining the NSG in 2004 and reinforcing stricter export controls. According to a November 2004 CIA report to Congress, China intercepted a shipment to North Korea of chemicals used in developing nuclear weapons.[31]

NORTH KOREA

Analytical discussion about North Korea usually generates more heat than light. This problem is largely due to the secretive nature of the regime and the consequent dearth of verifiable facts.

There are a very few consensus opinions among analysts that study the Stalinist state. One opinion that is generally accepted holds that regime survival is Pyongyang's first priority. Another one is that North Korea's nuclear weapon program is a bargaining tool as much as it is a deterrent. Almost everything else about North Korea's strategy and goals is a matter of disputed opinion.

Estimates of the number of nuclear weapons North Korea possesses vary depending on the source. The United States government estimated in 2002 that Pyongyang possessed one and possibly two nuclear weapons, while private analysts have expressed the number could be as high as twelve. John Negroponte, director of National Intelligence, declined to comment on the number of nuclear weapons that North Korea might have assembled during his testimony before the Senate Armed Services Committee in February 2006.[32]

Known Nuclear Installations[33]

A five-megawatt nuclear reactor is believed to be capable of expending enough fuel to produce about six kilograms of plutonium annually—enough for the manufacture of a single atomic bomb annually. In May 1994, North Korea shut down the reactor and removed about eight thousand fuel rods to reprocess into enough plutonium for four to six nuclear weapons.

Two (one fifty-megawatt and one two-hundred-megawatt) nuclear reactors are under construction. If completed, these reactors would be capable of producing enough spent fuel—two hundred kilograms of plutonium—for manufacturing nearly thirty nuclear weapons annually.

Known Delivery Systems

Nodong is the longest-range missile North Korea has deployed, with a 1,300-kilometer range.

Taepo Dong-1 is the longest-range missile North Korea has flight-tested. It has two stages (with an estimated range of 2,000–2,200 km) or three stages (with a range of either 2,200–2,672 or 2,200–2,896 km) and a warhead estimated at 700–1,000 kilograms—comparable in performance to the Soviet SS-4.

Taepo Dong-2 is a multistage missile with a 3,500-kilometer range. It is estimated that the Taepo Dong-2 could deliver a 650-kilogram warhead to Alaska, Hawaii, and the Pacific Northwest, or a much lighter warhead to most of the United States even though North Korea would not be able to develop a nuclear warhead lighter than 650–750 kilograms in the near term. In February 2005, Porter Goss, director of the CIA, testified before the Senate Select Committee on Intelligence that the Taepo Dong-2 is capable of reaching the United States with a nuclear weapon–sized payload.

Despite the apparent precision that citing numbers provides, no one knows if North Korea actually has any operational nuclear weapons or if its long-range missiles can hit a target smaller than the Pacific Ocean. The first missile tested did strike the Pacific Ocean east of Japan, but the second test failed to achieve even that modest goal and landed in the Sea of Japan.

Pyongyang certainly has a program to build nuclear bombs, but there is little evidence that the North Koreans have assembled a working weapon, much less the several weapons that some analysts predict. North Korea did test a nuclear device, but analysts are almost unanimous in assessing that the test was a technical failure.

Whether North Korea has fifty weapons or none, Washington has felt compelled to participate in round after round of negotiations in a frantic effort to denuclearize the Korean peninsula. A short history of proliferation negotiations is illustrative on how difficult it is to disarm North Korea.

In December 1991, Pyongyang signed the Joint Declaration on the Denuclearization of the Korean Peninsula with Seoul, which called for the implementation of a bilateral nuclear inspection regime to verify the denuclearization of the Korean peninsula.[34] That agreement was followed in January 1992 when North Korea signed a nuclear safeguards agreement with the IAEA, which allowed IAEA inspections into North Korean nuclear facilities in June 1992.

In January 1993, however, North Korea changed its mind and denied the IAEA access to two suspect nuclear waste sites and, subsequently, announced its withdrawal from the NPT in March 1993.

In response, the United Nations Security Council passed a resolution urging North Korea to cooperate with the IAEA and to implement the 1992 Joint Declaration. In October 1994, after several rounds of negotiations, the United States and North Korea concluded the Agreed Framework, under which North Korea agreed to

- freeze its gas-graphite-moderated reactors and related facilities;
- allow the IAEA to monitor the freeze;
- take steps to implement the Joint Declaration on the Denuclearization of the Korean Peninsula;
- remain a party to the NPT.[35]

In exchange, the United States agreed to

- construct two light-water power reactors;
- provide five hundred thousand tons of heavy fuel oil annually until the first reactor came online.[36]

At the time of the negotiations, intelligence reports indicated that the North Korean economy had collapsed and that the country was facing mass starvation. In fact, it is estimated that by 1998 more than a million people had starved to death. Many of the American participants that negotiated the Agreed Framework were aware of the severe economic crisis and continued the negotiations believing the regime would never survive long enough to benefit from its provisions.

Nevertheless, like an evil Energizer Bunny, the regime confounded the Americans first by surviving, then by admitting in October 2002 that it had retained a secret uranium enrichment program in violation of the Agreed Framework. Two months later, the U.S. government suspended heavy oil shipments to North Korea.[37] In January 2003, North Korea restarted plutonium-based nuclear facilities at Yongbyon, expelled IAEA inspectors, and announced its withdrawal from the NPT.[38]

In early 2003, the United States tried again to end North Korea's nuclear weapons program by proposing multilateral talks. In April 2003, an agreement was reached to hold talks including six countries, South Korea, North Korea, China, Japan, Russia, and the United States.

Four rounds of the "six-party talks" have so far taken place—in August 2003, February 2004, June 2004, and September 2005—and in the last round of talks, all the parties adopted a Joint Statement where North Korea committed to

- abandoning all nuclear weapons and existing nuclear programs;
- returning at an early date to the NPT and to IAEA safeguards;
- observing and implementing of the 1992 Joint Declaration of the Denuclearization of the Korean Peninsula.[39]

The other five parties agreed to

- provide energy assistance to North Korea;
- discuss at an appropriate time the subject of the provision of a light-water reactor to North Korea.[40]

At the end of the fourth round of talks in September 2005, the six parties agreed to hold a fifth round of talks in November 2005. However, when the time came, North Korea refused to return to the six-party talks unless the United States lifted sanctions against North Korean firms suspected of weapons proliferation and stopped accusing North Korea of counterfeiting U.S. dollars.

At the time of this writing, the United States continues to try to shepherd North Korea back to the Six-Party Talks. And because of a combination of pressure and sanctions from Beijing, Pyongyang has agreed to return to the process.

Nevertheless, the White House seems to miss the point that it should have gained from its own history of negotiating with Pyongyang. It doesn't matter if North Korea comes back to the six-party talks or signs a binding agreement, for North Korea nuclear weapons are much less a deterrent than a negotiating tool. If Pyongyang gives up its nuclear weapon program, then it surrenders its negotiating tool. What can the other five parties offer North Korea that is better than a nuclear bomb?

As stated at the beginning of this section, regime survival is Pyongyang's number one priority. North Korea cannot use its nuclear weapons without the sure knowledge that the United States retains sufficient nuclear options to destroy North Korea—and the regime with it. Furthermore, there is no reason to believe that Pyongyang will voluntarily surrender its nuclear program to the United States, China, or any combination of countries.

Since there is no reasonable expectation of North Korea using its nuclear weapons (if it has any), and Pyongyang will not negotiate in good faith, then there is no reason for the United States to continue negotiations or at least no reason to pursue negotiations with any urgency.

It is time for the United States to deescalate the rhetoric and scale back its negotiating effort. South Korea has more to gain or lose from North Korea than any other country in the world. South Korea is a stable democracy and has been a steadfast American ally for more than half a century. It is entirely appropriate that South Korea assume the lead in negotiations with North Korea. Washington should monitor, consult, and support, but avoid becoming directly embroiled in the negotiations.

The American role in stopping proliferation from North Korea should shift from begging and pleading with fifty-yuan dictators in Pyongyang, to active support and diplomatic strengthening of the Proliferation Security Initiative (PSI), beginning by asking South Korea to fully support the PSI. The "case-by-case basis" acceptance of PSI adopted by Seoul in 2005 gained it no gratitude from North Korea. Pyongyang called the decision an "unforgivable anti-national crime."[41]

Furthermore, the United States and South Korea should encourage Beijing and Tokyo to follow the same line. China and Japan's deference to South Korea in negotiations would limit North Korea's ability to manipulate the negotiation process. Moreover, Beijing and Japan's active participation in PSI would both severely curtail Pyongyang's ability to proliferate missile and nuclear technology or to strengthen its own programs.

NUCLEAR-ARMED INDIA

India's nuclear technology is not homegrown but was imported from the United States and its allies. Under the Eisenhower administration's "Atoms for Peace" program, the United States assisted nonnuclear states in the development of peaceful nuclear capability. From 1955, the United States trained foreign nuclear scientists and engineers and declassified thousands of reports on plutonium processing and other nuclear related information.[42] In 1955, members of the U.S. Joint Committee on Atomic Energy visited India to promote the peaceful use of atomic energy.[43]

Prime Minister Jawaharlal Nehru succeeded in persuading the international community to make Homi Bhahba (father of India's nuclear establishment) president of the first United Nations Conference on the peaceful use of Atomic Energy, held in Geneva in July and August 1955. This conference facilitated the flow of U.S., Canadian, and British assistance to the Indian nuclear programs in the mid-1950s.[44]

In 1955, the British assisted the construction on India's first reactor, the 1 MW Apsara research reactor, and Canada agreed to supply India with a powerful research reactor—the forty-megawatt Canada-India Reactor (CIR). Between 1955 and 1974, India sent more than a thousand scientists and engineers to the Argome Laboratory School of Nuclear Science and Engineering in Illinois and other facilities for guidance on the design and operation of their nuclear facilities.[45]

In February 1956, Washington supplied twenty-one tons of heavy water for this reactor, now dubbed the Canada-India Reactor, U.S., or CIRUS.[46] Acquisition of CIRUS was a turning point for India's nuclear weapons ambitions. The reactor was a design ideal for producing weapons-grade plutonium and was also extraordinarily large for research purposes.

CIRUS produced the plutonium used in India's first nuclear test in 1974, provided the design prototype for India's more powerful Dhruva plutonium production "research" reactor, and is directly responsible for producing nearly half of the weapons-grade plutonium currently believed to be in India's stockpile. Although U.S. cooperation on the CIRUS project was granted on the understanding that the reactor would only be used for peaceful purposes, there were no international safeguards available to regulate and verify the use of transferred technology.

After India's 1974 nuclear weapon test, the United States, together with Russia, China, and other countries that produced nuclear technology formed the Nuclear Supplier's Group. The goal of the NSG was to prevent exports of commercial or civilian nuclear technology or dual-use technologies from being diverted to weapons programs of other countries. For thirty years, U.S.-Indian nuclear technology transfers stopped.

India tested its nuclear weapons again in 1998, which brought on a storm of condemnation for New Delhi, but shortly afterward both the Clinton and Bush administrations began to seek out ways to cooperate with India, a de facto nuclear power that shared American values and interests.

In July 2005, President George Bush and Prime Minister Manmohan Singh agreed to the Next Step for a Strategic Partnership (NSSP) in which the United States and India agreed to civilian nuclear and space cooperation. This agreement, if implemented, would run counter to the spirit of the NPT. The NPT encourages cooperation in the civilian nuclear power field only with nonweapons states designated by the treaty in exchange for clear commitments by those states not to seek nuclear weapons.

In the past, the United States has withheld nuclear cooperation and severely limited defense cooperation with countries openly seeking nuclear weapons. The new willingness of the United States to engage in cooperative activities in the civilian nuclear power field with a state outside the NPT raises questions about the future of U.S. nuclear nonproliferation policy.

With all that said, New Delhi has many policies that serve broader American interests and demonstrate respect for nonproliferation goals:

India has no record of proliferating nuclear technology to other countries.
India is a democracy.
India and the United States have a sophisticated and mutually beneficial defense relationship.
India has agreed to separate its civilian and military nuclear facilities and place its civilian reactors under IAEA safeguards.
India declared a unilateral moratorium on testing nuclear weapons.

Despite India's appearance as a shining model of moderation and stability, there are perception issues with India's nuclear weapons programs that, if not properly addressed, could ignite a regional arms race.

The primary purpose of Pakistan's nuclear deterrent is India. Islamabad has largely accepted that New Delhi needs a minimum nuclear arsenal, but Islamabad asserts that India should not substantially exceed Pakistan's deterrent in size or capability.

There are also three U.S. policies toward India that unfavorably affect Islamabad's security perceptions. First, India and the United States are cooperating on regional missile defense, perhaps someday neutralizing Pakistan's nuclear deterrent.

Second, the proposed U.S.-India nuclear deal excludes eight of India's nuclear reactors, including its fast-breeder reactor. Fast-breeder reactors are known to be inefficient at creating nuclear energy, but very efficient at creating weapons-grade fuel. Islamabad is afraid that without international controls, India will continue to produce nuclear weapons until India has an overwhelming advantage.

Lastly, the United States is not including Pakistan in a civilian nuclear deal or selling it the high-tech weaponry Islamabad feels it needs for a conventional military deterrent. Pakistan is already insecure about India's much greater size, and now Islamabad worries about an American alliance with its greatest enemy.

With that said, Islamabad practices many dangerous policies that worry and annoy Washington.

Pakistan has an extensive nuclear proliferation network, and its belated efforts to stop proliferating nuclear weapons technology will not recall technology already spread to North Korea and Iran.

Pakistan is not a democracy. President Pervez Musharraf's claim that only continued army control can keep Pakistan together is a self-serving sham.

The United States and Pakistan have a long and mutually beneficial defense relationship, but Pakistan's past support of terrorist groups and its current ineffectual attacks on the same groups are the reason the United States wants a defense relationship with Pakistan.

Nevertheless, it is in America's interests to reassure Pakistan and the international community that criteria-based second-track policy does not present open-ended exceptions to qualifying nonweapon states. Properly crafted legislation and treaties should establish criteria that reward countries that comply with NPT goals and punish those that do not. More specifically, second-track negotiations should reassure Islamabad that Washington will not permit New Delhi to use its nuclear deal with the United States to dominate Pakistan or accelerate the arms race in Asia. More importantly, the United States retains its objectives of eliminating nuclear weapons.

WHAT THE UNITED STATES SHOULD DO

This section will bring us back to the central question of this chapter: what should the United States do to contain the burgeoning number of nuclear weapon states, and how does it engage with de facto nuclear powers without surrendering American nonproliferation goals?

First, the United States should develop criteria for engaging de facto nuclear states. Second, the United States must develop a more robust means to contain nuclear proliferators.

Engagement with de facto nuclear states that meet American criteria can include military-to-military contacts, conventional arms sales, missile defense cooperation, and joint military exercises, but in deference to the nuclear nonproliferation goals and treaty obligations of the United States, under no circumstances should cooperation extend to nuclear weapons and delivery systems designed for nuclear weapons.

The criteria should require the following:

- *A stable democracy and rule of law.* Democracy is not a shallow political ideology but a necessity for an effective nonproliferation regime. Of the current ten de jure and de facto nuclear weapon states, the ones with the best nonproliferation records are the democracies. The United States and its allies did assist India in developing its nuclear industry and indirectly its weapons program, but when India tested in 1974, cooperation halted, and the democracies moved to try and block further technology transfer. With that said, India has no record of passing nuclear technology to other countries. All the nondemocratic nuclear weapon states, on the other hand, are aggressive and indiscriminate proliferators.
- *A record of not proliferating nuclear technology and a demonstrated respect for the international nuclear nonproliferation regime.* India has no record of transferring nuclear technology to any other country—consistent with the NPT. India declared a unilateral moratorium on testing nuclear weapons—consistent with the Comprehensive Test Ban Treaty (CTBT). India has demonstrated an interest in participating in PSI. It is American reluctance to accept a country that is not an NPT member that has delayed India's participation in PSI activities.

- *Not a state sponsor of terrorism.* The nexus of state-sponsored terrorism and nuclear weapons are America's greatest nightmare.
- *Maintenance of a firm separation between civilian and military nuclear programs and outside technology transfers provided only to commercial nuclear power reactors.* Commercial power reactors are an area where the United States can accomplish multiple goals with de facto nuclear powers. An energy trade deal with India, for example, should include provisions that prevent India from subsidizing its civilian reactors and prevent the United States or other nuclear suppliers from providing nuclear technologies or facilities at prices below the cost of production. Without government assistance, a nuclear power plant would not be economically viable if it were diverting its resources to expensive military projects, like building more bombs. At the same time, a trade agreement that eliminated government subsidies and allowed India's power plants to operate for profit would force substantial reform in India's energy sector and aid in the country's economic development.
- *Pursuit of nonaggressive security policies.* This criterion addresses the fundamental security pretexts for developing nuclear weapons in ways that will encourage de facto nuclear states to abandon or reduce their nuclear weapons programs. For example, the threat posed by Pakistan is one of many reasons India has for possessing nukes, but India is Pakistan's only reason for possessing nuclear weapons. The criteria would require India to engage in substantive negotiations to resolve disputes.

  India does meet this criterion. The ongoing armistice at the line-of-control and Kashmir border talks between Pakistan and India are making remarkable progress. Although neither country is close to making a fundamental compromise on Kashmir, they have reached a range of agreements on other matters, particularly on controls for their nuclear weapons.
- *A ceiling on production of fissile materials.* Arm control advocates assert that this agreement, when implemented, will "free up" India's domestic capacity to produce the fissile material (highly enriched uranium and plutonium) needed to build nuclear weapons.[47] The Bush administration's proposed legislation to permit the implementation of the agreement with India addresses this issue by conditioning U.S. support for India's civil nuclear program on India's assistance to the United States in concluding a multilateral Fissile Material Cut-off Treaty.

> Ultimately, the size of India's nuclear arsenal depends on more than just the volume of fissile material it is capable of producing. India's perception of the threats it faces and its military doctrine regarding the possible use of nuclear weapons are at least as important. This issue is best addressed in the second track of the two-track nonproliferation policy proposed in this chapter. The broader purpose of the second track is to address the underlying security concerns that prompted India to obtain nuclear weapons in the first place, with the long-term goal of addressing India's security concerns in a way that it concludes that it no longer needs nuclear weapons. Clearly, the second track agenda should address the threat and doctrinal issues.

The flipside of cooperative de facto nuclear states like India are the wholly uncooperative de facto weapon states like North Korea and Iran. When negotiations fail, then more direct methods must be employed. The PSI was formed to coordinate diplomatic, law enforcement, intelligence and, when needed, the militaries of cooperating countries to disrupt shipments of weapons of mass destruction, their components, or the facilities or machinery to produce them. Currently, seventy countries give support to PSI, but the countries of the Asia-Pacific are slow to join.

PSI is not yet a permanent feature of the international nonproliferation regime. The NPT and NSG, although extremely useful, have demonstrated limits to their abilities to control the spread of nuclear weapons. PSI supplements those treaties by coordinating the participating countries to disrupt shipments through direct action, including stopping ships at sea.

It should be a priority of the United States to strengthen the authority of PSI in international law to permit PSI cooperating countries to intercept air, sea, or land shipments, if they are suspected of carrying contraband cargoes across international boundaries. The United States should work to increase the number of participating countries in the Asia-Pacific, particularly, India, China, Japan, South Korea, and Indonesia. Finally, the United States and the participating countries should consider the creation of a permanent coordinating body, under the auspices of the IAEA in its enforcement and coordinating functions.[48]

The end of the Cold War brought into existence arms control treaties that have dramatically decreased the overall number of nuclear weapons in the world. Unfortunately, at the same time, the number of states that possess nuclear weapons has doubled. Furthermore, the technology to build nuclear weapons is now sixty years old, and the number of countries with the industrial sophistication and resources to build nuclear weapons increases year after year.

Adopting a criteria-based formula for engaging de facto nuclear states will reward responsible countries without giving that country a free ride on its future behavior. Furthermore, it will permit the United States and the international community to maintain their long-term proliferation goals.

• 5 •

Pirates of the South China Sea

> The existence of the sea means the existence of pirates.
>
> —Malayan proverb

> It will be more easy to raise ships and men to fight these pirates into reason, than money to bribe them.
>
> —Thomas Jefferson

The United States is the world's largest trading nation, and more than half its trade is with Asia. Coincidentally, Asia is also the world's worst area for maritime piracy. During the 1990s, the number of pirate attacks in Asia increased steadily year after year, which worried business and government alike about the negative effect this lawlessness would have on trade in the region. After 9/11, the perception of the security situation changed for the worse as policymakers speculated about the possibility of terrorists adapting the methods of maritime pirates to hijack a ship and use it to cause catastrophic damage.

In June 2000, I published my first paper on piracy in Southeast Asia, warning that the growing number of piracy attacks would threaten maritime trade and specifically warning that piracy would affect insurance rates and other costs to countries that can least afford it. I was not alone. Lloyd's List International, the International Maritime Bureau, the OECD, Aegis Defense Services, and a host of other maritime or security-interested organizations also warned Asian governments that piracy, terrorism, and official corruption were growing and were affecting business in the region.

Although some countries, like Singapore, heeded these calls and implemented comprehensive plans to thwart pirate attacks in their waters, other countries did little else than complain and deny the problem. For example, before October 2002, the Indonesian government ignored or belittled warnings that terrorists were operating in Indonesia, and the government took little or no action until after the Bali bombing, the deadliest terrorist attack after 9/11. Jakarta and many countries for whom the Malacca Straits are vital seaways continued to ignore timely warnings about terrorist dangers. Increasingly, piracy was seen to be a phenomenon of deteriorating law and order and was connected with terrorism and official corruption.

Then in June 2005, the Joint War Committee (JWC), a group of London-based insurance companies that measure risk, listed the Malacca Straits as a "war risk" area, thus driving up insurance rates for carriers and shippers transiting the straits.[1] This correction to the risk assessment stimulated regional governments to stop the foot-dragging and to produce a solution to reduce pirate attacks in the Malacca Straits. Although regional military action affected only the Malacca Straits, the fact that there was any result at all shows that market stimulus offers a lesson on how maritime piracy can be controlled in the region.

The solution to reducing piracy to manageable levels is to address both cause and effect.[2] Governments need to understand the causes of maritime piracy to craft strategies to combat it. Maritime businesses, on the other hand, need to explain the effects of maritime crime in order to induce government motivation to resolve it; and if explanations fail to elicit the proper response, then a judicious application of market stimulus—as the insurance industry did when it raised insurance rates—can focus government attention.

DEFINING THE CAUSES

By way of explaining terms, the three components of maritime industry most affected by maritime crime are the shippers (manufacturers that own the cargo), carriers (companies that own the vessels), and insurers of the ships and cargoes.

According to the International Chamber of Commerce's International Maritime Bureau (IMB), incidents of maritime piracy have more than quadrupled over a ten-year period, going from 90 reported attacks in 1994 to 445 attacks in 2003. But these numbers are misleading. Most acts cited in the annual IMB reports on maritime piracy are not classic boarding and hijacking of a merchant vessel on the high seas. Instead, nearly two-thirds of the attacks in 2003 occurred while the ships were stationary in port and are thus better classified as sea robbery. The report fails to mention the most costly crime to the maritime transportation industry: extortion by port authorities. Maritime terrorism is also overlooked; the reports of terrorist attacks are lumped together with reports of dockworkers stealing paint cans.

The current definition of piracy is completely inadequate as a tool for policymakers. According to Malaysia's deputy prime minister, Datuk Seri Mohd Najib Tun Razak, "At present the IMB groups all forms of piracy under one category of piracy. Malaysia, Indonesia and Singapore feel that acts of piracy should be separated according to the crime committed."[3] Najib is right, and to meet his challenge to provide a useful definition for maritime crimes, the United Nations Internal Maritime Organization (IMO) and IMB should revise their existing definitions of piracy to include four categories of maritime crimes: extortion, sea robbery, piracy, and maritime terrorism.

EXISTING DEFINITIONS

There are two definitions of piracy today; the first is the United Nations Convention on the Law of the Sea (UNCLOS) definition used by the IMO:

> Piracy consists of any of the following acts:
>
> any illegal acts of violence or detention, or any act of depredation, committed for private ends by the crew or the passengers of a private ship or a private aircraft, and directed:
>
> on the high seas, against another ship or aircraft, or against persons or property on board such ship or aircraft;
>
> against a ship, aircraft, persons or property in a place outside the jurisdiction of any state;
>
> any act of voluntary participation in the operation of a ship or of an aircraft with knowledge of facts making it a pirate ship or aircraft;
>
> any act of inciting or of intentionally facilitating an act described in subparagraph (a) or (b).[4]

The UNCLOS definition is too narrow, restricting acts of piracy to the "high seas" and "outside the jurisdiction of any state." In 2003, only 122 reported pirate attacks, or 27 percent of actual and attempted attacks against vessels, took place on the high seas. The rest of the attacks occurred in ports and territorial waters well inside the jurisdiction of a state.

The International Chamber of Commerce IMB offers another definition of piracy:

> An act of boarding or attempting to board any ship with the apparent intent to commit theft or any other crime and with the apparent intent or capability to use force in the furtherance of that act.[5]

The IMB's definition is far too broad and includes any attack or attempted attack on a ship, whether it is anchored, berthed, or at sea. The IMO attempted to close the definition gap by using both the UNCLOS and IMB definitions.[6] But even using these two definitions still does not account for extortion by port officials, nor does it differentiate maritime terrorism.

There is a substantial difference between the tactics and kinds of organizations that commit sea robbery and the tactics and weapons used by pirates that board ships while the vessel is underway. Additionally, corrupt port officials and terrorists represent separate categories of criminal activities with their differing objectives and tactics. The problem is more than semantics because the definition of the crime affects, and in some cases determines, the agency or government that is responsible to deal with it.

A careful analysis of the data provided by the IMB, the United Nations International Maritime Organization (IMO), and additional sources demonstrates that the problem of crime at sea is not adequately defined. As stated previously, in order to quantify the threat to the maritime industry and to maritime security, there needs to be four categories of sea-based crimes that world leaders can use to create policies that will resolve the actual problem.

Crimes against ships should be placed into four categories:

- Extortion—against vessels by port authorities
- Sea robbery—that takes place in port while the ship is berthed or anchored
- Maritime piracy—against ships underway and outside the protection of port authorities in territorial waters, straits, and the high seas
- Maritime terrorism—a politically motivated attack against a maritime target by non-state actors

Extortion

On October 8, 2004, Malaysia's deputy prime minister Najib said, "Stopping [a vessel] for the sake of extortion does not constitute international terrorism."[7] Najib is correct, but his comments do not sufficiently clarify the problems caused by the extortion of vessels. Although figures are unavailable, anecdotal evidence suggests that extortion by corrupt port authorities is the most expensive crime perpetrated against merchant vessels. In March 2004, another senior Malaysian official, whose responsibilities included maritime issues, said that maritime piracy, as defined by the IMO and IMB, was only a nuisance. The Malaysian official stated that the most costly maritime crime was corruption by port authorities, particularly in Indonesia.[8]

Although corruption and extortion in ports takes many forms, it is a simple procedure. Port officials merely accuse vessels of an environmental or safety violation and then hold the ship in port until it pays the fine or a bribe. Appealing a fine can take days or weeks to resolve. While the ship is anchored in port, it is incurring port costs of up to $10,000 a day. Additionally, the vessel's cargo is delayed with the ship. The consequence is that the shippers and carriers, whose profit margins are razor-thin, prefer to pay the fine, no matter how improper it may be.

The story doesn't end with petty corruption. Sand dredging is big business with a global market of over $10 billion a year. Much of the sea-sand is exported from Indonesia's Riau province. The Indonesian navy is allegedly involved in a protection racket for a cartel of Indonesian dredging businesses. These activities came into conflict with the central government, and the upshot was that at least seven foreign-owned dredgers, with license to operate from the provincial government, were seized by the Indonesian navy and tied up in port for months.[9]

The IMB, in its report entitled "Port State Control," recognized that delays in port are a problem, but the report buries the issue in dense bureaucratic language and euphemisms. For example, the title of one section is "Reporting Procedures on Port State Control Detentions and Analysis and Evaluation of Reports."[10] In classic UN language, the report does not identify countries or ports that unduly delay vessels but instead simply says, in paragraph twelve, "the matter should be further discussed."[11]

The IMO is working to establish uniform worldwide standards to "improve the uniformity of inspection and reporting practices for port State control and promote exchange of information."[12] But it should go a step further: the IMO and IMB should publish reports identifying ports that regularly cause undue delay and publish instances of corruption or collusion, just as they report piracy and sea robbery. Both IMO and IMB should issue warnings to carriers, shippers, and insurers identifying ports that frequently delay vessels.

Sea Robbery

Today, 65 percent of all reported attacks on merchant vessels are committed while the ship is berthed or anchored in port. Attacks usually target the ship's stores and safe and the crew's personal valuables and rarely its cargo. Typical reports of port-related piracy read more like police blotter reports than high seas battles. For example, on January 29, 2003, while berthed at Wharf D in Panjang, Indonesia, "pirates" boarded the bulk carrier *Alberto Topic*: "While berthed, about eight pirates mixed in with stevedores and boarded. They broke padlocks of storerooms and tried to steal engine spares. Alert crew raised alarm and pirates jumped overboard. One pirate received serious injuries whilst jumping overboard and he was hospitalized."[13]

On March 1, 2003, "pirates" boarded the bulk carrier *Love Me Tender* while berthed in Sabah, Malaysia, and "stole ship's stores and property from the forepeak store. Port authorities and police were informed."[14]

Although these robberies are unfortunate, most raids on stationary vessels in ports seldom involve violence. The tools and equipment used in sea robbery are no more sophisticated than crowbars and sledgehammers, which robbers use to break into lockers so that they can steal ship stores. Crimes committed in ports against stationary ships should be categorized as sea robbery and therefore should not be weighted with the more histrionic term *piracy*. Adding these petty crimes to reports on piracies both exaggerates the problem and blurs efforts to make policy. Local law enforcement agencies and port authorities should differentiate piracy from sea robbery and implement port security policies that address the security weaknesses identified by the IMB's reports on sea robbery.

Piracy

Whether a ship is on the high seas or in territorial waters, successfully boarding and attacking a ship while underway requires more organization and equipment than robbing a stationary ship in port. Additionally, to ensure a good return on the extra investment in equipment, the pirates need better intelligence to assure that their target has something worth stealing.

Boarding a moving ship is far more difficult than boarding a stationary one in port. In 2003, pirates boarding stationary ships (anchored or berthed) were successful 90 percent of the time, but they were only successful in 58 percent of their attempts to board a steaming vessel.[15] Pirates often use guns when attacking ships underway because the vessel must be slowed or stopped before boarding is possible.

As a result of the increased firepower, there are significantly more deaths and injuries in attacks against ships underway. In 2003, only two crewmembers were killed, and two went missing from the 242 sea robberies that took place in ports. Of the 210 ships attacked while underway, however, there were 13 hijackings, 193 hostages taken, 19 crewmembers killed, and another 38 people missing. The incident reports are also far more hair-raising. For example, on April 8, 2003, the general cargo ship *Trimaggada* was transiting the Malacca Strait, and

> several pirates in three fishing boats fired on the ship from both sides, and forced the Master to stop engine. The Master sent a distress message. Pirates boarded the ship and gathered all crew on deck. They took hostage the Master, Chief Officer and Chief Engineer and took them off the ship. The 3rd Officer reported to the Indonesian Navy. A Navy boat arrived and escorted the ship to Belawan anchorage. Hostages were subsequently released upon payment of ransom.[16]

Pirates frequently appear to have intelligence about the ships they are hijacking. For example, on August 28, 2003, the bulk carrier *Regina V* was boarded while steaming off Bintan Island, Indonesia, and

> six masked pirates armed with guns and knives boarded the ship from a speedboat. They went to bridge, tied up Duty A/B, took hostage 3/O, assaulted him and forced him to knock on Master's door. Master heard the noise and escaped thru porthole with ship's cash. The pirates knew how much cash was on board and they wrote down the figure on paper. They broke the Master's door and ransacked his cabin and also crew cabins. The pirates tied up some of the crew and assaulted C/E and 3/O many times and threatened crew with guns. The pirates left at 0015 LT with crew personal effects and ships equipment.[17]

Better equipment, arms, and intelligence imply a more complex level of organization than that exhibited by sea robbers. Combating these sophisticated transnational criminal organizations will require international cooperation. The UNCLOS definition of piracy, however, limits piracy to attacks on the "high seas," leaving out almost half of all acts of piracy against ships underway. Of the 210 reported attacks against ships underway in 2003, attempted and committed, 88 (42 percent) occurred in some country's territorial waters. According to UNCLOS, article 111, "Right of Hot Pursuit," a foreign navy/coast guard or maritime police vessel is prohibited from pursuing a suspected pirate vessel into another country's territorial waters. The pirates, on the other hand, recognize no such ban on their movements and will use any country's territorial waters to elude pursuers.

To remedy the definition gap, the UN could expand the UNCLOS definition of piracy to include attacks on all ships underway on the high seas and in territorial waters. Additionally, article 111 could be amended to permit hot pursuit of suspected pirate vessels by foreign naval air and sea vessels into territorial waters with notification to the responsible authorities.

Another solution would be for countries plagued by pirate attacks, such as Indonesia and the Philippines, to negotiate treaties with their neighbors and allies to coordinate air and sea patrolling and to permit hot pursuit of suspected pirate vessels into their territorial waters by foreign air and sea vessels that comply with the requirements set forth in the treaty.

Maritime Terrorism

Terrorists use their maritime assets to accomplish three objectives: to attack against shipping for purpose of creating fear, to smuggle arms and other contraband, and to raise funds through piracy. Although these types of activities are not yet substantially disrupting sea lanes, terrorists are demonstrating a growing sophistication and competence in naval attacks, which should be a cause for worry among policymakers around the world.

Two examples of early maritime terrorism were the attacks against the USS *Cole*[18] and the French oil tanker *Limburg*.[19] These two tragic and widely publicized attacks did little to alert the world to the fact that terrorists were targeting ships. Nor did they cause the IMO or IMB to modify their definitions or policies on pirates in order to address the new threat to the world's sea lanes. In fact, the IMB does not report deaths caused by terrorists as piracy. In the IMB annual report on piracy for 2001, the IMB noted "that of the 72 casualties in 2000, 57 deaths were due to attacks by terrorists rather than pirates, namely 17 sailors died on the USS *Cole* and 40 deaths were due to a bomb explosion aboard a ferry in the Philippines. Thus the deaths due to piracy in 2000 amounted to 15."[20] Using this logic, the IMB can claim that terrorists are not involved in piracy since any time a terrorist attack occurs, the IMB simply classifies it as something other than maritime piracy. This might be useful if the IMB had a separate category for terrorists, but at present, the IMB does not separate terrorist attacks from its other piracy reports.

Al Qaeda's attacks in 2000 and 2002 were relatively simple missions from a naval perspective, but with devastating consequences. The IMB's 2003 reports demonstrate that terrorist groups are developing more sophisticated tactics, vessels, and weapons to carry out their missions. For example, on October 26, 2003, an Indonesian terrorist/insurgent group, known as GAM, intercepted a fishing trawler, PKFA 8588, in the Malacca Straits.

> While underway, several armed uniformed men suspected to be GAM rebels in a fishing boat hijacked the fishing trawler and sailed it towards Indonesian waters, where Indonesian Marine Police confronted them. A shoot-out ensued in which two of the suspected GAM members on board the trawler were shot dead and another was injured. Several others in the boat escaped. The crew of the trawler and the suspected GAM members were taken for investigation.[21]

Sri Lankan terrorists, Liberation Tigers of Tamil Eelam (LTTE), operate their own navy, Sea Tigers, to commit acts of terrorism and piracy and to smuggle weapons. Two examples of suspected LTTE incidents demonstrate their suicidal brutality and potential to harm the world's shipping. On March 10, 2003, a Sri Lankan navy patrol boat northeast of Mullaitivu, Sri Lanka, approached an unidentified general cargo vessel: "While underway, the ship was in[ter]cepted by a patrol boat and ordered to stop. When the ship ignored the warning, the patrol boat opened fire. In a deliberate attempt, crew detonated explosives and sank the ship."[22] On March 20, 2003, the Ufauan-U 225 fishing trawler was steaming sixteen miles off Chundikulam, Sri Lanka, and "was attacked with rocket propelled grenades. Nine crew were rescued and 18 were missing."[23]

A separate category for reports about attacks from terrorist groups and identification of ports and regions where terrorists operate would substantially assist national policymakers in their antiterrorist efforts.

Inadequate definitions of maritime crimes have largely influenced the creation of inadequate state solutions that focus on the more fascinating-to-the-media crimes of high-seas piracy, rather than on the more numerous and costly crimes that occur in port.

The vision of battling pirates at sea is particularly stimulating to the world's sailors. In testimony to Congress on March 24, 2004, Admiral Fargo proposed a Regional Maritime Security Initiative (RMSI) to get control of security in the Malacca Straits. In dramatic language, he declared, "The ungoverned littoral regions of Southeast Asia are fertile ground for exploitation by transnational threats like proliferation, terrorism, trafficking in humans or drugs, and piracy." Indonesia and Malaysia both reacted negatively to the statement and strongly asserted their sovereignty over the Malacca Straits, and RMSI disappeared.

Nonetheless, the navies of these countries offered their own naval patrol schemes to combat high seas piracy. In July 2004, the governments of Indonesia, Malaysia, and Singapore agreed to step up naval patrols in the Malacca Straits. Despite these declarations and meetings, there was no decrease in attacks in the Malacca Straits in 2004 or decline in sea robbery in Asia's ports.

THE EFFECTS OF PIRACY ON THE MARINE BUSINESS COMMUNITY

In his excellent study on the response of the marine insurance industry to piracy and terrorism, Martin Murphy argues that the London insurance market has become less worried about cause and more concerned about defining the effects of piracy. "It now takes the view that if the effects of piracy and terrorism are broadly the same then for all intents and purposes they are the same."[24] But what are the effects?

The costs of piracy on business are manifold and frequently hidden. There are the direct costs of stolen or damaged property. These costs are largely unknown because they usually fall inside the "deductible" level of insurance policies and shipmasters rarely report these losses, partially from fear of rising insurance costs.

Corruption among port authorities is an enormous cost to the carriers, but the selection of the victim is frequently arbitrary, subject to political whim, and sometimes difficult to distinguish from legitimate law enforcement. Thus, it is not found calculated in any published form.

Then there are the costs of injured or killed crew. It's somewhat macabre to put a dollar amount on human life, but nonetheless, the increased deaths and injuries from maritime crimes are costing carriers and insurance companies more money every year as pirate attacks become more violent.

Another rising cost is from kidnap for ransom. These kinds of ship hijackings are the fastest-increasing maritime crime in Asia. Insurance companies rarely pay ransom, but they do pay all related costs such as transportation and accommodations for specialists who negotiate the release of the victims. Ultimately, somebody does pay the ransom, and that must be added into the gross losses due to piracy and maritime crimes.

Last is the problem of evaluating the cost from maritime terrorism. Terrorists want to achieve two things: to surprise and to cause as much damage as possible. From the point of view of the insurance company, those characteristics make assessing risk very difficult. Actuary tables are based on predicting risk from historical data. Terrorists intend to achieve surprise by attacking in places not attacked before, so historical data simply do not help.

Since the eruption of piracy and terrorism as maritime business hazards, the insurance industry had struggled unsuccessfully to assess the risk. Many of the different crimes were covered under different categories. For example, ship seizures by the Indonesian navy were covered under a war policy, but the frequent kidnapping for ransom of ship's crews fell not with war underwriters but under mutual Protection and Indemnity Clubs.[25]

Finally, in 2005, realizing that the current system was inadequate, the London insurance companies' Joint War Committee conducted sweeping changes to its list of areas at risk. In addition to the factors already included in war risk assessment, such as seizures and confiscations, the JWC also considered "the difficulty of differentiating piracy from terrorism, the increased use of violence, the employment of more sophisticated tactics and methods, the under estimated potential for catastrophic loss and, because of terrorism's unpredictability, the inappropriateness of assessing future risk on the basis of past losses."[26] The most important change that came about from the review was to add the Malacca Straits to the list of areas at risk in June 2005.

Needless to say, the addition of the Malacca Straits to war risk areas was not welcome in Asia's capitals. Despite the protestations of surprise and dismay, the governments of the region, especially Indonesia, did significantly step up naval patrols in the straits. Regional governments maintained that the increased patrolling decreased pirate attacks on ships in the Malacca Straits in 2005, falling to twenty attacks in 2005, down from sixty in 2004,[27] and there were no attacks in the Malacca Straits in the first quarter of 2006.

The reduction in attacks in the Malacca Straits is not due solely to increased naval patrols. The reduction partially reflects the devastation caused by the December 26, 2004, tsunami that flooded many of the most notorious pirate coasts, killing, or at least displacing, many pirates and their ships and boats. Furthermore, the subsequent humanitarian relief effort was led by a huge number of foreign navy vessels all operating in the straits. There was also a political element to the reduction of attacks when on August 15, 2005, the Indonesian government signed a peace treaty with the Free Aceh Movement (GAM). GAM was suspected of involvement in some pirate attacks in the northeastern part of the straits, and its accession to the peace process eliminated its reasons to participate in piracy.

Further disassembling reports that the Malacca Straits are suddenly safe is that piracy in the South China Sea, which is at the eastern mouth of the

Malacca Straits, did not significantly decrease. Reports of attacks that occurred and attempted attacks dropped from 113 in 2004 to 97 in 2005.[28] Then attacks increased again in the first quarter of 2006 to 25 compared with 23 the year before.[29] Furthermore, predation continued on vessels in ports, accounting for 62 percent of 2005's attacks in the South China Sea.

Also, alleged corruption among port authorities remained active. For example, in August 2005, a Croatian ship was seized and the crew held at gunpoint when Indonesian officials accused them of using improper travel documents. In September 2005, the carrier paid a $1 million "bail" for possible court costs and fines (it was losing $2,200 a day in port costs), to free the ship, even after an Indonesian court ruled in the company's favor.[30]

There is, however, one lesson that can be derived from the analysis: the governments littoral to the Malacca Straits, when properly motivated, can marshal their resources and reduce maritime crime in a specific location. If the countries of Southeast Asia were motivated to implement a comprehensive antipiracy strategy, they could reduce maritime crimes down to manageable levels. The problem is eliciting the requisite motivation before the regional economies are significantly damaged or crippled by uncontrolled maritime crime.

CONCLUSION

Under the current reporting system used by IMB and IMO, maritime terrorist attacks are not differentiated from other attacks. Instead, they are lumped together with common criminal activities, hindering efforts to identify terrorist attacks from piracy or robbery. Furthermore, extortion by port authorities is not published in any form.

Beyond the physical danger to seamen and the loss of property, the rising costs associated with piracy and imposed on shippers, carriers, and insurers threaten America's diplomatic efforts to fight terrorism and reduce trade barriers.

As the United States lobbies to reduce trade barriers in Asia, these increased costs from piracy serve as a nontariff barrier to trade. In addition, the added insurance costs and safety risks for trading in particularly dangerous ports act as an indirect economic boycott, restraining companies from conducting business with many of America's friends or allies that are least able to afford direct efforts to combat the piracy.

• *6* •

Trade and American Foreign Policy in Asia

With Kelly S. Dillon

> "Most economic fallacies derive from the tendency to assume that there is a fixed pie, that one party can gain only at the expense of another."
>
> —Milton Friedman

One of America's most important soft power tools is trade promotion. Trade helps grow the United States economy; it develops the economies of America's trade partners; and it motivates countries to seek peaceful resolutions to problems in order to maintain mutually beneficial trading relationships and participation in a rules-based trade relationship binds governments to the rule of law.

Because of the somewhat arcane nature of the global trading system, this chapter will spend some time on how trade promotion works, how it helps American foreign policy in Asia, and what measures should be taken by the government to achieve American goals in Asia. We will also examine some (but not all) of the peculiarities in trade with Asia and how U.S. policy should address those problems.

Trade will be critical to U.S. policy toward Asia in the twenty-first century. As with any foreign policy tool, trade is not one-size-fits-all. Asia contains two of the world's freest economies in Singapore and Hong Kong and two of the world's most repressed economies in North Korea and Burma, with varied degrees of development and liberalization in between. Successful trade policy with Asia will require that policymakers utilize all the tools of trade promotion to create mutually beneficial, rules-based relationships. These closer commercial ties will create new opportunities and overall higher living standards in both Asia and the United States.

Free trade agreements (FTAs) between the United States and Asia are flourishing in the region. However, some countries, like China and India, are not likely candidates for FTAs. Therefore U.S. policy must also focus on the World Trade Organization (WTO) and the enforcement of commitments. Successful policies in the Asia region will include the negotiating of more bilateral and regional agreements, encouraging those countries that are not yet WTO members to join, and continuing to advance multilateral agreements, while ensuring that all obligations undertaken in the WTO are fulfilled. As agreements flourish between Asian countries as well as with countries outside Asia, it is important for the United States to continue to involve itself in the region in order to secure economic opportunities for U.S. businesses.

To accomplish America's trade agenda with Asia, Congress should grant permanent trade promotion authority to the office of the president so that trade negotiations can smoothly and predictably transition administrations. Also, U.S. policymakers, led by the United States Trade Representative (USTR), need to expand the government's policy and negotiating capacity; expand its research and enforcement capacity; and open an Asia-Pacific regional office with the mandate to strengthen regional engagement and station more trade experts and negotiators in embassies located in the capitals of major trading partners, such as China, India, Japan, Korea and throughout Southeast Asia. Given its vital mission to create new market opportunities for U.S. businesses, USTR is underfunded. In order for USTR to expand trade negotiations with Asia and around the globe, Congress must increase USTR's funding.

Lastly, to act as a bridge between the eventual realization of a comprehensive global trade deal through the WTO and the current messy, but necessary, maze of bilateral and regional trade agreements, the United States should pursue a Global Free Trade Association for all countries, regardless of their geographic position, which share a commitment to free trade and capital movement.

THE BENEFITS OF TRADE

America's most misrepresented foreign policy tool is trade. For Americans, international trade generates wealth, spurs domestic innovation, and increases economic efficiency by providing lower costs to consumers. For America's allies and trading partners, trade strengthens the rule of law and spurs economic growth more than any other form of foreign aid.

Despite its manifest benefits, trade is not without its critics. Foreign trade is blamed for job losses, a general decline in thc manufacturing base, and lost capability to manufacture critical defense goods. In fact, the opposite is true. Increased foreign trade (1) provides more jobs in the United States, (2) greatly increases the output of the manufacturing sector, and (3) subsidizes the American defense industry.

Importing low-cost goods and raw materials helps American labor and the manufacturing sector by increasing productivity. Between 1950, when the average American tariff was at 40 percent, and 2000 when tariffs had fallen to about 4 percent, American annual imports grew from $9.1 billion to $1 trillion. Despite this 13,000 percent increase in imports, American manufacturing jobs grew from 15.2 million to 18.5 million over the same period. Furthermore, American manufacturing output has grown on average 6.2 percent a year since 1960, and total output now stands at $1.5 trillion.[1]

Nevertheless, lack of access to Asia's burgeoning markets does create trade imbalances. Enforcement of WTO rules and comprehensive trade agreements with major Asian markets, such as China, ASEAN, and India would dramatically increase American exports to those countries as well as develop their markets.

The other myth of foreign trade and globalization is that it endangers national defense industrial independence. Some analysts point to American dependence on foreign-manufactured silicone chips and suggest that the United States should protect or subsidize American silicone chip production. However, every dollar spent on propping up outdated manufacturing infrastructure, capabilities that can be reproduced in any number of countries friendly or allied with the United States, is a dollar not spent on new research and development. "Instead, the United States should allow this old technology to be produced elsewhere so that its resources will be freed to finance development of the next generation of computing. Adversarial nations will be forced either to lag behind or to devote resources to keeping up with U.S. producers."[2]

More important, the United States is the largest exporter of arms in the world. Foreign purchases of American arms reduce costs of those arms to the American military by increasing economies of scale and thus decreasing the overall cost for each item manufactured. For example, it is cheaper per airplane to manufacture 250 airplanes than just 100. Furthermore, foreign purchases of American weapons subsidize the expensive research and development phases of arms purchases.

In fact, some allies contribute directly to R&D in order to influence the direction of weapon development. The best example of this new phenomenon is the F35 Joint Service Fighter. There are eleven countries contributing to the development of the aircraft, including Australia and Singapore, and they are committed to purchasing and sharing production of the fighter. The sharing of development expenses and economies of scale in manufacturing reduce costs and increase competitiveness of American arms.

The United States is the world's leading exporter, and trade creates one-quarter of the U.S. GDP. American exports are enhanced by trade agreements. According to the USTR, "Trade agreements level the playing field and encourage foreign governments to adopt the sorts of open and transparent rulemaking procedures, and non-discriminatory laws and regulations."[3]

Because of the value of trade agreements the United States has completed and continues to pursue a myriad of different types. The USTR remains committed to multilateral liberalization through the WTO but also actively seeks both regional and bilateral FTAs. In addition to FTAs, USTR participates in dozens of bilateral investment treaties (BITs) that focus on protecting private investment in countries where investor rights are not already protected through existing agreements.[4] Finally, there exists a host of trade and investment framework agreements (TIFAs), which establish a framework for expanding trade and resolving outstanding disputes between countries. TIFAs are often a first step to establishing an FTA.

INTERAGENCY NATURE OF U.S. TRADE POLICY

Trade policy is a multiagency responsibility. Section 242 of the Trade Expansion Act of 1962 established the interagency nature of U.S. trade policy. This interagency organization is known as the Trade Policy Staff Committee (TPSC) and is led by USTR. The trade representative is a Cabinet member who serves as the president's principal adviser, negotiator, and spokesperson on trade issues. The five permanent members of the TPSC are the Departments of Commerce, State, Treasury, Agriculture, and Labor. In addition, USTR invites other agencies such as Justice, Defense, and the Environmental Protection Agency to participate. Subsequent Trade Acts instituted the private sector advisory committee to ensure that U.S. commercial interests are reflected in trade negotiations.

The TPSC is a time-consuming process, but it is critical to the overall success of U.S. trade policy. The process utilizes the expertise of other agencies, allowing USTR to focus on coordinating and negotiating trade policy. When a negotiating position is established, the negotiators know that they are speaking on behalf of all interested executive branch agencies and that the position is in line with U.S. legal, regulatory, and policy frameworks.

WORLD TRADE ORGANIZATION

The WTO was created in 1995 at the conclusion of the Uruguay Round as the successor to the General Agreement on Tariffs and Trades (GATT). There are currently 149 members of the WTO, which account for 97 percent of the world's trade. Since the GATT/WTO came into existence, world trade has increased on average of 6 percent and is twenty-two times as big in 2000 as it was in 1950.

The WTO is the international organization that sets the global rules of trade. The mission of the WTO is to liberalize global trade or "ensure that trade flows as smoothly, predictably and freely as possible."[5] The trade agreements reached by the participating countries are administered by the WTO, but ultimately the WTO is not so much a regulatory body as it is a forum for participating countries to negotiate the global rules of trade.

Trade rules are reached through a series of negotiations called rounds. The first round sought mainly to reduce tariffs, but as the GATT developed and more countries joined, each round sought to deepen global integration. The WTO operates by consensus, and nothing is approved until everything is approved when negotiating a new round.

The Uruguay Round, which lasted from 1986 to 1994 and resulted in the creation of the WTO, was the last successfully completed round. The Uruguay Round also concluded agreements on trade in the service industry in an agreement called General Agreement on Trade in Services and covers 22 percent of the world's trade and 70 percent of the U.S. economy. The other landmark agreement was the Trade-Related Aspects of Intellectual Property Rights (TRIPS) that protects many facets of intellectual property rights, including copyrights, trademark, and sound recordings.

After concluding the Uruguay Round and in the wake of the 9/11 terrorist attacks on New York and Washington, the WTO countries launched a new round of negotiations in Doha, Qatar. The Doha Round, also called the Doha Development Agenda, had the ambitious goal of liberalizing the most politically charged industry: agriculture. The original plan was to conclude negotiations by January 2005. Unfortunately, the Doha Round reached an impasse in 2003, and on July 24, 2006, Director General Pascal Lamy suspended negotiations because the gaps between major players (which included India) on agriculture remained too wide. It is very unlikely that countries will reach a comprehensive agreement before the deadline is passed.

TRADE PROMOTION AUTHORITY

Few Americans realize how much the United States drives the global trade agenda. The negotiation deadline for the Doha Round was set by the WTO to accommodate the congressionally established limits of President Bush's trade promotion authority, or TPA, which expires on July 1, 2007. The major reason for declaring the Doha Round a failure was because the negotiators could not reach an agreement before the deadline of December 2006, and TPA would expire before an agreement was ready to present to Congress.

The time limit of TPA also hinders the completion of FTAs currently under negotiation. The United States and Thailand were negotiating an FTA, but after expending a considerable amount of effort in negotiations, USTR was forced to dump Thailand because a domestic political crisis in Bangkok threatened the timetable. USTR added South Korea and Malaysia, but TPA deadlines force a rapid pace on negotiations that can normally last years.

TPA was the successor to the "fast-track" legislation which Congress allowed to lapse in 1994. The President was without Congressional trade negotiation authority between 1994 and the creation of TPA in 2002. During that time, the United States fell behind other trading powers in negotiating trade agreements and ultimately lost its competitive advantage in favorable trade agreements. For example, before 2000, the United States had signed only three comprehensive free trade agreements, since 2002 Congress has approved FTAs with Australia, Bahrain, Chile, Jordan, Oman, Morocco, Singapore, Peru, the five member South African Customs Union (Botswana, Lesotho, Namibia, South Africa, and Swaziland), and the six parties to Central American free trade agreement (Costa Rica, Dominican Republic, El Salvador, Guatemala, Honduras, and Nicaragua). The countries with which the United States has passed or is negotiating TPAs comprise America's third-largest export market that together purchased $78 billion in American goods and services in 2004. Taken together, these countries are the world's sixth-largest economy.[6]

Enacted as part of the trade act of 2002, TPA permits the president to present a trade agreement to Congress but limits Congress to a yes or no vote.

Because of the politically contentious nature of trade agreements this "up" or "down" approach is virtually the only way to get a trade agreement past Congress without amendment. A congressional amendment to trade agreement would have to be approved by all members of the WTO thus restarting the negotiating process. That does not mean that Congress has no input; in fact, the TPA requires close consultation between the president and Congress during the negotiation process, but without TPA there is little likelihood that Congress would approve the Doha Round trade agreement.

Although USTR has been masterful at using the TPA-enforced deadline to extract concessions from lagging countries, there are a number of countries important to American trade and regional foreign policy that USTR was forced to block from trade agreements because USTR could not reasonably close negotiations before TPA expired.

One of these countries is Indonesia, the largest economy in Southeast Asia, the largest Muslim country in the world, the world's third-largest democracy, and a front-line state on the global war on terrorism. A comprehensive trade agreement with Indonesia would promote a basket of American national interests in Asia. Greater trade between the United States and Indonesia would enhance economic success for the new democratic government, further undermine popular support and the recruiting base of terrorist groups, and strengthen Indonesia's capacity to resist pressure from China.

CHINA

The specter of China economically dominating Asia and turning most Asian countries into vassals to China's economy is a very real fear across the region. In a speech delivered to the National Committee on U.S.-China Relations, then Deputy Secretary of State Robert Zoellick was speaking of American businesses, but he could have been speaking for every government in the Asia-Pacific when he said that they "are concerned that mercantilist Chinese policies will try to direct controlled markets instead of opening competitive markets."[7]

To avoid the region falling under the thrall of the Chinese economic juggernaut, the United States must first encourage China to become a responsible member of the international trading system then assist the other countries of the Asia-Pacific to develop strong, independent, but globally integrated economies.[8] This strategy can best be accomplished through negotiating then enforcing comprehensive trade agreements.

When I visited China in April 1990, the most common form of transportation on the streets of Beijing was bicycles. Even then, however, China was already four years into a fifteen-year-long negotiation process to join the WTO. On December 11, 2001, China became the 143rd member of the WTO. As a mixed reward to the vision of China's leaders to persist in the complex negotiations, China is now the world's third-largest trading nation, after the United States and Japan, but the smog-choked streets of Beijing are packed with motor vehicles of all description.

China's economy grows at a phenomenal rate of more than 10 percent a year. China has emerged as a powerhouse in the world economy, and trade between the United States and China has moved from the periphery to center stage for both countries. Only Canada and Mexico trade more with the United States than China.

It is a consistent theme of this book that despite China's great power status, it does not participate in international organizations except in the narrowest pursuit of its own interests, nor does Beijing enforce the rules that support the international system that China seeks to dominate. China exhibits the same pattern of behavior in its participation in the WTO. Despite the evident benefit China derives from the WTO, Beijing has not joined many of the WTO trade arrangements and is apathetic about enforcing the rules it did accept.

An example of the way China fails to enforce WTO rules is the trade in wood products. Chinese manufacturers of furniture and other wood products use country-of-origin loopholes to launder lumber obtained illegally from other countries.[9]

In order to preserve what's left of its own devastated forests Beijing banned domestic logging. The domestic logging ban sparked a dramatic increase in imports of primary forest products, and China is now the world's third-largest importer of lumber after Japan and the United States.[10]

Demand is driven both by domestic requirements of the construction industry and for China's rapidly expanding furniture manufacturing sector that exports wooden furniture to the United States, Japan, Europe, and the rest of the world. The "loophole" is that even though the wood is imported, once it has been processed into furniture, the rules of origin allow China to mark it as "Made in China." In effect, Chinese manufacturers are laundering illegally harvested lumber from Burma and Indonesia.

Besides busting WTO rules, China's illegal logging also undermines U.S. foreign policy objectives in Southeast Asia by propping up corrupt and unaccountable militaries. Most of the income derived from illegal logging in

Burma and Indonesia ends up in the pockets of generals. In Indonesia, the military's extragovernment sources of income inhibit the ability of the democratic government to institute professional reforms in the Indonesian armed forces. In Burma, the military runs the country, and allowing China to plunder the country's natural resources provides Burma's generals with sufficient income to defy the wishes of its people and the international community.

China's trade in illegal lumber is just the tip of the iceberg for American trade and foreign policy concerns. The service industry comprises 80 percent of the American economy. The backbone of the American service industry is its intellectual creativity. Whether it is piracy of software, entertainment, audiovisual products, or Internet-related materials, the protection of American intellectual property is key to continued American prosperity.

USTR rates intellectual property right (IPR) enforcement as "China's greatest shortcoming."[11] The threat of U.S. trade sanctions and the use of WTO mechanisms to enforce the trade rules forced Beijing to take action to enforce Chinese and WTO rules on IPR piracy, but USTR concedes that China's commitment to protection of American intellectual property continues to "fall short."[12]

It should be a United States priority to compel China to live up to its WTO obligations and to participate in the rules-based international trading system consistent with its economic and political benefit. In its top-to-bottom review of U.S.-China relations, USTR makes a number of recommendations, including expanded enforcement capacity, expanded information-gathering capability, expanded in-country negotiating capacity, increased coordination with trading partners, strengthened regional cooperation, and an increased focus on regulatory reform in China.[13] These solutions are smart, creative, and targeted at the problems of trade with China. The only deficiency is that these new capabilities should be applied to more of Asia's giants.

INDIA

Although India is a founding member of GATT/WTO and was a full participant in the Uruguay Round of negotiations, before 1991, India's economy was a socialist anachronism; most industries were government owned, with Soviet-style central planning segregated by five-year planning cycles. As a result, not only were Indians desperately poor, but India made almost no mark on international trade. India's population is estimated at more than a billion people, or almost 20 percent of the world's population, but in the first half of the 1990s, India's exports comprised only 0.5 percent of world exports.

The government of India recognized the expanding gap between its moribund economy and the rapidly developing economies of other Asian countries, particularly China, and in 1991, New Delhi began a process of reform aimed at joining the global marketplace. The result of these ongoing reforms was strong economic growth, averaging around 6 percent through the 1990s and 7 to 9 percent in the new millennium.

In 2003, Morgan Stanley economists predicted that economic reforms and globalization of the service industry, particularly the IT industry, will be the driving force propelling India to a trillion-dollar economy by 2010.[14] Morgan Stanley cited India's "vast English-speaking" population, with high levels of mathematical skills, and advanced education system as valuable assets to India. There are three hundred million people in India's middle class, the same size as the entire population of the United States, and the education system is adding two hundred thousand engineers every year. When this enormous reservoir of skilled workers and consumers are tapped by the global economy, a trillion dollars will likely be only a milestone in India's future growth.

There are some hurdles to India's integration into the global marketplace. Unlike China, India is slow to sign agreements that open its economy, but fastidious in its international obligations. In IPR enforcement, for example, India has met its TRIPS Agreement obligations. In many cases, India's legal system already provided significant protection to intellectual property. For example, India's Copyright Act of 1957 needed only minor amendment in 1999 to fulfill India's IPR obligations.

Perhaps because New Delhi actually expects to adhere to the agreement it signs, India balks when it comes to making concessions at the WTO. For example, although current U.S. agricultural tariffs are 12 percent compared with India's 114 percent, Kemal Nath (India's Trade Minister) blamed the U.S. for the failure of the Doha agricultural agenda because Washington was "insisting that developing countries open up their markets. . . ." Observers also noted Nath's apathy during the negotiations, commenting on his late arrivals and early departures from the July 2006 negotiations in Geneva.

Furthermore, India's emergence as a leader of the developing countries in the latest WTO round makes it absolutely necessary for U.S. policymakers to work with India on both the multilateral and bilateral levels to achieve meaningful trade liberalization that benefits both countries. Despite the enormous potential of the Indian economy, almost all trade engagement is through the WTO, and there are few bilateral trade agreements between the

United States and India. For example, the U.S. bilateral investment treaty program (BIT) is important for promoting bilateral market oriented policies and exports in numerous countries around the world, but there is no BIT with India.[15] Another bilateral tool to promote trade is the TIFA, which is used primarily with countries that are in the beginning stages of opening their economies—like India—but there is no TIFA with India.

India is an important—in fact, vital—future market for American goods and services, and it should be an important priority with USTR, but there is little evidence that the White House or Congress is focusing on integrating India into the world economy. Nor is India taking enough initiative to deepen its economic relationship with the United States. This problem can be partially reconciled if all of the measures that USTR wants for China are also applied to India, but instead of needing to focus on enforcement of existing agreements the regional and national USTR offices could focus on integrating India's massive economic potential into the global market.

Measures to integrate India's economy should include expanding negotiating capacity in country; for example, USTR should post a senior trade official at the embassy in New Delhi. Additionally, the Foreign Commercial Service should also expand its presence at the embassy to collect information on current and future Indian trade issues, as well as increase high-level meetings between U.S. and Indian trade officials.

REGIONAL TRADE AGREEMENTS

One of the most memorable sound bites of part-time presidential candidate Ross Perot was made during the 1992 presidential campaign when he warned voters to listen for the "giant sucking sound" as American jobs moved down south if the North American Free Trade Agreement (NAFTA) was ratified. Despite the resonance of Perot's prediction in the minds of many Americans, Congress ratified NAFTA, and it has been an unqualified success for the American economy.

Here are a few figures from USTR:[16]

- From 1993 to 2005, trade among NAFTA countries (United States, Canada, and Mexico) grew by 173 percent.
- Merchandise exports from the United States to Mexico and Canada grew faster—133 percent—than U.S. exports to the rest of the world, at 77 percent.

- The average unemployment rate for the ten years before NAFTA was 7.1 percent and averaged only 5.1 percent for the first ten years of NAFTA.
- U.S. industrial production rose by 28 percent for the twelve years before NAFTA and grew by 49 percent for the first twelve years of NAFTA.
- And these new jobs were not low-paying jobs. Compensation, meaning salaries and benefits, grew at an average annual rate of 2.3 percent after NAFTA, compared with before when compensation grew only 0.4 percent annually.

In the Asia-Pacific, the United States has not been as successful in forming effective trade regimes. The biggest and most important economic meeting is the Asia-Pacific Economic Cooperation forum (APEC). Formed in 1995, APEC was intended to integrate the Asia market in advance of the WTO. But since 9/11, APEC has become little more than a forum to discuss the war on terrorism, and no significant trade measures have resulted from APEC meetings.

In October 2002, the Bush administration announced the Enterprise for ASEAN Initiative (EAI). Recognizing that the countries of ASEAN collectively comprise the United States' fifth-largest trading partner,[17] the EAI seeks to deepen the economic and trade relationship that the United States has with the region. The goal of the EAI is to create a network of bilateral FTAs with the ten members of ASEAN. The EAI gives ASEAN countries the flexibility to move at their own speed toward an FTA with the United States, but ultimately all FTAs must meet the same high standards of the U.S.-Singapore FTA to enter into force.[18]

While the EAI is a good step toward linking the countries of ASEAN more strongly to each other and to the United States, the U.S.-Singapore FTA remains the only FTA in force. It is hoped that negotiations with Malaysia will conclude prior to the expiration of President Bush's trade promotion authority. In order for the EAI to be successful, the United States must patiently work with the less developed countries like Cambodia and Laos on WTO entry as well as push to continue trade talks with the more advanced economies of Indonesia, the Philippines, and Thailand.

BILATERAL TRADE AGREEMENTS

A comprehensive global trade agreement should remain the United States' principal objective, and the WTO should remain its main global trade forum. However, the WTO membership is too large, its objectives too comprehensive, and its consensus decision making process too cumbersome to expect an early realization of global free trade. Free trade agreements are negotiated with the WTO in mind and ultimately must be approved by the WTO. Regional and bilateral treaties are designed either to enhance existing WTO provisions or to overcome or bypass weaknesses in the global trade regime. The only regional trade forum the U.S. belongs to in Asia, APEC, has atrophied due to many of the same problems that affect WTO and the Bush administration's tendency to use the APEC leader forum as a pulpit to harangue Asia-Pacific leaders about the war on terrorism.

Starting with President Bill Clinton and accelerated by President Bush, the United States has sought to overcome the multilateral trade agreement problem through bilateral trade agreements. Unfortunately, in the Asia-Pacific region, the United States is not pursuing bilateral trade agreements with sufficient vigor. For example, it has signed thirty-nine BITs, but only three—Bangladesh, Mongolia, and Sri Lanka—are with Asian countries. Similarly, the United States has signed many TIFAs, but only a handful are with Asian countries, and Congress has approved only two in the Asia-Pacific, Singapore and Australia.

Despite the paucity of trade agreements in the region, there are examples that demonstrate the immense possibilities of a trade strategy. For example, since the 2002 U.S.-Vietnam bilateral trade agreement (BTA) was ratified by Congress, Vietnamese total exports have soared 83 percent, from $14.4 billion to $26.5 billion. In addition to the United States, Vietnam has expanded its export markets to countries it had not traded with prior to the U.S.-Vietnam BTA agreement. This includes several Middle Eastern, Latin American, and African countries.[19]

Vietnam is not the only country to experience remarkable economic growth after a trade agreement with the United States; the same phenomenon is seen with other countries that have closed trade agreements with the United States. The advantage of an American trade deal is not just lowering trade barriers on a list of products; instead, agreements negotiated by the USTR include structural changes in the developing country's economies that create efficiencies and permit rapid economic growth even without great surges in foreign investment.

Furthermore, bilateral trade agreements have significant collateral benefits for American foreign policy. For example, both India's and Pakistan's economies were ranked among the "mostly unfree" nations in the *Wall Street Journal*/Heritage Foundation's *Index of Economic Freedom*. Pakistan scored slightly higher at 3.33 to India's 3.49,[20] compared with the world median of

3.04 and the Asia-Pacific median score of 3.28. Both countries maintain crippling trade protection practices, but there is also a growing—in fact, a cascading—desire among their policymakers, businesses, and average citizens to both increase their participation in the global economy and improve cross-border trade. A U.S. BTA with both countries would significantly benefit all three countries.

Pushing trade agreements in Asia will not only improve U.S. trade with those countries but most likely favorably affect cross-border trade between Asian countries as well. With all that said, bilateral and regional trade agreements are not ends in themselves but intermediary steps toward a comprehensive, rules-based global trading system under the WTO. The problem with all measures short of a global system is that they tend to skew trade. For example, even though the United States has FTAs with Australia and Singapore and both countries have FTAs with one another, those FTAs do not constitute a common free trade agreement, and trade among the three countries is still a discrete bilateral relationship. To partially resolve this problem, the Heritage Foundation has recommended a global free trade association.

GLOBAL FREE TRADE ASSOCIATION

In the 2001 *Index of Economic Freedom*, the Heritage Foundation proposed a free trade association to promote "a new trade agenda for a new global economy: an agenda that—unlike today's agenda, which rewards protectionism and trade laggards—actually unites countries that unilaterally open their economies."[21] The Global Free Trade Association (GFTA), as it is known, was not proposed as a substitute for the WTO, but as a more tiered approach that does not tie the entire global trading system to its slowest member. The biggest hole in the GFTA, as proposed by the Heritage Foundation, is that it establishes artificial criteria to join and does not account for the dynamic growth of bilateral trade agreements.

In today's global trading system, many countries already have FTAs with the United States and also have FTAs with other countries. The United States has thirteen FTAs, including Australia, Canada, Chile, Israel, Jordan, Mexico, Morocco, and Singapore, and is negotiating with Korea and Malaysia. Meanwhile, Singapore has concluded eleven FTAs, including Australia, Jordan, India, Japan, Korea, New Zealand, Panama, ASEAN, and a Trans-Pacific FTA that includes New Zealand, Brunei, and Chile. For its part, Australia has four FTAs with the United States, New Zealand, Singapore, and Thailand. One can see that many of the same countries are negotiating FTAs with each other, and it demonstrates the possibilities of expanding the existing web of bilateral FTAs to global free trade association without inventing new criteria and with a minimum of negotiations.

A GFTA would advance its agenda in step-by-step negotiations. First, countries that already have FTAs with the United States would have a round of trade liberalization negotiations adopting "best practices" already agreed to in the group; then further rounds would be extended to other countries already bound in FTAs with the founding group.[22] Finally, the growing prosperity of the GFTA countries would attract additional countries and lead the way for breaking the deadlock of WTO negotiations.

CONCLUSION

As stated repeatedly in this book, it is important to embed Asia in the rules-based international systems. China and India, for example, are essentially free riders on the global trading system, they benefit from the rules that protect their trade, but they selectively enforce the rules of the system. China hardly enforces IPR at all, and India has earned a reputation as spoiler at WTO negotiations by leading factions that resist agreement.

To use Robert Zoellick's widely accepted idea, the countries of Asia must become stakeholders in the international trading system. Without these giants enforcing and expanding the system, it will eventually break down. No system can exist when its largest components break the rules that hold it together.

For its part, the United States needs to expand its capacity to negotiate bilateral and regional trade agreements and to better monitor compliance with WTO and other trade agreements. In order to accomplish that goal, the office of the USTR must have a larger budget and post senior trade officials with the embassies of the largest economies of Asia, including China, Japan, South Korea, Indonesia, and India. The senior officials at all agencies involved in U.S. trade policy also need the personnel to conduct extensive information gathering on the respective country's economy.

USTR should either open a regional Asia-Pacific office or post officials to embassies to increase coordination with other trading partners and to strengthen regional engagement. This regional USTR office should be colocated with the regional assistant secretary described in chapter 3 and charged with advancing the U.S. trade agenda by expanding regional trade agreements, enforcing compliance with existing agreements, and thereby strengthening the rule of law and regional resilience to terrorism and pressure from China.

To integrate the Asia-Pacific strategy with America's global national interests, Congress should grant the president permanent trade promotion authority. And the president should direct USTR to open the first round of trade liberalization negotiations to create a global free trade association. The founding members would include all the interested countries with which the United States and its trading partners already have FTAs.

• 7 •

Unification of the Korean Peninsula

> There is nothing like dream to create the future. Utopia today, flesh and blood tomorrow.
>
> —Victor Hugo, *Les Miserables*

One of the most important events that will occur in Asia during the twenty-first century will be unification of the Korean peninsula. Not only will it free the millions of Koreans enslaved by the Kim family dynasty, but unification and how it occurs will affect the U.S.-Asia Pacific alliance system, ballistic missile defense, U.S. relations with Beijing, and relations between Korea, Japan, and China. Furthermore, depending on how it occurs, unification will either disrupt or be a great enabler of trade and economic growth for the whole region. Unification will also affect global humanitarian aid and refugee programs.

The focus of this chapter is to identify the challenges to U.S. policy presented by Korean unification and offer policy prescriptions to guide American policymakers through the unification transition and toward the new united, postdivision Korean government.[1]

ASSUMPTIONS

Because of the host of unknown factors involved in the eventual unification, I will conduct this analysis with two assumptions. The first assumption relates to the "when" of unification. I chose fifteen years because after that amount of time, the international situation will have changed so much from the current alignment as to make policy prescriptions made today outdated. Many of the recommendations, such as maintaining the alliance, will still be valid, but one cannot presume too much about the future.

The second assumption is that the responsibility of unification will fall on the shoulders of the government of the Republic of Korea (ROK) in Seoul. This assumption relates the "how" of unification. Scholars and defense planners generally ascribe to three main scenarios for unification: a gradual unification through mutual agreement, a sudden unification resulting from the implosion of the Democratic People's Republic of Korea (DPRK) government, and a violent unification following a war.[2] In all of these scenarios, the ROK, with its capital in Seoul, is the most likely successor to today's two states. Lastly, Seoul is the historic capital of Korea and no matter the nature of the unification, the prevailing powers will most likely choose Seoul as the unified country's capital.

SITUATION ON THE KOREAN PENINSULA

The disparities in size and power between North and South Korea are tremendous. The population of South Korea is twice that of North Korea, 48 million to 23 million. The *CIA World Fact Book* estimates North Korea's GDP at $40 billion and stagnant, if not shrinking,[3] while South Korea's economy will soon top $1 trillion when measured by purchasing power parity (PPP), and it is growing rapidly.[4]

The DPRK (North Korea) was created at the end of World War II. Japan had been the colonial master since 1905, and when it lost the war and withdrew its forces from the Korean peninsula, the Soviet Union and the United States delineated their respective occupation zones at the thirty-eighth parallel. The rest is the predictable history of twentieth-century communist dictatorships marked by failed economies and political repression, except the DPRK dinosaur has managed to survive into the twenty-first century. South Korea, on the other hand, evolved from dictatorship to democracy and developed a large and vibrant market economy.

Most communist-era countries were redundantly named People's Republics or Democratic Republics, yet none of them possessed a representative government. North Korea's official name, Democratic People's Republic of Korea, is triply redundant and even more repressive than its communist cousins.

North Korea's first dictator, Kim Il Sung, died in July 1994 and was succeeded by his son, Kim Jung Il, who remains in power to this day. Although no lightweight when it came to economic mismanagement and barbaric political repression, Kim Il Sung has been outpaced by his son.

During the 1970s and 1980s, like many communist economies of the era, North Korea's economy stagnated, buoyed up only by subsidies from the Soviet Union. The Soviet Union cut off subsidies in 1991, and one year after Kim Jung Il ascended the throne, the DPRK's economy collapsed, resulting in the starvation of as many as three million North Koreans. Droughts and flooding were blamed for the famine, but make no mistake: North Korea's economic disaster is man-made. The population survives only because of international handouts, but widespread undernourishment remains, and attendance at school has reportedly fallen as starving children scrounge for food instead of studying (see table 7.1).

After five years of ignoring the economy, in 2002, Kim Jung Il instituted some modest reforms, but mismanagement, corruption, and widespread skepticism retard their implementation. Skepticism is prevalent on both sides. The DPRK government is suspicious that economic reform will weaken political control, while potential investors are leery because North Korea regularly defaults on loans and never loses an opportunity to cheat a friendly investor.

In fact, an estimated one thousand investors or businesses either went bankrupt or incurred substantial losses as a result of doing business with North Korea.[5] Hyundai's experience investing in a tourist project was a warning to other companies. Hyundai was once one of South Korea's largest companies, but it lost a reported $1.5 billion to North Korea in reported "licensing" and other costly pay-offs trying to help the DPRK develop a scenic area to attract South Korean tourists.[6] Hyundai fired its CEO, Kim Yoon-kyu, in charge of Hyundai's North Korean businesses, for questionable business practices and drastically cut back operations in North Korea. In 2006, the DPRK closed the remaining Hyundai offices in retaliation for ROK cutting off food aid to North Korea over the missile tests.

Kim Jung Il's special talent is causing the death of millions through the criminal mismanagement of the economy, but he does not neglect to use direct action against people suspected of opposing his regime. North Korean prisons are reportedly clogged with tens of thousands of people, where as many as 25 percent die every year.[7] Deadly experiments on prisoners include gas chambers and poisoned food.[8] There are ever-increasing reports of other horrors against prisoners coming from North Korean refugees.

Table 7.1. Operational Expenditures: Selected Asian Countries (thousand dollars)

			2001		
Country	*Development*	*Relief*	*Special Operations*	*Bilateral*	*TOTAL*
Cambodia	1,171	26,140	—	—	27,312
China	11,687	—	—	882	12,569
India	17,889	3,747	—	—	21,636
Indonesia	—	15,710	—	—	15,710
North Korea	—	233,515	—	—	233,515
Sri Lanka	637	3,224	—	—	3,861
Vietnam	182	12	—	—	194
			2002		
Country	*Development*	*Special Relief*	*Operations*	*Bilateral*	*TOTAL*
Cambodia	1,301	16,333	—	1,608	19,242
China	12,657	—	—	1,837	14,494
India	9,817	434	—	—	10,251
Indonesia	—	11,060	—	—	11,060
North Korea	—	101,879	796	60	102,735
Sri Lanka	2,899	4,865	—	—	7,764
Vietnam	—	—	—	—	—

Source: World Food Programme, *Annual Report 2002*, annex 3, 38–39, www.wfp.org/policies/annual_reports/documents/2002_wfp_annual_report.pdf.

In every measure of humane accomplishments, the Seoul-based ROK is far more successful than the Pyongyang-based DPRK. Infant mortality rates under the DPRK are three times that of ROK-born babies, and adult life expectancy is shorter (71.65 years vs. 77.04 years) in the north. Furthermore, the World Food Programme estimates that more than 60 percent of North Korean children are either below weight or stunted by lack of food.[9]

Because of the brutal economic and political conditions in North Korea, refugees are on the move across the country despite the police state's restrictions on unofficial travel. Because militarization of the north-south border prevents the passage of refugees, they generally choose to flee to China. Estimates of the number of North Korean refugees in China range as high as 300,000, of which a very small number successfully flee China's police state for South Korea. Another 250,000 of internally displaced people (IDP) are believed to be wandering homeless in North Korea.

There are no South Korean refugees; instead, people flock to the country to work. There are 235,000 foreigners working legally in South Korea, and another 180,000 are believed to be working there illegally.

These same disparities carry over into the military. Although North Korea spends as much as 25 percent of its gross national product on the military, it is still only able to muster a military budget less than 20 percent of South Korea's annual defense expenditures. North Korea has managed to scrape together greater numbers of tanks and artillery than South Korea, but largely by not retiring (or repairing) ageing equipment. South Korea's armed forces, on the other hand, are qualitatively far superior, integrating the world's latest technology and training into the armed forces. Given the overwhelming advantages of the ROK over the DPRK, it is difficult to imagine any scenario where North Korea prevails over South Korea.

SCENARIOS

There are a number of published scenarios on how unification of the Korean peninsula might take place. They can be grouped into three rough categories: reform, collapse, and war. In the reform scenario, North Korea begins a process of economic reforms that lead eventually to a gradual and peaceful unification. The collapse theory is that North Korea does not reform and fails; unification comes about through South Korea occupying or annexing North Korea. The war scenario postulates a war on the peninsula that would eventually result in reunification.

Reform

The reform theory is the more desirable, but it is less likely than the collapse theory. ROK president Kim Dae Jung's "Sunshine Policy" was based on the reform theory. Kim Dae Jung permitted South Korean investment in the north, such as Hyundai's Mount Kumgang tourist deal; provided unconditional humanitarian assistance; and tried to increase direct communications between families divided by the governments. Although President Kim Dae Jung quite rightly saw this as a policy to bring about gradual changes to the DPRK, Kim Jung Il appears to have seen it the same way and thus interpreted the Sunshine Policy as a dangerous threat to his regime.

Part of the success of the DPRK regime in remaining in power is its ability to convince North Koreans that the ROK is a hopeless failure and viciously hostile to North Korea. DPRK leaders evidently believe that a dose of "sunshine" on the vast differences between North and South Korea will not flatter the DPRK leadership and expose decades of propaganda as a monument of lies. Thus, the DPRK views accepting South Korean humanitarian aid, engaging in talks with South Korean leaders, and allowing North Koreans to visit with South Koreans as destabilizing to North Korea.

The reform scenario is dependent on engagement with North Korea, but no country, even patrons such as Russia and China, have regular meetings with the Dear Leader. In fact, the weird personality cult surrounding Kim Jung Il precludes normal engagement. The cult of personality confers all kinds of mystical powers on Kim Jung Il. North Korean newspapers unashamedly report cherry blossoms blooming out of season on his birthday, and he is reportedly able to influence the weather. North Korean propagandists claim he has written five of the world's greatest operas and shot eleven holes in one the first time he golfed.

In Asia, golfing is a popular activity for national leaders to engage each other in an informal setting. Because of possible exposure of his actual golfing abilities, it hardly seems likely that Kim Jung Il would participate in a golf game watched by the world press. The Dear Leader rarely travels outside North Korea and has never participated in an event that might cast doubt on his mandate from heaven.

The six-party talks—involving North and South Korea, Japan, China, Russia, and the United States—is also a reform scenario policy. The objective of the talks is to denuclearize the Korean peninsula and to eventually normalize relations with the DPRK. Although each of the six countries views these objectives in a slightly different way, the process of engaging North Korea assumes that Kim Jung Il will participate in the negotiations in good faith—despite all experience to the contrary.

Ultimately the reform scenario rests on North Korea voluntarily undertaking substantive reforms to its economy. Despite some signs that North Korea recognizes the problem, there is no indication that the DPRK government view reforms as necessary or prudent to its survival.

Collapse

The collapse scenario postulates that North Korea will, like Eastern Europe and the Soviet Union, collapse under the weight of its own contradictions and the ROK would move in and pick up the pieces as West Germany did in East Germany. In fact, a 1997 study by the Korean Unification Ministry found that the North Korean system should have collapsed in 1992.[10] So what happened?

By any standard, North Korea is a failed state and survives only on the handouts of countries not well disposed to the DPRK. Additionally, illicit activities such as currency counterfeiting and drug smuggling make up a significant portion of its budget, reportedly earning at least $500 million to $1 billion annually. The World Food Programme provides hundreds of millions of dollars of relief assistance every year. Japan, South Korea, and the United States also provide hundreds of thousands of tons of food aid. China is believed to provide fuel assistance and purchases North Korea's meager commodities and trade goods.

Despite its vulnerability to the whims of philanthropy of the international community and its restraint in some cases from seeking criminal prosecution, the DPRK continues to demand foreign assistance in the most strident and insulting terms, a tactic the Economist Intelligence Unit calls "militant mendicancy."[11]

Examples of North Korea's militant mendicancy abound. For example, when Hyundai provided ten thousand cattle to North Korea free of charge, the North Koreans demanded that they keep the trucks they were transported in, too. In another outrage, in September 2005, the U.S. Treasury Department blocked Banco Delta Asia, in Macao, from doing business with American financial institutions because the bank was accepting North Korean counterfeit U.S. dollars. In retaliation, North Korea refused to return to the six-party talks. When the United States neither declined to back down from its position nor offered concessions to the DPRK to get them to return to the six-party talks, North Korea tested its long-range Taepodong II missile in July and a nuclear device in October 2006 as an implicit threat to the region and the United States.

It is not difficult to imagine that the international community will eventually tire of these antics and stop providing aid. In fact, following the missile and nuclear tests, South Korea, Japan, the United States, and even China cut off humanitarian aid, and both China and Russia voted for a United Nations Security Council resolution opposing North Korea's missile and nuclear weapon programs. How long North Korea's decrepit economy can survive without aid and under increasing surveillance on its criminal activities remains an open question.

The collapse theory rests on three assumptions: first, that North Korea will not reform; second, that the current situation is unsustainable; and third, that the DPRK will not resort to armed conflict. There are few signs that the DPRK will undertake substantive reforms, and the political and economic situation continues to deteriorate. The next section will examine the possibility of armed conflict.

War

The last of the scenarios, unification as a result of a war, is the most deadly and the least likely of the three scenarios. The U.S. Army's Deputy Chief of Staff for Intelligence commissioned a Rand Corporation study to consider this possibility. The authors, Jonathan Pollack and Chung Min Lee, conclude that the only way the DPRK would choose war is if "its other policy options were exhausted, and systemic atrophy reaches unmanageable levels."[12] Pollack and Lee argue that the military option would be suicidal for Kim Jung Il personally and North Korea in general, but because of the state's overwhelming focus on military preparation, the war option could not be ignored.

Reinforcing that argument, Kim Jung Il tends to choose brinkmanship over diplomacy, and there is a possibility of war through miscalculation. As discussed earlier, in order to display his ire at financial sanctions and lack of American concessions to his demands in the six-party talks, Kim Jung Il fired off seven missiles on July 4, and tested a nuclear device in October 2006. Although both the nuclear missile launches were a political and technical failures, the tests did demonstrate that the Dear Leader prefers military options, however unsuccessful they might be.

Furthermore, it is not unknown in history for national leaders to choose war as a means to distract public attention from failed domestic policies. Therefore, it is in the range of possibilities that the DPRK would choose to conduct a campaign of confrontation and brinkmanship in order to distract the nation from another famine, and through miscalculation convince South Korea the preparations were genuine, thus setting off a war—intended or not. Also, if the government of North Korea experienced a crisis so severe that Kim Jung Il believed his hold on power or personal survival was at risk, he may order his army to attack in a desperate attempt to regain control of the country.

However it starts, a war on the Korean peninsula would be deadly, and Seoul, which is in missile and long-range artillery range of the border, would be hit hard. Despite the disparities in capability between North and South Korea, initial success by North Korea cannot be discounted. There are numerous historical examples of smaller, lesser-equipped forces having great initial success; the Confederate armies in the American Civil War and the Japanese and German militaries in World War II are some examples. Nevertheless, no matter if there are early battlefield victories, the remorseless accounting of logistics would quickly grind down the Korean People's Army (KPA).

The KPA's ageing and undermaintained equipment will break down quickly. Tanks and trucks must have fuel, and North Korea has very little. There is so little fuel in North Korea that commercial satellite photos and eyewitness accounts show the roads almost empty of vehicle traffic even in the middle of the day. The implication is that even if the KPA has hoarded sufficient fuel for an attack, the drivers are insufficiently trained to operate the vehicles, thus increasing the number of maintenance-related breakdowns and vehicle accidents clogging North Korea's flimsy road network.

The KPA artillery is quantitatively strong, but artillery needs logistical support, too. The KPA has already dug in 90 percent of its guns close to South Korea's border, but there is no reason to believe that KPA artillery arm is any more efficient than the rest of the country, and a considerable number of their guns and missiles will probably not work properly at the critical moment. The tank fleet is no better. The KPA still retains a large number of World War II–era Russian T-34s in its front-line inventory, and few of the other available tank models are younger than the fathers of soldiers driving them.

Finally, initial military successes would actually work against the KPA. If the KPA were to push far into South Korea, then guns, tanks, crews, fuel, and ammunition would have to be moved forward at considerable logistical effort. The underfed, underweight, and underequipped soldiers would have to fight and maintain discipline during a protracted march across South Korea. One can only imagine what KPA soldiers might think as they march through a land undeniably richer than their own. History is replete with examples of military offensives, successful at the outset, slowing, stopping, and even disintegrating when soldiers stop to scavenge, loot, and desert.

Furthermore, there is no reason to believe that the KPA has any generals like Stonewall Jackson (United States), Tomoyuki Yamashita (Japan), or Erwin Rommel (Germany). North Korea has not fought a war in fifty years and officer promotions are based on political considerations, not military prowess. Their South Korean and American opponents, on the other hand, are professional soldiers with considerable tactical and operational training and experience.

It is far more likely that the ROK armed forces will repel the initial attack and then move into the North Korean border area to stop the rain of missiles and artillery on South Korea and to gain control of the DPRK's nuclear weapons (if there are any). Since 90 percent of the KPA is massed along the border and they lack the logistical ability to flee with their weapon systems intact, ROK army occupation of the northern side of the demilitarized zone would effectively destroy the KPA. At that point, there would be no significant forces between the South Korean army and the Chinese border, and the ROK government would have to decide whether and how to occupy the rest of the Korean peninsula.

How Nuclear Weapons Affect the War Scenario

The DPRK claims to have built a number of nuclear bombs. Pyongyang does not permit the IAEA or any other national or international organizations to examine its nuclear reactors or weapon stockpile, so there is no means to verify this claim. Nevertheless, North Korea does have the nuclear reactors and technology to create nuclear devices and has tested a nuclear bomb and the delivery systems to use them. No matter how unsuccessful these tests were, the international community must assume that Kim Jung Il does possess nuclear weapons and the means to use them.

Having a nuclear bomb and using it are two entirely different issues. At the most, North Korea may have as many as twenty crude weapons and demonstrably unreliable and imprecise delivery systems. The United States, on the other hand, has thousands of nuclear warheads with missile systems precise enough to deliver them uninvited to Kim Jung Il's dinner table. If North Korea were foolish enough to use its nuclear weapon against an ally of the United States, such as Korea or Japan, then Washington, D.C., would be bound by treaty and common sense to retaliate.

It is an unfortunate fact that nuclear weapons are large explosive devices, and inside their blast radius, nuclear explosions do not discriminate between the guilty and the innocent. Kim Jung Il, his family, friends, cronies, dog, and tens of thousands of his unwitting subjects will die in the event of a nuclear war. Kim Jung Il and his military advisers know these facts and cannot escape their logic. There is no reason to believe that either Kim Jung Il or anyone inside his inner circle are suicidal, so there is every reason to believe that Kim Jung Il intends his nuclear weapons as bargaining devices only and would never dare use them.

It remains incumbent on the international community, however, to denuclearize the Korean peninsula.

THE OTHER PLAYERS

China, Japan, Russia, and the United States all have important strategic interests in the unification of the Korean peninsula. During any unification scenario, each of these players will seek to protect those interests. Briefly examining those interests will assist in determining American policy toward unification.

China

There is a significant and opaque gap between what China says and what China does with North Korea that makes it difficult to assess the nature of the relationship. According to Chinese diplomats speaking unofficially on the margins of international conferences, despite the fact that China literally holds North Korea's pursestrings, Beijing has been unable to translate that position into influence over Pyongyang.

Beijing claims to have tried to prevent Pyongyang from developing either ballistic missiles or nuclear weapons. Beijing also encourages the ideologically communist North Korea to adopt the Chinese model of economic development, but all to no avail.

As stated in chapter 3, China began nuclear cooperation with North Korea as early as 1959, but Beijing became suspicious that North Korea was developing nuclear weapons at a nuclear waste site in Yongbyon in 1987. China reportedly halted all transfers of nuclear technology and withdrew its nuclear technicians from North Korea. Since then, Beijing has refused to provide any nuclear-related assistance to Pyongyang. Nevertheless, the nuclear weapons technology discovered in North Korea's nuclear program, including large numbers of centrifuge machines to produce weapons-grade uranium, has its origins in Chinese assistance to Pakistan's nuclear programs. It seems unlikely that Islamabad would have passed on Chinese-origin nuclear technology in such quantities to North Korea without Beijing's knowledge and consent.[13]

China's missile assistance to North Korea began in the 1970s. Throughout the 1980s and 1990s, China transferred short-range ballistic missiles and production technologies, assisted North Korea in a long-range ballistic missile project, and trained North Korean engineers.[14] The long-range Taepodong-2 reportedly replicated in large part the Chinese CSS-2 intermediate-range ballistic missile. China insists, however, that it is no longer helping North Korea and in August 2002 promulgated a comprehensive missile-related export control system, similar in scope to the Missile Technology Control Regime (MTCR).[15]

In July 2006, when the world already knew North Korea had a missile on the launch pad, but still had not fired it, China publicly demanded that Pyongyang not test its missile. After North Korea tested anyway, China assisted in the adoption of United Nations Security Council resolution condemning North Korea's missile test. And in October when North Korea was preparing to test a nuclear device China publicly and vehemently opposed the test, but again Pyongyang defied Beijing and tested anyway. Publicly humiliated, Pyongyang's communist patrons in Beijing again assisted in the creation of another UN resolution but stopped short of tough sanctions. Beijing's public stance against Pyongyang, but its apparent reluctance to punish Kim Jong Il's defiance, adds to the confusion over China's intentions with North Korea.

China's interests, however, go beyond the Korean peninsula. The People's Liberation Army (PLA), China's armed forces, believe that it is on the verge of or perhaps already engaged in a global Cold War with the United States. There are almost forty thousand American military men and women in South Korea as part of the fifty-year-old alliance. The PLA fears that a North Korean collapse could bring American soldiers to China's borders.

In the late 1990s, I worked in the Pentagon and once played escort for a visiting PLA delegation led by a Chinese general who was a veteran of the Korean War. During the lunch conversation, the possibility of a North Korean collapse came up, and an American general asked about China's reaction to such an event. The Chinese general was visibly shaken by the question. He first spoke quietly through his translator, acknowledging that he had recently been to North Korea and that North Korea was in bad shape. He did not deny the possibility of a collapse, but then he started speaking louder and gesticulating toward the American general in a stop gesture, saying in English, "No more Task Force Smith! No more Task Force Smith!" He was referring to the original American wartime intervention into Korea in July 1950, named after its commander, Lieutenant Colonel Charles Smith.

The general's meaning was obvious to everyone at the table: in the event of a war or North Korean collapse, China does not want American forces crossing into North Korea. China, however, does not place the same limits on itself.

China demonstrated its ambivalence toward the sanctity of Korea's borders in February 2002 when Beijing sponsored the "Northeast Project." The goal of this project is to define or resolve various "problems" related to the history, geography, and ethnicity of certain provinces in northeastern China bordering Korea. The research has largely focused on the Kingdom of Koguryo

(37 B.C.–A.D. 668), which is also one of Korea's three original kingdoms. Although China made no official claim to North Korea as Chinese territory, Chinese scholars determined that Koguryo was absorbed into ancient China and is integral to China's modern borders. Even North Korea was shocked by China's declaration and accused China of "manipulating history for its own interests."[16]

South Korean scholars, politicians, and citizens see a far more sinister plot. The borders of Koguryo, as drawn by Chinese scholars, have a suspicious similarity with today's modern division between North and South Korea. Many South Koreans believe that China is setting the historical stage for absorption of North Korea in the event of a collapse.

South Korean fears about China's intentions are firmly grounded in historical precedent. Throughout Korea's long history, China frequently exercised control over the Korean kingdoms through its tributary system. Most recently, China invaded Korea in 1951, attacking American and ROK troops that had defeated the North Korean army and were pursuing the defeated remnants to the Chinese border. Significantly, Chinese forces were amassing on the border before American and ROK troops had crossed the thirty-eighth parallel.

Beijing's interests in North Korea reflect China's vision of itself as a great power. In any unification scenario, China will seek recognition of its regional dominance from the new government in Seoul, similar to the tributary relationship it once exercised on the peninsula. In pursuing that goal, China will seek to

- control the reunification process in any of the scenarios;
- keep American and foreign troops out of North Korea and hopefully move them off the peninsula all together;
- break the U.S.-Korean alliance;
- aggravate animosities between Korea and Japan;
- denuclearize the Korean peninsula; and
- demand recognition of the borders as China defines them. China has a large ethnic Korean population, swelling daily with North Korean refugees, and it will not want a unified Korea claiming Chinese territory. Beijing may want to define the border farther south of its current border with North Korea.

In any scenario except "reform," China will most likely use the ensuing disorder as an excuse to send troops into northern Korea. Beijing has not hesitated to use the PLA in Korea, as well as in Tibet, India, and Vietnam, and to enforce its maritime territorial claims in the South China Sea. Once they arrive, the presence of Chinese troops will become a powerful bargaining chip for Beijing as it deals with Seoul. China will put the price of withdrawal at dissolving the American alliance and denuclearization of the peninsula, and Beijing may still attempt to redraw the boundary farther south. The Republic of Korea must be prepared to make the price very high for China intervening where it is not wanted.

Japan

Japan and Korea are geographically close and share a long and bumpy history. Koreans retain painful memories of Japanese occupation and resent Japan's reluctance to admit to or apologize for its actions in Korea before and during World War II. With all that said, Japan is South Korea's largest trading partner, and Tokyo shares Seoul's concerns about a peaceful unification of the peninsula.

For Tokyo, North Korea's intransigence and militancy are both scary and an opportunity to rid itself of post–World War II constitutional restrictions on its armed forces. In 1998, North Korea fired a Taepodong missile over Japan, which landed in the Pacific Ocean on the other side. The missile test simultaneously proved that North Korea cannot deploy a working long-range missile and scared the Japanese enough to begin the process of loosening constitutional restrictions on its military.

Japan is restricted by its constitution to a self-defense force, rather than a professional military, and from participating in collective defense. Although China is a major long-range concern in Tokyo, North Korea's rogue behavior provides Japan with a convenient excuse to reform its military institutions. The recent nuclear and missile tests have served to accelerate the process. The United States also wants a normal Japanese armed forces to help participate in the ever-changing security threats and humanitarian crises in the Asia-Pacific region.

With all that said, Japan's concerns about North Korea are not fallacious or a veneer for anti-Chinese policies. Tokyo quite sincerely does not want a North Korean missile, especially a nuclear-tipped one, landing in or near Japan. Furthermore, North Korea has kidnapped Japanese citizens, holding them hostage for decades, and some died while in DPRK custody. KPA navy vessels intrude into Japanese waters and spy on Japanese ports. Finally, most Japanese, for humanitarian reasons alone, would like to see North Korean reform. Official Tokyo would dearly love to see a reform and peaceful reconciliation scenario, but it fears the war scenario or the costs of a collapse.

- For South Korea, Japan is critical to the reunification process under any scenario.
- Japan is South Korea's largest trading partner, and this symbiotic trade relationship will sustain the Korean economy during and after unification.
- A reform scenario implies foreign investment in North Korea. Japan could be a major investor if North Korea should undertake economic reforms.
- A collapse scenario will require significant humanitarian and development assistance. Japan is the largest foreign aid contributor in Asia, donating $2.2 billion in 2004. Much of that aid and more could be channeled to Korea.

In the war scenario, Japan could play a major role in providing the ROK military with logistical support and intelligence sharing. In the East Sea, between Korea and Japan, Japan could provide direct naval assistance by protecting commercial shipping, missile/air defense, and cooperation in blockade enforcement. China's intentions toward a unified Korea could be less than favorable, and a friendly Japan could be a card Seoul can play in the diplomatic maneuvering during the reunification process. Unfortunately, historical animosities affect all aspects of Japan-Korea relations, but it is in the best interests of a unified Korea and a remilitarized Japan to resolve their differences.

Russia

Moscow's interests in North Korea are far more transparent and practical than Beijing's objectives and consequently far less threatening. The Russians have economic security and diplomatic interests.

During the Soviet era, North Korea accumulated a $3.8 billon debt. Russia wants to be repaid. Russia is interested in expanding transportation links, particularly rail links, with North Korea in order to gain commercial access to the peninsula's ice-free ports. In the Far East, Russia has as much as three hundred thousand kilowatts of surplus electrical power, and Moscow would like to sell that surplus to energy-starved North Korea.

Moscow's security interests are in restricting North Korea's nuclear and missile technology proliferation and denuclearizing the peninsula. Lastly,

Moscow is nostalgic for its superpower days, and the six-party talks offer Russia an opportunity to participate on the world stage.

Ultimately, if the unified Korea assumes DPRK debt and is open to trade, Russia will benefit from the rationalization of the relationship and will welcome unification.

America and Korean Unification

For the United States, the challenges of Korean unification are numerous, and policy prescriptions will have to be nuanced. American policy for all scenarios should assume that the Republic of Korea will be the successor state on the Korean peninsula and conform to the needs of the ROK. American interests are in a peaceful unified, sovereign, democratic Republic of Korea with a free market economy. The United States wants to retain the fifty-year-old alliance and a comprehensive free trade agreement with Korea.

In support of the reform scenario, the United States should seek a peace treaty between the United Nations and the DPRK that includes mutual recognition between both Koreas. Once there are a peace treaty and normal diplomatic relations between the ROK and North Korea, then the United States can normalize relations with the DPRK. Trade and security agreements can follow the success of diplomatic relations, but American agreements with the DPRK should stay a respectful distance behind ROK initiatives.

The United States needs to play a more active role in finding common ground between Japan and Korea. Convincing Japan to face up to the black marks, as well as the successes, of its historical legacy should be a major U.S. foreign policy goal. Koreans also must learn to forgive the Japanese for the brutal acts of their grandfathers and act in the best interest of a unified Korea. Developing confidence-building measures between these two East Asian democracies would significantly assist U.S. policy in the region.

Scenario 2 will not find conditions in North Korea the same as they were in East Germany in 1990. The collapse of the DPRK will most likely be accompanied by a major humanitarian crisis with a potentially hostile, confused, or distrustful population. The United States has considerable experience dealing with humanitarian disasters from Indonesia to Haiti. Nevertheless, coordinated plans with Australia, Japan, ROK, and other friends and allies would be invaluable when time is short during a crisis.

Furthermore, American and foreign military presence in northern Korea, at least until the ROK has firm control of its new borders, is likely to provoke a negative and unhelpful response from China. The United States and Korea must prepare a unified diplomatic strategy to engage China during the crisis. The heart of the unified position should be that American forces will not cross into northern Korea as long as the PLA remains on its side of the border.

Simultaneously, the United States and South Korean armed forces must plan and prepare for the latter's forces alone to restore order and distribute aid in northern Korea. These missions will not only include the logistical efforts of distributing aid but will also require ROK troops trained and experienced in peacekeeping, counterinsurgency, and border security missions.

The United States should share its experience in Iraq and Afghanistan in order to prepare the ROK armed forces for the situation in northern Korea. Furthermore, the ROK should be encouraged to participate in UN peacekeeping efforts to gain practical experience.

The war scenario will require robust military and diplomatic preparations. Militarily, the ROK armed forces must be prepared to

- repel a KPA attack;
- destroy KPA forces threatening Seoul and South Korea;
- seize nuclear weapons and any other weapons of mass destruction;
- occupy all of northern Korea;
- repel or expel any foreign forces that may enter North Korea uninvited;
- establish border control.

That is a tall set of missions for any army. The implied mission for the ROK is it must maintain a large, well-trained, and equipped military capable of accomplishing all those missions.

The diplomatic missions will be equally daunting. ROK diplomats will have to

- engage the United States in supporting ROK actions while avoiding a superpower confrontation;
- engage China by addressing Beijing's concerns about its border integrity and security, and gain Beijing's acquiescence to ROK military activities;
- gain United Nations support for ROK actions in northern Korea;
- leverage Japanese and other allied assistance.

These scenarios create a context for American military presence in South Korea. In any of the scenarios, as long as China stays on its side of the border, American presence in northern Korea would be unnecessarily provocative.

Nevertheless, the United States has a treaty obligation to the ROK. An American military presence in South Korea should be organized to provide a strong defense against KPA incursion and a follow-on offensive capability should the PLA intervene.

The types of troops needed to accomplish the first mission would be

- counterbattery, antimissile, and antiaircraft artillery;
- air superiority fighters to defeat the KPA air force over South Korea;
- substantial logistical bases, including prepositioned equipment for quickly building up offensive forces on the peninsula, should they be needed.

These forces are generally defensive in nature and thus not provocative. Offensive forces can be quickly deployed from the United States in the event of a war.

When I was a platoon leader in West Germany in the early 1980s, the biggest annual exercise was REFORGER, or "Return of Forces to Germany." The purpose of the exercise was to practice quickly deploying large American forces to Germany in the event of a Soviet attack. The same kind of exercise can be organized with South Korea in the twenty-first century. The purpose would be the same, to practice rapid deployment with the Korean armed forces and to serve as a deterrent by demonstrating to any potential adversaries the ability to rapidly provide offensive capability. This exercise would also allow a draw-down of offensive oriented forces permanently stationed in South Korea.

CONCLUSION

The United States must prepare now for Korean unification. Washington must develop policies that shape the diplomatic environment by bringing together the ROK and Japan and reassure China that an American alliance with Korea is not anti-Chinese.

The military environment can be shaped by stationing appropriately organized forces in South Korea and Japan. Furthermore, the Pentagon must engage the South Korean military in an active exercise program and ensure that the latest technology and doctrine are available to the ROK armed forces.

In the short term, as long as there are two Koreas, the United States must have policies for the DPRK. For North Korea, the United States should:

- avoid panicking about North Korean brinkmanship—wringing concessions from frightened world leaders is the objective of Kim Jung Il's antics;
- continue to investigate and sanction the DPRK on illicit activities such as currency counterfeiting;
- insist that all discussions with DPRK take place inside the six-party talks.

The reunification of the Korean peninsula will undoubtedly be a far more painful event than the fall of the Soviet Union and the reunification of Germany. Nevertheless, when it occurs, the United States must rise to meet the challenge and to lessen the burden on our longtime friend and ally, the Republic of Korea.

• 8 •

One China, Two Chinas, One Taiwan?

By John J. Tkacik Jr.

> What is necessary is to rectify names. . . . If names be not correct, language is not in accordance with the truth. If language be not in accordance with the truth, affairs cannot be carried out into success.
>
> —The Analects of Confucius, Book 13, Verse 3

Is there only one China? Are there two? Is the government of one China seated in Beijing and the other in Taipei? Or perhaps Taiwan is wholly independent from China? And if everyone agrees that Taiwan is independent "in fact" (de facto) from Chinese sovereignty, then what real difference does it make if it is "independent" in law (de jure)?

These questions are at the core of the China-Taiwan problem, a problem that has been an indigestible morsel of U.S. foreign policy at least since 1946 and that still causes recurring bouts of gastric distress among American diplomats at the United States Department of State to this day. The United States will be forced to answer these questions during the course of the next century.

HISTORY AS A GUIDE

The idea that Taiwan is "part of China" is a very recent one. "Formosa" was the name given the "beautiful" isle of Taiwan by sixteenth-century Portuguese explorers, and later Spanish and Dutch colonists adopted the name. When the Dutch founded their colony in southern Taiwan in 1624, Taiwan's population consisted almost exclusively of Austronesian or "proto-Polynesian" aboriginal peoples who belonged to several tribes, which were linguistically distinct and had never unified and never established any islandwide confederacy or institution.[1]

There is, in fact, considerable linguistic evidence that the island of Taiwan was the launching platform for the Polynesian expansion into the Pacific islands via the Philippine islands as early as the second millennium B.C.[2] This supposition is consistent with Taiwan's geographic position at the northern end of the Philippine archipelago.

Since its aboriginal peoples lacked any form of government recognizable to European eyes, Taiwan was what in seventeenth-century international law would be termed "*terra nullius*"—a populated land without government and hence susceptible to claim by an established state willing to institute civilized governance. Although Taiwan had theretofore been regularly visited by merchants and fishing fleets from China, Japan, and Okinawa, none had the will nor inclination to bring Taiwan (Formosa) under formal state rule. In fact, China's Ming Dynasty instituted a formal "ban on sea trade" with islands beyond the Chinese coast—including Taiwan—which encouraged pirates from China and Japan to raid coastal China from Taiwanese bases.[3]

In the early seventeenth century, the Dutch controlled what is now Indonesia, the Spanish controlled the Philippines, and the Portuguese had been granted an imperial Chinese (Ming) writ to control piracy from their base in Macau. The Dutch established their base in southern Taiwan in 1624 and, after obliging a Spanish settlement in Northern Taiwan to disband in 1642, continued as the sole rulers of Taiwan until 1662. While the Dutchmen were minding their own colonial business on the island of Formosa, the Chinese Empire was once again (it happens in China once every two to three hundred years or so) under increasing continental pressure from non-Chinese barbarians, this time from Manchuria. By 1644, the Manchus completely subdued China and established themselves as the "Qing" ("Clear" or "Pure") Dynasty to replace the Chinese "Ming" ("Brilliant") Dynasty in 1644.

In 1662, Dutch rule ended at the mouth of cannon barrels aimed by a pirate admiral by the name of Zheng Chenggong (known in Dutch chronicles as "Koxinga"), whom the Dutch assumed, despite common knowledge that his mother was Japanese, was a "Ming" Chinese loyalist still at odds with the invading Manchus. Zheng, who died soon after his capture of Taiwan, established an independent "administration [that] exercised full authority over Taiwan and dealt with foreign countries as a sovereign nation."[4]

The Manchus finally assumed sovereignty over Taiwan in 1683 as part of their suppression of the Rebellion of the Three Feudatories (*sanfan zhi luan*) in southern China when Zheng Chenggong's son, Zheng Jing, joined the rebellion against the Manchus. A Manchu-organized fleet ventured into the Taiwan Strait and soundly defeated Zheng Jing's flotilla. According to Taiwanese historians, the Qing emperor Kangxi himself admitted that Taiwan had never belonged to either the Manchus or China. But "Taiwan is a small pellet of land. There is nothing to be gained by taking it, and no losses in not taking it"—except, of course, that it harbored anti-Qing pirates.[5] In 1723, Kangxi's son, the Emperor Yongzheng, solemnly intoned that "from ancient times, Taiwan has not been part of China. My holy and invincible father brought it into the territory."[6]

For the next two centuries, the Qing imperial court in Beijing considered Taiwan more of a nuisance than an imperial asset. In Taiwan, "the state was saved the expense of initial pacification of the natives . . . because it inherited the system of taxation and control created by the Dutch and continued by the [Z]hengs."[7] Chinese colonists only began to move into Taiwan's northeastern plain in the early nineteenth century, and the first Chinese magistrates arrived in 1810. Even so, the rest of Taiwan was populated by "uncivilized" barbarians over whom the Qing government, even as late as 1871, declined to accept responsibility—especially when it came to protecting foreign seamen whose ships wrecked on eastern Taiwan's aboriginal coastline. Then, following the Sino-Japanese War of 1894–1895, China turned its title to Taiwan over to Japan "in perpetuity"—rather than give up Chinese sovereignty over Qing dynastic homelands in Manchuria. The Japanese view of the Chinese cession of Taiwan was that Li Hongzhang "always considered Formosa a curse to China and was exceedingly pleased to hand it over to Japan."[8]

Japan's subsequent colonization of Taiwan in 1895–1945 brought the island a political, social, and economic culture quite alien to China's. And by the end of World War II, Japanese policies to assimilate Taiwan into metropolitan Japan were much more enthusiastic than imperial China's efforts.[9]

At the end of World War II, Taiwanese in general welcomed the arrival of Chiang Kai-shek's troops as occupation forces. But as we will see later in this chapter, the brutality, venality, and corruption of the Chinese occupation troops and their arrogant attitude toward the Taiwanese quickly led to division between the Taiwanese and Chinese and to the "February 28 (1947) Uprising." Significantly, the period of the Chinese Civil War (1945–1949) is the only period since 1895 when the same government ruled both China and Taiwan, and it was perhaps the saddest period in Taiwan's history.

TAIWAN IN THE CIVIL WAR

Although the ultimate disposition of the island of Taiwan was a matter of debate for much of the war, U.S. and British diplomats finally agreed at Cairo in November 1943 that "territories Japan has stolen from the Chinese, such as Manchuria, Formosa, and the Pescadores, shall be restored to the Republic of China."

That intent was indirectly affirmed in July 1945 at Potsdam where Allied leaders declared only that Japanese sovereignty would be restricted to the four home islands "and such minor islands as we determine." But while "Manchuria" seemed to be considered Chinese territory on the date of Japan's surrender, Taiwan's status was still unclear. When General MacArthur issued his surrender orders of September 2 to Japan's armed forces via the Imperial General Staff, he specified that "senior Japanese commanders and all ground, sea, air, and auxiliary forces within China (excluding Manchuria), Formosa, and French Indochina north of sixteen degrees north latitude shall surrender to Generalissimo Chiang Kai-shek." Clearly, MacArthur, at least, saw that Chinese territory included "Manchuria" (where Japanese forces would turn their swords over to the Soviet Red Army, which already occupied the territory) but not "Formosa." The surrender, by the way, was to be "on behalf" of the victors, the United States, Britain, Russia, Australia, and China. To some, these remained significant legal points, the importance of which would begin to emerge a year and a half later.

In late September 1945, General Chen Yi, former governor of Fujian province with a spotty warlord background who was at the time serving as secretary-general to Chiang's cabinet, was named governor of Taiwan and arrived in Taipei on October 23. Two days later he declared a formal "retrocession" of the island to Chinese sovereignty. But with all of Chiang's best soldiers busy fighting the communists on the Chinese mainland, Chen Yi's troops were notably ill disciplined, uneducated, and poor and tended toward theft and abuse. Almost immediately, the social situation on Taiwan began to deteriorate.

The orderly, prosperous, and well-policed Japanese colony descended quickly into semichaos after battalions of Chinese soldiers began to show up in November. By March 1946, American newspaper readers found front-page accounts of Chinese plunder in Taiwan. A Scripps Howard journalist reported that the Chinese state monopoly on Taiwan rice sent local prices soaring 1,000 percent, with similar price hikes on other monopolized commodities such as coal, sugar, and salt. Whatever former Japanese businesses the government couldn't absorb was quickly confiscated by the KMT party itself. Newspapers, movie theaters, radio stations, and the like, all guaranteed the KMT a propaganda lock on information.

But there is no denying that a substantial number of Kuomintang Party cadres who accompanied the occupying army were idealistic professional political organizers. They moved quickly to prepare elections for the Taiwan provincial People's Political Council (PPC). They organized local PPC elections in February–March 1946 and arranged for the PPC to meet in formal session on May 1, 1946.

The Taiwan PCC spent that first ten-day session examining a vast spectrum of administrative corruption and incompetence, including police abuse and extortion, a collapse of the public health system, unpaid teachers and university staff, appropriation of public corporations, intimidation of journalists and editors, the failure of the government to pay its bills (China National Aviation Corporation cut off scheduled air service to Taiwan for a month for failure of the occupation administration to pay its debts), refusal to put local Formosans in government positions, and widespread looting of commercial shipments. The delegates assailed the Taiwan Military Garrison commander for permitting his troops to engage in massive and indiscriminate looting (he stalked out of the session without replying).[10]

In a report to the State Department, the embassy in Nanking specifically noted that the Nanking government's representatives met with

> outspoken and forceful criticism from an articulate and intelligent body of local representatives, spokesmen for a public whose general level of education and information is considerably higher than the average for the mainland from which the government officials come. Attempts to limit debate, questioning and criticism and to slur over important but embarrassing problems met with spirited opposition.[11]

It is clear that throughout 1946, Formosans readily adapted to the concept of representative democracy and awaited the new constitution with optimism and anticipation. But the Kuomintang was not yet ready to confer democracy to Taiwan. On January 10, 1947, Governor Chen Yi announced that the mainland Chinese were advanced enough to enjoy the privileges of constitutional government, but because of long years of despotic Japanese rule, the Formosans were "politically retarded" and not capable of self-government in an "intelligent manner."[12]

It was too much for the Taiwanese. Sporadic demonstrations erupted throughout the island. And on the evening of February 27, six policemen tried to arrest a woman for selling contraband cigarettes at a stall in the square at Taipei train station. A crowd of angry onlookers surrounded the police, and when one officer struck the woman, the crowd heckled the police. When a policeman's gun went off, killing a bystander, the crowd set upon the police. The next day, February 28, 1947, some three thousand Taiwanese marched in demonstration to the tobacco monopoly headquarters and then on to Governor Chen's office. A government guard fired into the crowd, killing one of the protesters—a killing that sparked a paroxysm of violence throughout the city against mainlanders. Immediately, the "2–28" rioting spread down the island, engulfing most of the bigger cities in turmoil that lasted for days.

The demands of the Taiwanese rebels included an end to corruption, reforms of the monopoly systems, and greater home rule for Taiwanese, and indeed some demonstrators wanted the Chinese off their island altogether. Some even approached American consular officials in Taipei about the possibility of establishing a United Nations trusteeship government for Taiwan, preferably administered by the United States, which had also taken over administration of Japan's nearby Ryukyu Islands.

The rebellion was suppressed—during the course of which perhaps ten thousand Taiwanese were seized and executed, with another eight thousand to ten thousand rounded up and shot in the ensuing months. The dead included prominent Taiwan political leaders whose only crime was to attempt to mediate the uprising. But the thousands of dead (generally reckoned at eighteen thousand out of a population of six million) included prosperous businessmen, college students, landowners, and the elite of Taiwan's society.

After February 28, the island was put under martial law. Taiwan was not allowed to hold elections until 1950, and no new elections for National Assembly or Legislative Yuan members until 1969—and then only for assemblymen and legislators from Taiwan.[13] The wanton corruption of the KMT administration in Taiwan, which led to the February 28 Uprising and the bloody pogrom against Taiwanese elites that followed, was a deep embarrassment to the United States. The American ambassador in Nanking was obliged to portray U.S. support for Chiang's regime as aid to a democracy under siege from a communist rebellion.[14]

So disturbed were American policymakers about the abuse of the Taiwanese people, newly liberated from the Japanese colonial yoke, at the hands of Governor Chen, his venal KMT cadres, and his ill-led soldiers that they began to back away from the idea that now Taiwan was, in fact, sovereign Chinese territory. Most American diplomats accepted that the immediate postwar policy intention for the disposition of Taiwan was to reunite it with China. After the 2–28 pogroms, however, this no longer seemed to be a prudent idea.

On April 11, Acting Secretary of State Dean Acheson declared that the transfer of sovereignty over "Formosa" to China "has not yet been formalized." The 2–28 uprising was also a wake-up call to Chiang himself who, by 1949 had begun to realize that his regime would be spending an extended period of exile on the island of Taiwan. Chiang was already under notice that the United States did not yet regard Taiwan as under formal Chinese sovereignty—although it was "legally administered" by Chiang under the terms of the Japanese surrender. Accordingly, Chiang realized that his minions needed to clean up their respective acts if they were to retain any durable international legitimacy on the island.

On the one hand, Chiang felt constrained to ratchet up the repression of Taiwanese dissent and most especially the ever-growing (but subterranean) sentiment for "Taiwan Independence" from China. On Taiwan, a "White Terror" (as opposed to a communist "Red Terror") reigned that was fairly effective in making political opposition unhealthy for natives. On the other hand, Chiang's bureaucrats implemented a rather sweeping land reform program that limited landholdings, gave excess acreage to tenant farmers, and compensated landowners for the confiscation of their properties with share ownership in local Japanese industries and businesses that had been appropriated by the mainland occupying authorities. Politically astute Taiwanese landowners were able to wrangle shares in the nationalized firms, and the "land to the tiller" program ingratiated the new KMT regime to the disaffected poor tenant farmers in Taiwan. The land reform also infused the economy with new capital, which revitalized enthusiasm for entrepreneurship.

By the end of 1949, it became clear to Chiang on Taiwan that he was not going to "retake the Mainland" from the Communists anytime soon. To make matters worse, Chiang was left in no doubt that the United States intended not to lift one finger in his defense should Mao's forces invade. On January 12, 1950, Secretary of State Acheson gave a seminal foreign policy speech accusing Chiang of squandering his support among the Chinese people.[15] Chiang was, in Acheson's words, "a refugee on a small island off the coast" of China. The United States, Acheson stated flatly, was committed only to defending a "defense perimeter" in the western Pacific that fanned from the Aleutian Islands, through Japan to the Philippines—leaving Taiwan and South Korea outside the pale. Chiang's army began to dig in on Taiwan's beaches for an expected communist invasion across the Taiwan Strait—scheduled, intelligence officials estimated, for August 1950. And then a miracle happened.

TAIWAN AND AMERICA'S STRATEGIC INTERESTS IN THE PACIFIC

Late at night on June 25, 1950, communist armies of North Korea under Korean People's Army commander Kim Il Sung, fully armed, supplied, and fueled on direct orders from Moscow, trained and commanded by Soviet military advisers (who disappeared into the background just weeks earlier), struck out across the formal postwar line of demarcation at the thirty-eighth parallel between the Soviet occupied zone in the north and the American zone in the south. In Washington and throughout the west, Marshal Kim's attack was a clear case of communist aggression. It fit a pattern of Moscow-directed aggression in Eastern Europe, the Berlin Airlift, the Greek civil war, guerrilla fighting in Turkey, not to mention the communist victory in China.

Within forty-eight hours, President Truman ordered the U.S. Seventh Fleet into the Taiwan Strait with orders to prevent either side from taking advantage of the situation to attack the other. With the Korean War, Taiwan suddenly reemerged in the U.S. political consciousness as "Free China" though it was far from "free" in the American sense of the word.

Truman called on the "Chinese Government on Formosa" to cease all hostilities against the mainland, and stated that "the determination of the future status of Formosa must await the restoration of security in the Pacific, a peace settlement with Japan, or consideration by the United Nations." The United States delegation to the United Nations asserted on August 25, 1950, that "the actual status of the island [Taiwan] is that it is territory taken from Japan by the victory of the allied forces in the Pacific," that the "Chinese Government was asked to take the surrender of the Japanese forces on the Island. That is the reason the Chinese are there now."

Ten days after the U.S. Army entered the North Korean capital at Pyongyang, and barely a month after the American amphibious landing at Inchon routed and ultimately destroyed the main force of the North Korean Army, on the night of October 16, 1950, eighteen divisions of "Chinese People's Volunteers," about two hundred thousand men,[16] slipped "all at once" across the Yalu and proceeded stealthily by secondary roads and trails to wooded staging areas to await their initial offensive.[17] By November 24, there were "a total of 450,000 Chinese troops in Korea, including 380,000 combat fighters." And with that, the Chinese communist armies began the first of five bloody campaigns that would push the American, South Korean, and UN forces back south of the thirty-eighth parallel several times over the next six months.

Mao Zedong and Chiang Kai-shek were rivals to the throne of China, Mao in the northern capital and Chiang in exile offshore. The matter of Chinese sovereignty over Taiwan was a matter of regime legitimacy in both Beijing and Taipei. As long as a rival authority existed in Taipei, Beijing considered the Chinese Civil War to be unfinished. And the longer Chiang's regime was confined to the island of Taiwan, the more tenuous was the legitimacy of his own rule.

Americans were sympathetic to neither side. Their main criterion for supporting Chiang was American national interests. The San Francisco Peace Treaty, which formally tied up loose ends from Japan's surrender, could reasonably have resolved the matter of Taiwan's sovereignty, but the United States delegate (and future secretary of state) John Foster Dulles argued that the situation in the Pacific was so uncertain that "the wise course" on Taiwan was "to resolve doubts by invoking international solvents other than this treaty." The British delegation agreed that "the treaty itself does not determine the future of these islands."

Even Chiang's own foreign minister, who signed a separate peace treaty with Japan in April 1952, had to admit to the Legislative Yuan, the Chinese parliament in exile in Taipei, that Taiwan was not—legally speaking—Chinese territory. "In fact, we are controlling [Taiwan and the Pescadores islands] now. . . . However, the delicate international situation makes it that they do not belong to us," he explained, adding that "under present circumstances, Japan has no right to transfer Taiwan and the Pescadores to us; nor can we accept such a transfer from Japan even if she so wishes."

Through the Korean War, the question "Who Lost China?" became one of many campaign slogans with which the Republicans thwacked the Truman administration. With former General of the Army Dwight D. Eisenhower's victory in the 1952 presidential election, Taiwan soon became the recipient of massive amounts of new American military and economic aid—which this time Chiang spent more wisely and effectively than he could ever have hoped in the chaos of the postwar Chinese mainland. Land reforms increased agricultural production, and by the early 1960s, Taiwan's government implemented a new industrialization strategy to foster rapid export-led growth for three decades to come.

A "littoral defense line in the western Pacific" remained the centerpiece of U.S. policy in East Asia until President Richard Nixon's historic opening to China in July 1971. Nixon and his national security adviser, Henry Kissinger, stressed by the Vietnam War and Soviet nuclear threats to China, lost sight of America's core strategic interests in the Pacific Ocean to focus on the more immediate threat of Soviet expansion and hegemony on continental Asia. China, to them, was a potential counterweight to the USSR on the Eurasian landmass.

TAIWAN'S EXPULSION FROM THE UNITED NATIONS

Until 1971, the Republic of China in Taipei, not the People's Republic in Beijing, continued to hold the Chinese seat in the United Nations Security Council. In March, Pakistan's president Yahya Khan had broached the subject of a hypothetical Nixon visit to China during a trip to Beijing, and he told Nixon that the Chinese leadership had responded favorably. The stage was set for Kissinger's secret visit to Beijing in July 1971. In the meantime, China quietly rounded up support for a resolution sponsored by Albania, which would remove Taipei's representative from the Security Council and seat Beijing's.

Expulsion from the United Nations was a dash of cold water on Generalissimo Chiang Kai-shek's hopes that his "Republic of China," operating in Taipei, would ever again return victorious to mainland China. At the UN expulsion, some of Chiang's top foreign policy aides immediately foresaw a diplomatic imperative of splitting Taiwan from China in the international context.

ROC's vice minister Yang Hsi-kun had been present in New York when the fateful United Nations vote was tallied and watched in horror as the Tanzanians danced in the aisles, the Algerians embraced, and the Albanians quietly shook hands when China's victory was announced. He wasted no time exiting the building and returning to Taipei for conferences with Chiang Kai-shek and his advisers.

In the summer of 1971, while Beijing's support in the United Nations metastasized across the General Assembly, Chiang's top aide, Presidential Office Secretary General Chang Chun, conferred in Tokyo with Prime Minister Eisaku Sato and former prime minister Nobusuke Kishi. The advice from two of Japan's most powerful politicians was blunt: "the only hope for the future of the Republic of China was to adopt a course of separation, giving up all Mainland claims and pretensions."

There is ample evidence that, had the United States not opened channels to China in 1971, the United States would have continued to push its "dual representation" model for Beijing and Taipei in the United Nations. The international community would have welcomed it. Certainly Japan was supportive, as were a number of other major nations. Beijing would have resisted but no doubt in the end would have accepted a UN seat under protest.

Like so much in history, however, if one thing had happened, another would not have. The catch-22 for a "Chinese Republic of Taiwan" was that President Chiang in Taipei would have accepted it only if he had actually been expelled from the United Nations, and the People's Republic would never have allowed an independent Taiwan Republic unless it had been a fait accompli before the PRC took over the Chinese seat on the United Nations Security Council. Once Taiwan had absented itself from the UN, it was never going to get back in.

Five years later, as President Gerald Ford's secretary of state, Henry Kissinger had a chance to muse about the risks inherent in a policy that accepted that Taiwan is "part of China." On October 29, 1976, Kissinger said to his top China aides, "If Taiwan is recognized by us as part of China, then it may become irresistible to them. Our saying we want a peaceful solution has no force: it is Chinese territory. What are we going to do about it?" Arthur Hummel, then assistant secretary of state and later ambassador to Beijing, responded, "Down the road, perhaps the only solution would be an independent Taiwan."

The international context of the 1970s was such that China remained a minor strategic power and an even more diminutive trade power whose global diplomatic footprint was faint.

At the beginning of the China initiatives in 1971, then-California governor Ronald Reagan had been deeply unsettled by Nixon's summary treatment of Taiwan. Because of Reagan's impeccable credentials as a friend of Taiwan, Nixon sent him as a "special envoy" to Taipei to convince Chiang of America's continued goodwill. Before his departure across the Pacific, the California governor declared that Nixon "has been blunt in his declarations that we will not under any circumstances desert an old friend and ally . . . give anything away, or betray our honor. If I am wrong, and that should be the result—time then for indignation and righteous anger."[18] Reagan later consoled himself with the thought that 140 Soviet ground force divisions on the Chinese border damped Moscow's temptations for adventures in the Middle East and Europe.

Nixon's now-historic "Shanghai Communiqué," issued ironically on February 28, 1972, further muddied American interests in a Taiwan that would be separate from China: "the United States acknowledges that all Chinese on either side of the Taiwan Strait maintain there is but one China and that Taiwan is a part of China. The United States Government does not challenge that position."

Six years later, President Jimmy Carter normalized relations with Beijing in December 1978 with yet another communiqué, which affirmed that "the Government of the United States of America acknowledges the Chinese position that there is but one China and Taiwan is part of China."

The U.S. Congress was appalled at the way President Carter dumped a longtime friend and ally, Taiwan, for China. So much so that the Congress adopted an unprecedented piece of legislation, the Taiwan Relations Act (TRA) drafted on the assumption that while the Carter administration agreed that it had "acknowledged the 'Chinese position' that Taiwan is part of China," but emphasized that "the United States has not itself agreed to this position."[19] Accordingly, the TRA treats Taiwan as a nation independent of China for the purposes of domestic U.S. law: "[w]henever the laws of the United States refer or relate to foreign countries, nations, states, governments, or similar entities, such terms shall include and such laws shall apply with respect to Taiwan."[20]

But the real significance of the TRA was in its statement of U.S. policy:

> (b) Policy
> It is the policy of the United States—
>
> (1) to preserve and promote extensive, close, and friendly commercial, cultural, and other relations between the people of the United States and the people on Taiwan, as well as the people on the China mainland and all other peoples of the Western Pacific area;
> (2) to declare that peace and stability in the area are in the political, security, and economic interests of the United States, and are matters of international concern;
> (3) to make clear that the United States decision to establish diplomatic relations with the People's Republic of China rests upon the expectation that the future of Taiwan will be determined by peaceful means;
> (4) to consider any effort to determine the future of Taiwan by other than peaceful means, including by boycotts or embargoes, a threat to the peace and security of the Western Pacific area and of grave concern to the United States;
> (5) to provide Taiwan with arms of a defensive character; and
> (6) to maintain the capacity of the United States to resist any resort to force or other forms of coercion that would jeopardize the security, or the social or economic system, of the people on Taiwan.

This policy statement, for all practical purposes, substituted what could be called a "quasi-alliance" with Taiwan (by virtue of section 2[b][6], which articulates a formal defense commitment to Taiwan)[21] for the soon-to-be defunct U.S.–Republic of China Mutual Defense Treaty of 1954.[22] Again, China reacted angrily to the TRA, but President Carter, facing a veto-proof margin of congressional support, signed it into law. It remains the law of the land.

President Ronald Reagan was uncomfortable with the regime in Beijing and went out of his way to treat Taiwan with dignity and warmth. In 1982, President Reagan's "six assurances" to Taiwan's president Chiang Ching-kuo (son and heir to Chiang Kai-shek, who died in 1975) reconfirmed America's "long-standing" policy of not recognizing Chinese claims to sovereignty over Taiwan. He promised that his administration "will not interfere . . . or prejudice the free choice of, or put pressure on, the people of Taiwan" on their relationship with China. But by 1992, the Washington China-policy bureaucracy had begun to articulate something called a "One China Policy," an abbreviated wording that had the unfortunate effect of miscommunicating to Beijing the idea that the United States accepted China's territorial claims and, as a matter of international law, would have to acquiesce in China's sovereign right to use force to recover territory in rebellion.[23]

The administration of President George W. Bush has been very uneasy with democracy in Taiwan. Bush's China policy has been beset with distractions and anxieties around the globe, not to mention a war in Iraq and another in Afghanistan, perennial crises in the Levant, and of course the psychotic blustering of a nuclear-armed North Korea. It seems that the Bush foreign policy system can only handle a finite number of crises at a time, and the president himself was said not to want a "China in-box" that would further clutter up his desk. Accordingly, his aides adopted the simplest method of keeping a China in-box empty—they pressured Taiwan's democratically elected leadership to suppress their desire to deny that Taiwan is part of China.

It was conventional wisdom in the second Bush administration that Taiwan's president Chen Shui-bian was a "troublemaker" who agitated for "Taiwan Independence" for purely political advantage; that Chen was trying to get the United States into a war with China, from the rubble of which an independent Taiwan would emerge; and that Chen intended to fight for Taiwanese independence "to the last American" (words hauntingly identical to the America-Firsters' attacks on Winston Churchill in 1941).

Set aside the notion that Chen seeks Taiwan independence purely for "political advantage," that he is willing to sacrifice the well-being of his own country to achieve it, or that he hopes the United States will protect his island in a war but does not intend for Taiwanese to fight or suffer the predations of war—but logically, it cannot be all three. The Bush administration—which staked its "national security strategy" on the global expansion of democracy—had a remarkably tin ear when it came to democracy in Taiwan. But to understand this, one must first examine what Taiwan's new democracy is all about.

U.S. INTERESTS IN TAIWAN AND CHINA

In the broad matrix of America's geostrategic stake in the Asia-Pacific region, Taiwan may indeed be "small" compared with China, but as an East Asian power, it most emphatically is not "small" at all. It is a very substantial member of the community of Asian democracies in its own right.

Taiwan is a crucial element in the new geostrategic structure of the Asia-Pacific as the magnitude of China's military might catches up with its economic and trade power. Taiwan is one of democratic Asia's major nations; its exports rank third after Japan and South Korea, and it is one of America's top ten export markets, taking about $22 billion in U.S. goods in 2005—slightly more than half the value of total U.S. exports to China that year.

Taiwan's population is slightly larger than Australia's. And, if Taiwan were a member of the ten-nation Association of Southeast Asian Nations, it would be ASEAN's biggest economy and largest military spender. So, demographically, Taiwan is indeed a major East Asian nation.

Finally, the United States has a large political stake in the island's success. Taiwan is a poster child for democracy in Asia, it is a long-term (albeit "unofficial") American defense partner, and it is a strategically significant piece of real estate in the Pacific Rim. The United States has provided security assurances to Taiwan against Chinese threats for over a half century.

Aside from the obvious political interests the United States has in ensuring the survival and success of democracy in Taiwan, there are vital economic interests as well. For example, Taiwan's semiconductor industry is the world's most advanced, according to a report in February 2005 by the Pentagon's Defense Science Board.[24] According to that same report, the Pentagon gets a substantial volume of vital microchips from Taiwan's chip "fabs." Meanwhile, the report adds, America's microchip production capacity is diminished—with only one U.S. chip fab able to produce "trusted and classified" chips for U.S. defense needs.

UNDERSTANDING THE FORMAL CHINA-TAIWAN POLICY

Three things American political leaders must first understand are (1) what U.S. policy toward Taiwan actually is, (2) how the name "our one China policy" undermines its effectiveness, and (3) what animates a bureaucratic antipathy toward Taiwan in the face of China's pressures against Taiwan and the United States.

The formal, diplomatic stance of the United States toward Taiwan is to "take no position on the question of Taiwan's sovereignty."[25] Of course, in a rather Zen-like way, to "take no position" is indeed to take a position because having no position cedes the argument to those that do have a position. That aside, it should be obvious that the United States certainly does have very important strategic, political, economic, and defense interests in preventing one of Asia's smaller democracies—and one of America's traditional allies in Asia—from being threatened and pressured by Asia's largest dictatorship into an annexation that it does not want.

Thus, a political union between Taiwan and China cannot possibly be in America's interests on any level. Unhappily for democratic Taiwan, China's communist regime claims sovereignty over the island and threatens catastrophic war should Taiwan's people formally and democratically repudiate Beijing's claim.

Washington accommodates the Chinese regime by assiduously ignoring the issue—and by pressuring Taiwan's leaders not to make too much of it, either. But the incoherence of this stance lies in its conflict with U.S. policy clearly mandated in the Taiwan Relations Act of 1979.[26]

To the credit of the George W. Bush administration, it has tried to rearticulate a somewhat conditioned position that insists that the United States is committed to "our one-China policy" and "opposes" any move by China or Taiwan to "change unilaterally" the "status quo *as we define it.*"[27]

On April 21, 2004, came a glimmering of this position in a public statement by Assistant Secretary of State for East Asia and Pacific Affairs James Kelly, who enumerated for the House International Relations Committee the "core principles" of U.S. policy in the Taiwan Strait.

- The United States remains committed to *our* one-China policy based on the three Joint Communiqués and the Taiwan Relations Act;
- The United States does not support independence for Taiwan or unilateral moves that would change the status quo *as we define it*;

- For Beijing, this means no use of force or threat to use force against Taiwan. For Taipei, it means exercising prudence in managing all aspects of cross-Strait relations. For both sides, it means no statements or actions that would unilaterally alter Taiwan's status;
- The United States will continue the sale of appropriate defensive military equipment to Taiwan in accordance with the Taiwan Relations Act; and
- Viewing any use of force against Taiwan with grave concern, we will maintain the capacity of the United States to resist any resort to force or other forms of coercion against Taiwan.[28]

Indeed, Secretary Kelly admitted at the April 21 hearings that, when it came to "our" one-China policy, he was "not sure [he] very easily could define it." Nonetheless:

> I can tell you what it is not. *It is not the One-China policy or the One-China principle that Beijing suggests*, and it may not be the definition that some would have in Taiwan. But it does convey a meaning of solidarity of a kind among the people on both sides of the Strait that has been our policy for a very long time.[29]

Sadly, this is as close as a State Department official has ever gotten to defining "our one China policy," in private or in public. Nor, as it happens, has any U.S. official ever "defined" the "status quo *as we define it*."[30]

One part of the Taiwan policy canon that also received Kelly's special mention was President Ronald Reagan's "six assurances":

> Our position continues to be embodied in the so-called "six assurances" offered to Taiwan by President Reagan. 1) We will neither seek to mediate between the PRC and Taiwan, nor 2) will we exert pressure on Taiwan to come to the bargaining table. Of course, 3) the United States is also committed to make available defensive arms and defensive services to Taiwan in order to help Taiwan meet its self-defense needs. We believe a secure and self-confident Taiwan is a Taiwan that is more capable of engaging in political interaction and dialogue with the PRC.[31]

But Kelly lost count of the Reagan six assurances when he neglected to mention the fifth assurance, that "the U.S. has not altered its position regarding sovereignty over Taiwan," and the sixth, which promised that "the U.S. will not exert pressure on the Republic of China to enter into negotiations with the PRC."[32] Instead, Kelly continued, "And we expect Taiwan will not interpret our support as a blank check to resist such dialogue."

Kelly's last phrase, however, ran counter to the Reagan assurances that the United States will not "exert pressure on Taiwan to come to the bargaining table" with the Chinese communists. Why, pray tell, would the U.S. expect Taiwan to "interpret" the Reagan assurances as anything else *but* a "blank check" to resist dialogue, if the democratically elected leaders of the people of Taiwan choose to resist dialogue?

Congressional suspicion about an undefined "our one China policy" and "status quo as we define it" is straightforward. Both reflect a deep uneasiness in Congress and among the American public with an executive branch policy that, on its face, seems to concede that democratic Taiwan should be "one" with China's dictatorship. The prototypically "diplomatic" replies from State Department officials are equally revealing. There is no policy—at least not that they could speak of, no doubt for fear of antagonizing Beijing.

CHINA'S CALCULUS FOR WAR OVER TAIWAN

China, unlike the United States, is quite forceful in asserting its agenda. China's irredentist rhetoric of "unification" has become alarmingly bellicose since the late Marshal Ye Jianying pronounced a "fundamental policy of striving for peaceful reunification" in September 1981.[33] On August 31, 1993, just in case anyone was under any illusions that Beijing had accepted the Cold War status quo, the Chinese State Council issued a white paper that asserted flatly that "there is only one China in the world, Taiwan is an inalienable part of China, and the seat of China's central government is in Beijing"; that wishes for Taiwan's reunification with China "have not come to fruition for reasons such as interference by some foreign forces"; that, in fact, "the Taiwan question and the responsibility of the United States"; and that "the Chinese Communist Party is ready to establish contact with the Chinese Kuomintang [KMT] at the earliest possible date to create conditions for talks on officially ending the state of hostility between the two sides of the Taiwan Straits and gradually realizing peaceful reunification." The repository of true authority over Taiwan, the CCP believed, was not the people of Taiwan, still less the government of the "Republic of China," but rather the "Chinese Kuomintang Party."[34]

By February 2000, the Beijing regime sensed a need to be a bit more categorical about the status of Taiwan's so-called government.

Since the KMT ruling clique retreated to Taiwan, although its regime has continued to use the designations "Republic of China" and "government of the Republic of China," it has long since completely forfeited its right to exercise state sovereignty on behalf of China and, in reality, has always remained only a local authority in Chinese territory.[35]

But Beijing was quite a bit more strident, even hysterical, as it pondered the possibility that, in less than a month, Taiwan's voters could elect a proindependence president. The new white paper dismissed the idea of "so-called controversy about democracy" as "an excuse for obstructing the reunification of China" and a "scheme to deceive compatriots in Taiwan and world opinion."

And to make certain Taiwan's voters got the message, the white paper drew its red lines defining the circumstances under which China would use armed force against Taiwan:

> If a grave turn of events occurs leading to the separation of Taiwan from China in any name, or if Taiwan is invaded and occupied by foreign countries, or if the Taiwan authorities refuse, *sine die* [which is Latin for *wu xianqi* or, in English, "without a date certain"], the peaceful settlement of cross-Straits reunification through negotiations, then the Chinese government will only be forced to adopt all drastic measures possible, including the use of force, to safeguard China's sovereignty and territorial integrity and fulfill the great cause of reunification.[36]

Drastic was the operative word. Four days before the Taiwan election in March 2000, Chinese premier Zhu Rongji heatedly advised Taiwan voters to cast their ballots in the presidential election with a "cool head" or risk "not getting a second chance." The normally staid, sober-minded Chinese premier said that "Taiwan Independence Forces" gain strength daily as the election nears, and he was "unusually direct" in serving notice that "we cannot accept Taiwan independence, that's our bottom line, and it's the heartfelt demand of China's 1.2 billion people."

Working himself into near-hysterics in a briefing for foreign reporters on March 14, the Chinese premier hissed that those who argued that China did not have the missiles, ships, or aircraft to invade the island had misread history, and the Chinese were ready to "shed blood" to prevent Taiwan breaking away.[37] In all likelihood, Premier Zhu was under severe pressure within the Chinese leadership that was willing to sacrifice China's trade relations with the West—especially the United States—on the Taiwan issue, and Zhu's emotions were more likely a reflection of his alarm at the economic costs of rash behavior of the Chinese Politburo than of the political costs of rash decisions by the Taiwanese electorate.

Of course, Chen Shui-bian was elected, and China had to put up with it. There ensued four more years of Chinese histrionics, and in March 2004, Chen was reelected. Three days before Chen's second inauguration, on May 17, 2004, China's foreign ministry proclaimed that China would "crush" Taiwanese independence moves "at any cost,"[38] comments that the White House spokesman declared "have no place in civilized international discourse."[39]

A year later, on July 14, 2005, Chinese major general Zhu Chenghu, dean of foreign students at the People's Liberation Army National Defense University, at the request of China's foreign ministry, briefed a group of foreign journalists all of whom had their voice recorders humming on the table before them, saying, "If the Americans are determined to interfere, [then] we will be determined to respond." He added that "we Chinese will prepare ourselves for the destruction of all of the cities east of Xi'an. Of course the Americans will have to be prepared that hundreds . . . of cities will be destroyed by the Chinese."[40]

General Zhu's comments were a culmination of Chinese threats that had built up over the previous several months. The 2006 Pentagon report on China's military power points out that General Zhu's views are widely shared in the PLA and at the very least are emblematic of an ongoing debate on nuclear strategy within the military.[41] One of my colleagues at the Heritage Foundation (and now chair of the U.S.-China Economic and Security Review Commission) who has known General Zhu for more than a decade, Larry Wortzel, observed that one objective of the Chinese leadership "is to put enough doubt in the minds of the American public that they will think it's not worth going to war over Taiwan."[42]

A few months prior to General Zhu's threats, in March 2005, China's National People's Congress had passed legislation called "The Statute against Splitting the Nation," article 8 of which declares

> In the event that the 'Taiwan independence' secessionist forces should act under any name or by any means to cause the fact of Taiwan's secession from China, or that major incidents entailing Taiwan's secession from China should occur, or that possibilities for a peaceful reunification should be completely exhausted, the state *shall* employ non-peaceful means and other necessary measures to protect China's sovereignty and territorial integrity.[43]

The use of the word *shall* (*dei*) in the last sentence is a mandate to action. Article 8 also directs that "the State Council and the Central Military Commission shall decide on and execute the non-peaceful means and other necessary measures," without the need for further reference to the National People's Congress. Nowhere in the legislative history of the Chinese Statute, however, is there any clue to the meaning of "splitting the nation" or "incidents entailing Taiwan's secession," or just what might be an example of "incidents entailing Taiwan's secession," or how anyone would know when "possibilities" for "peaceful reunification" would be "exhausted." This is a problem because Taiwan has already functioned for over a half century as an independent political entity from China and already considers itself de jure separate from the People's Republic of China.

It is difficult to imagine a situation in which Taiwan could engage in any additional substantive "incidents entailing secession" than it already has; therefore, the "statute," in effect, proclaims that a *casus belli* already exists without requiring further action by Taiwan. In short, this "statute" is not any kind of law recognizable in the Western democracies.

"WAR AVOIDANCE": A SENSIBLE STRATEGIC OBJECTIVE FOR WASHINGTON?

Although the United States has never had the reputation for cringing in the face of war threats from strategic adversaries who seek to dominate America's friends and allies—or anyone else, for that matter—there has arisen over the past decade a "China exception" in American doctrine about nuclear war. Apparently, American policymakers who understood during the Cold War that "mutual assured destruction" was the price to pay should the Soviet Union have attempted similar adventurism, believe that China's military leadership—as personified by General Zhu Chenghu—is completely psychotic. Under General Zhu's scenarios, the very rapid and drastic escalation of a war with China over Taiwan would be very difficult to control, yet many in the Washington foreign policy bureaucracy are persuaded that China will, in fact, risk nuclear war. If it were otherwise, such threats from China would be no more effective on them than Soviet threats were to America's Cold Warriors.

Many thoughtful (but perhaps naive) commentators point out that the Taiwan issue could become a *casus belli* in a Chinese war against the United States.[44] They argue that nothing is worth getting into a war with China, and consequently the United States should abandon any security commitments to Taiwan save to provide Taiwan arms should the Taiwanese feel like fighting

China all by themselves. I am told often that America's paramount national interest in the Taiwan Strait area is to "avoid a war." Taiwanese strategists have a similar view. A former Taiwan vice minister of national defense used to begin his briefings with the statement "Taiwan's overarching defense policy is the prevention of war." To which I would point out, to both my American and Taiwan colleagues, that if that's your "overarching defense policy," then the cheapest way to implement that policy is to surrender.

International relations scholars and bureaucrats alike tend to forget their academic training. Modern "war avoidance" theory centers on the proposition that democracies do not make war on each other but rather are themselves the targets of aggression.[45] Henry Kissinger pointed out in his first published book, *A World Restored*, that in an international system where "peace" is made the highest priority, the system is at the mercy of its most ruthless member, and there is an overwhelming incentive to appease the demands of the most ruthless member regardless of how unreasonable they are.[46] Kissinger's model predicts that China will use its constant threats of war over Taiwan as a means to an end because it sees influential forces in the United States and other nations that value "peace" more than they value democracy in Taiwan.

When one considers how much China has enmeshed itself in the international manufacturing supply chain, however, it is clear that war isn't any more in the interests of the Chinese Communist Party leadership than it is in America's. It is inconceivable that the Beijing regime would ever challenge the United States in Taiwan unless, of course, it was absolutely convinced that the United States would back down. Consequently, its strategy in the Taiwan Strait is a multidimensional one—military, political, economic, and psychological—designed to induce America to back down.

China is financing a very rapid expansion of its military, particularly its navy, in order to give the appearance that it will soon be in a position to inflict heavy pain on the U.S. Navy in the Pacific. With a certain amount of huffing and puffing, Beijing believes that it can present Washington with a calculus that says, "The pain I could suffer from a Chinese naval strike is greater than the pain I would suffer from the loss of Taiwan; hence, I will cut my losses and quit ahead of time."

So, presented in this way, "Taiwan Independence = War" is an unpalatable policy equation.

One logical U.S. counterresponse would be to present China with a similar calculus with an added disincentive—something that says, "The pain China will suffer from increasing threats or even military action against Taiwan will be far greater than leaving Taiwan alone, independent or not independent." Or, simply put, the United States should posit a new strategic equation on the Taiwan issue:

(war) = (economic devastation) + (Taiwan's independence)

To be an effective response to China, of course, Beijing must believe that Washington is prepared to sanction China severely for military action. In addition, if Washington were also to proffer the likelihood that the United States would, actually, in the end, recognize the de jure independence of an invaded Taiwan, Beijing would be faced with an even more unpalatable conundrum: how could it be sure that threatening military action against Taiwan would not itself ultimately result in an internationally recognized independent Taiwan?

Unfortunately, the State Department's habit has been to insist that America's commitment to Taiwan is no more than a "responsibility under the Taiwan Relations Act."[47]

TAIWAN'S DEFINITION OF ITSELF

A crucial element in determining "island" Taiwan's future is understanding how Taiwan's people view themselves and supporting them in that view. For the years between 1988, when Taiwan president Lee Teng-hui came to power, and 2000, when he retired (and his successor was defeated in that year's presidential elections), Taiwan's people had formed a substantial consensus on their future as separate from China. Since then, that consensus has been strained, both by external pressures from China as well as the United States and other fellow democracies, and by internal pressures against resisting China's pressures exacerbated by the external ones.

One thing that the vast majority of Taiwanese believe is that Taiwan is presently independent from the People's Republic of China and has been since 1949. This infelicitous fact has been a burr in the saddle of America's China policy for thirty years, and no doubt it will continue to be for years to come precisely because few American officials in authority have devoted any thought to a desirable end state of the Taiwan-China calculus.

China, on the other hand, considers Taiwan to have been deeded over to Chiang Kai-shek's regime in 1945, and therefore, since the People's Republic succeeded Chiang's regime in 1949 (and in the United Nations in 1971), Taiwan's real estate is communist property.

Taiwan's "Republic of China" has always considered itself both de facto and de jure separate from the "People's Republic of China," and since 1992, it has constitutionally cut itself off from the People's Republic by statutorily disenfranchising all residents of the mainland who otherwise would have "Republic of China" citizenship.

In 2000, a proindependence candidate was elected Taiwan's president by nearly 40 percent of the popular vote (in a three-way race), and he was reelected with a shade more than 50 percent in 2004. Taiwan's long-standing official description of its own status is that it and the People's Republic are "two sovereign, independent and mutually non-subordinate nations."[48] In 1999, Taiwan's previous president described his country's relations with China as "special state-to-state relations,"[49] and the current president said in August 2002 that "there is one nation on each side of the Taiwan Strait." As of September 2005, Taiwan's official description of itself is "The Republic of China *is* Taiwan."[50]

Unlike the leadership of Communist China, Taiwan's political leadership is not monolithic. Democratic Taiwan's political leaders on both sides of the so-called Green-Blue[51] divide are getting progressively anxious as China's military expansion builds steam, as China begins to use its economic clout to deepen Taiwan's economic dependence on China, and as China's Communist Party ratchets up pressure on Taiwanese businessmen with investments in China.

Taiwan's proindependence "Greens," led by President Chen Shui-bian, are nervous that China's military power will further weaken support in Washington for Taiwan. In their agitation, they believe they must trumpet ever more loudly Taiwan's separate democratic identity from China. That identity, for them, has become a fundamental element of state legitimacy. Hence their sense of urgency in abolishing governmental institutions, like the National Unification Council and the National Unification Guidelines, that imply that unification with China is Taiwan's state doctrine.

For the moderates in the "Blue" camp, however, their "state legitimacy" rests on a claim that Taiwan's Republic of China—not the communists' People's Republic—has sovereignty over all of China, from the Pacific coast to the western deserts of Xinjiang. Their vision of a future China is one where the democratic ROC eventually supplants the totalitarian PRC—or that the PRC regime democratizes, and the ROC can then unify with it. In the decades or centuries until China's democratic millennium, however, they are content to acquiesce to Beijing's claim that the PRC (as "China") is sovereign over Taiwan.[52] Moreover, because they have no intention of challenging

Beijing's assertion that Taiwan cannot be "independent," some "deep Blue" politicians question the need for a robust defense and seem willing to entrust Taiwan's security to Beijing's goodwill.

TAIWAN AND CHINA IN THE TWENTY-FIRST CENTURY

At the beginning of 2006, new worries were beginning to arise about the direction of Taiwan and corrosive effect that incoherent U.S. policies are having on the resolve of Taiwan's people.

On January 29, Taiwan's president Chen Shui-bian made some unscripted comments about the continued utility of the "National Unification Council" (a public council designed to consider possible modes of future unification of democratic Taiwan with communist China). President Chen told a Lunar New Year's gathering that day "everyone now calls for, encourages, demands to know whether the national unification council and the guidelines should or should not be dismantled (*feichu*)" and opined that

> everyone knows the National Unification Council has become just a name on a sign, and if a store not only has a sign that no one can see, and moreover has nothing to sell, then what kind of 'common unification' shall such an establishment, such a National Unification Council, such a set of National Unification Guidelines, be able to achieve? . . . the principle of "one China" . . . is profoundly problematic (*feichang you wentide*).[53]

Since mid-2002, the Bush administration had tried to gain Chinese acquiescence for U.S. moves on North Korea, Iraq, Afghanistan, and the war on terror, by trying to keep the Taiwan issue out of sight. For Bush National Security Council aides and the State Department, this meant leaning on Taiwan's president to keep silent when China touted claims of sovereignty over the island. In President Chen's first inaugural address on May 20, 2000, at the suggestion, if not insistence, of the United States, he made five pledges, including "the abolition of the National Unification Council or the National Unification Guidelines will not be an issue."[54] The first blow-up over these pledges came when President Chen outlined a new "One Country on Either Side of the Strait" (*yibian yiguo*) formulation on August 3, 2002, just as the United States was courting Chinese support (or at least nonopposition) for the United Nations Security Council.[55]

But concerns are misplaced. Beijing, after all, is the *real* problem. Beijing's so-called Anti-Secession Law was itself an open-ended declaration of a *casus belli* against Taiwan. Unfortunately, the official U.S. reaction—at least in public—was muted. The most the State Department spokesman could say was "we believe it to be unhelpful."[56] "Unhelpful," indeed. Yet Washington's reaction to Beijing's "law" was far milder than its abuse of Taiwan's leader for far less serious transgressions. And the U.S. government must understand that so long as Taiwan refuses to acknowledge Beijing's sovereignty, Beijing's long-term strategy is to isolate Taiwan in the international community to the most extreme extents possible.

In short, China has done nothing—and intends to do nothing—to requite Taiwan's outreach. By the time of his November 2005 visits to Japan and China, President Bush is said to have become so dismayed by Beijing's sustained hostility toward Taiwan's leaders that he inserted a paragraph praising Taiwan's democracy into his Asia policy speech in Kyoto[57]—a paragraph that surprised every China watcher in Washington, including those in the White House.[58] The receptivity of Taipei's "elected leaders" to a dialogue with Beijing's unelected ones is unquestioned. Beijing simply refuses.

CRUCIAL QUESTIONS

Before moving on to specific questions about the direction of Taiwan policy, the U.S. administration must reach a consensus on whether "war avoidance" by itself makes sense as a strategic objective of the United States; on whether China, or any totalitarian regime, can ever be deterred from ultimately using military force except with unified and firm push-back from the democracies of the world presumably bolstered by coherent American leadership. If firmness and unity among the nations of the international community of democracies are needed, do American policies regarding the Taiwan Strait have the perverse effect of encouraging China's bellicosity rather than assuaging it?

At the very least, the United States must counter Beijing's relentless campaign to isolate Taiwan economically and politically by strengthening U.S.-Taiwan trade ties and strongly encouraging allies and other democracies to include Taiwan in international efforts on health, transportation, nonproliferation, counterterrorist, and disaster relief.

A U.S. free trade agreement with Taiwan would be a good place to start. Membership—even as an "observer"—in other formal and informal international organizations like the World Health Organization, the International Civil Aviation Organization, the International Maritime Organization, and the various informal nonproliferation groups like the Australia Group (on chemical weapons) and the Missile Technology Control Regime, and in refugee and relief "core groups" would benefit the international community and provide Taiwan with enhanced international legitimacy. In turn, Taiwan's enhanced legitimacy would provide extra deterrence against China's constant threats of force against Taiwan.

Taiwan's legal status, as a matter of international law, has gone unratified since 1945. Japan formally renounced "right, title and claim" to Taiwan in its instrument of surrender at the end of World War II. It was occupied by the Chinese Nationalist Army in October 1945 and became a haven for the Nationalists' government in exile after their defeat in China's civil war. Taiwan was saved from certain Chinese communist occupation by the Korean War, which obliged President Harry Truman to position the U.S. Seventh Fleet in the Taiwan Strait. And, in the absence of an international treaty formally transferring sovereignty from a defeated Japan to anyone else, the question of who "owns" Taiwan has been in diplomatic limbo since 1945.[59]

This situation presents a historic opportunity for the people of Taiwan to choose their future. Whether they want to be a part of China, become independent, or choose some other future, it should be the choice of a democratic people and not part of an international backroom deal. The clear and stated policy of the United States should be to do everything necessary to allow the people of Taiwan to decide their future.

• 9 •

The Asian Space Race and the Masters of Infinity

The future ain't what it used to be.

—Yogi Berra

At the end of the twentieth century, the United States could brag of winning almost every major aerospace laurel, from first flight to putting men on the moon. In the 1960s and 1970s, the National Air and Space Administration (NASA) was planning manned missions to Mars and beyond. Although the Soviet Union placed second, during the twentieth century, it also won many "firsts" in space, such as the first man in space. West Europeans did not launch an indigenous manned mission, but Europe participated with the American and Soviet efforts, including thirty-nine European astronauts flying on either Soviet or American missions. The rest of the world contented itself with watching American achievements on television.

The twenty-first century, however, already portends a significantly different future than most people imagined as they watched Neil Armstrong plant an American flag on the moon. From the end of the Apollo program until 2004, American efforts in manned space exploration have been limited to discovering more expensive ways to orbit the Earth. America's foremost competitor, the Soviet Union, dissolved in 1989. Russia, the successor state, lost its empire and the resources to compete in space. As for the new Europe, after four centuries of achievement in science and exploration, the ancient empires of Europe found a comfortable retirement in the European Union and seem no longer interested in embarking on another national adventure.

Instead, the countries of Asia have stepped into the starting blocks of a new space race. China, Japan, India, and South Korea all have ambitious space programs. China has already launched men into space. Japan and India are developing manned space programs, and South Korea is investing in a space program. Many of Asia's smaller or less developed countries have space programs, too, and can be expected to make their mark during the twenty-first century.

THE ASIAN CHALLENGE

China became the third country to launch a man into space when China's first twenty-two-hour manned space mission was successfully completed in October 2003. Two years later, in October 2005, China sent two men into Earth's orbit for five days for additional experiments and data collecting. Beijing announced in April 2006 that Shenzjou-7, China's third manned spacecraft, will carry three astronauts for preliminary work on a Chinese space station shortly after the 2008 Olympics.[1] These achievements have triggered a race among Asian countries. The participating countries will be China, India, Japan, and South Korea, all racing to develop cheaper, more efficient ways to put humans into space.

Not only is China first off the mark, but it will likely set the pace in the early years. China has already successfully tested six Shenzhou space capsules, including the two crewed capsules in 2003 and 2005. The Shenzhou (Divine Vessel) capsule can carry up to three Chinese "taikonauts" into space. Modified and improved from Russia's Soyuz model, the Shenzhou has an "orbiting module" that has its own solar panel and independent flight control system to remain free-flying in space several months after the crew's landing back on Earth.[2] The rocket bearing the capsule is the Long March, which has had twenty-seven consecutive successful launches by 2006.

The Shenzhou-7 mission in 2008 will comprise space station–building drills to be followed by a launch of a cosmic experimental capsule capable of accommodating astronauts' short-term stays,[3] and it will eventually lead to the construction of a twenty-ton space station[4] assembled from linked orbiting modules. The Long March rockets currently cannot heave large components into space due to their smaller lift capacity compared with space shuttles.[5] Consequently, the Chinese are developing a new heavy lift rocket called the CZ-5. In addition, the Chinese have adapted the U.S.-Russian designed APAS-89 docking system that is compatible with the International Space Station (ISS).

China's ambitious program includes sending taikonauts to the moon and eventually establishing a base there. Chief of the China National Space Administration (CNSA) Luan Enjie's remarks in March 2003 uncovered China's three-phase unmanned lunar program "Chang'e," whose first phase of circumnavigating and mapping the moon is expected to be completed by 2010.[6] Phases 2 and 3 will involve a landing of robotic explorers and retrieval of soil samples by 2020.

China's space activities are expected to surpass those of Russia and the European Space Agency within a decade.[7] Rank conscious Asians will applaud the success of a fellow Asian country, but the specter of Chinese preeminence will spur them to pursue programs of their own. The contenders are already positioning themselves.

INDIA

Most Americans probably don't realize India has a space program, but India has been in the space exploration field since 1962 and has developed a sophisticated space-going organization called the Indian Space Research Organization (ISRO). Furthermore, India feels that it is a peer competitor with China, and Beijing's manned program shames New Delhi's policymakers. They do not intend to break the bank to compete with China, but as India develops economically, there will be a commensurate escalation of its space ambitions.

ISRO operates with an annual budget of $600 million and twenty thousand employees.[8] In January 2003, India's prime minister Vajpayee announced that it was time for India to "send a man into space." In response to his call, in April 2003, ISRO announced plans to send an unmanned satellite to the moon by 2005 and to put an Indian astronaut on the moon by 2015. The realities of space flight have already intervened, and India's unmanned mission to the moon will not be launched until 2008. ISRO chairman Madhavan Nair said in May 2006 that India currently "has no plans to embark on manned missions to space" due to concerns about their immediate necessity and cost-effectiveness.[9] India attempted to get an astronaut on the space shuttle, but the shuttle program is closing, and all its missions are fully booked.

Nevertheless, India continues to move forward with its unmanned space probe programs, including the $100 million Chandrayaan-1, where ISRO and NASA are closely cooperating. Chandrayaan-1, New Delhi's first unmanned lunar satellite, is scheduled to be launched into moon orbit in early 2008 for a two-year-long survey of polar icecaps and mineralogical mapping. ISRO believes that India's available rocketry can launch a probe into lunar orbit, but manned missions will require development of a more capable rocket.

Moreover, in January 2006, Nair expressed India's interest in partnering with the United States and European countries in a space probe to Mars after the successful completion of the Chandrayaan-1 mission.[10]

JAPAN

Japan is already in space in a big way, and a 100 percent Japanese-manned mission is not far in the future. Realizing that space exploration was now in its grasp, in 2003, Japan combined three agencies that had previously divided the country's civilian space program into one, the Japanese Aerospace Exploration Agency (JAXA). JAXA's mission is to take a systematic and continuous approach to space exploration from basic research to practical application.

JAXA is not Japan's only space-interested organization; like all countries interested in space, the military component looms large. Spread among six ministries and agencies involved in space programs, Japan's space budget in 2005 reached $3.4 billion. Nearly one-third of it was allocated to the development of military reconnaissance and war fighting satellites, and another one-third went to JAXA for its space exploration programs.[11]

Japan's existing H-IIA rocket has the capacity to launch 10 tons into low-Earth orbit, sufficient lift to carry the 7.5-ton Soyuz spacecraft, the workhorse of the Russian space program. NSDA has a conceptual design for a made-in-Japan space capsule that could be rapidly developed with existing technologies.

In September 2005, Hayabusa, Japan's $170 million probe mission to the asteroid Itokawa, traveled 620 million miles and arrived successfully onto a three-mile orbit over Itokawa.[12] Though postponed until 2010 due to an unexpected thruster problem, Hayabusa's return will mark the world's first successful asteroid landing mission that will bring home samples and image data of the asteroid. JAXA's unmanned lunar orbiter mission SELENE will be launched in July 2007 to collect geological, mineralogical, and topographical information about the moon. SELENE will be carried on an H-2A rocket, which has been the core element of Japan's space program despite a crushing launch failure in November 2003, which led to the destruction of two spy satellites in midflight.[13]

Japan is not ignoring the commercial aspects of space. With the rise in energy costs, Japan has embarked on an ambitious experiment to beam microwave energy from satellites in space to a receiving station on Earth. JAXA plans to launch a satellite in 2010 that will open out a large solar array to transmit 100 kilowatts of energy to earth. By 2020, JAXA hopes to deploy sufficient satellite capability for a 250-megawatt station and a gigawatt-size solar generator by 2030.[14]

Despite these commercial expectations, Japan was stung by Chinese successes in manned exploration, and Tokyo is accelerating programs to prepare for launching its own manned missions. Japan's space program is characterized by its close cooperation with the United States. Through that cooperation, Japan is able to send astronauts into space on shuttle missions and the International Space Station (ISS). Japan is a major partner of the ISS, and intends to use it as a platform to develop its manned program. In 2006, Japan docked the Japanese Experimental Model (JEM), also named Kibo, the Japanese word for "hope," to the ISS. The Kibo facility has a crew compartment in which Japanese astronauts live and an exposed facility for conducting experiments in open space. The experiments include space medicine for humans living in space and testing equipment for future space activities.

The ISS is resupplied using Russian and American vehicles, but Japan plans to augment this capability with a vehicle of its own, the H-IIA transfer vehicle (HTV). The HTV will carry only supplies to the ISS, but it will be launched from a Japanese rocket and will serve as a test bed for the Japanese to gain practical knowledge and know-how for launching future manned spacecraft.

Confident in the reliability of its technologies and growing public support to meet the Chinese challenge, JAXA announced in March 2005 that it will seek a government decision on the technical development and construction of facilities for the establishment of an international human lunar base from the year 2015 and on, and it will embark on an initial phase of base establishment by 2025.[15]

KOREA

South Korea is the undisputed underdog in the Asian space race. South Korea embarked on the satellite business only in the late 1980s, decades later than the United States and Russia, with the establishment of the Korea Aerospace Research Institute (KARI). However, at the beginning of this century, the Republic of Korea government decided to become one of the top ten space-faring nations by 2015.

Since the launch of its first indigenous satellite on a U.S.-French mission in 1992, South Korea has sent nine satellites into space and plans to put three more multipurpose satellites into Earth orbit by 2009.[16] The Republic of Korea's space budget for satellite launching for the next five years will amount to $2.6 billion.[17] All these launches, however, have been on other country's launch vehicles. To be a space-faring nation, Korea needed to develop its own launch capability.

On August 31, 1998, North Korea attempted to launch a satellite on a Taepo Dong 1 ballistic missile, thus becoming the most impoverished country to join the world's most expensive national adventure. Pyongyang's satellite did not achieve orbit, but it did successfully provoke South Korea into accelerating its space program.

In 1999, the United States agreed to lift all restrictions on commercial rocket development with South Korea. On August 8, 2003, South Korean leaders broke ground on a brand new space center to be completed by 2007. The facilities at the center will include a satellite launch vehicle, launch control facilities, tracking radar, a launch vehicle assembly facility, a satellite test facility, and a space experience center.[18] To reach its 2015 goal, the government decided to short-circuit the development process and look for outside help to develop an indigenous launch vehicle. KARI, in cooperation with Russian scientists, is currently developing South Korea's first satellite launch vehicle, KSLV-1, which will be operational in 2007.

In September 2005, Seoul and Moscow signed an agreement of cooperation in space development, including a plan to put a first South Korean astronaut into space on a Russian Soyuz spacecraft by 2007—later delayed to 2008. The ministry of Science and Technology is contributing $6 million, and KARI is raising over $20 million from a broadcast company to support this project. The Republic of Korea government will select two final candidates to send to Russian training facilities by the end of 2006.[19]

Rhee Shang-hi, a member of Korea's National Assembly, founded a group called Young Astronauts Korea. Participating children attend space camps and read articles about Mars in the organization's journal "Science World." Rhee's goal is to instill Korean young people with the goal of putting Koreans in space.

The Republic of Korea's domestic aerospace industry, including the manufacturing of aircrafts, satellites, and rockets, generated $1.4 billion in 2003, about 0.25 percent of total domestic production.[20] Yet, the Korean government expects that the local market will grow to $5.8 billion by 2015, about 1 percent of the world market.[21] In light of the Korean achievements on both sides of the Thirty-eighth Parallel the Republic of Korea's determination to succeed in the space race should not be discounted.

OTHER SPACE PROGRAMS IN THE ASIA-PACIFIC

Australia, Indonesia, Malaysia, Singapore, Taiwan, Thailand, and Vietnam all have space programs. Although there is a considerable gap between these smaller programs and the budgets of the big four Asian space powers, they should not be overlooked. For example, Indonesia founded the National Institute for Aeronautics and Space (LAPAN) in 1963 and launched its first satellite in 1976.

These programs are generally managed with the same goals in mind as larger countries. The commercial aspects are strong, with many of the countries interested in developing advanced technology and manufacturing capability. Asia is the fastest-growing market for satellite services, and it is predicted to grow at least 9 percent annually through 2011 compared with Europe's expected growth at 6 percent or less.[22] And that business is not just spare change; the direct-to-home satellite TV revenues alone are expected to generate $15 billion in Asia between 2001 and 2011, compared with $20 billion in the United States.[23]

There is also a strong military content. Every country except Malaysia possesses ground stations for receiving satellite imagery. The regional militaries, including Malaysia, are financing significant portions of satellite remote sensing and communications.[24]

Lastly, a diminutive budget does not mean small ambitions. On May 19, 2006, Malaysia signed a contract with Russia to send two Malaysian astronauts to the ISS. The two Malaysians will be trained at Russia's cosmonaut training center and are expected to be on the ISS by September 2007.[25]

THE MILITARY AND POLITICAL MOTIVATIONS

National pride and international prestige are obvious benefits of a manned space program. In Beijing's communist party, policymakers need to justify continued authoritarian rule, achievements in a space program help buttress the nationalist credentials of the communist party. But there are other benefits that help compensate for costly space programs: scientific research, the development of commercial satellite launch industries, and the spin-off of money and technology to national aerospace industries. Another space race can spur economic development as well as scientific research for Asia and the rest of the world, but there are clear military applications as well. A country that can launch a person into space can use the same technology to launch a nuclear weapon and hit targets on another continent.

Military competition is a key factor in Asia's rocket development. Beijing wants to become a peer competitor of the United States and needs reliable intercontinental ballistic missiles to achieve that status. Also, China has other nationalist goals that require missiles. For example, the PLA keeps hundreds of missiles along the coast opposite Taiwan. The goal is to intimidate sufficient Taiwanese to prevent them from declaring formal independence.

For India, New Delhi frequently cites the Chinese threat. The Indian military's current deployed arsenal of missiles, called Agni-I, has a limited range, and because of its liquid fuel (a liquid-filled rocket has to be fueled at the time of launch, unlike a solid-fueled rocket, which is already fueled), it is slow to deploy. The Agni-I's 700 kilometer range means that India could only hit Tibet, which is not India's interest and does represent a deterrent to the Han Chinese in Beijing. The Indian military is developing Agni-II and Agni-III missiles with greater range and solid propellant that can both respond quickly to a Chinese missile attack and hit Beijing. The missiles booster was developed by ISRO.

Seoul and Tokyo worry about North Korea and beyond Pyongyang lies China, an ancient enemy to both countries. Missile proliferation across Asia worries the world. Nonproliferation treaties were designed to limit access to potentially dangerous technology, but that premise no longer holds.

After India tested its nuclear weapons in 1998, Russia stopped selling it rocket development technology, specifically in the area of cryogenic engines for the upper stage of rockets. Indians love to boast that Russia's action was the best thing to happen to them. They were forced to develop their own cryogenic engines, and now India is technologically self-sufficient. Furthermore, Pakistan's and North Korea's development and export of missile technology, in the face of intense international disapproval, show the ineffective reach of current nonproliferation agreements.

During the first space race, the United States and the Soviet Union ended up creating bilateral stability. In the Asian space race, the United States must seek multilateral stability across the Asia-Pacific region. The United States also must press on with missile defense development and encourage the participation of allied countries.

These Asian pioneers are moving ahead in other technologies besides space. China and India will bring on-line the next generation of fusion reactors in 2006 and Korea will complete its K-Star fusion reactor in 2008, a year before the United States expects to complete its next generation fusion reactor and eight years before France's effort.[26]

THE AMERICAN VISION

America's vision of its future in space is complex and reflects the nature of the American character. Strong national security concerns stand side by side with altruistic dreams of peaceful exploration of space; nationalist drive to be the first and the best is softened with the knowledge that American achievements represent all mankind; and hardheaded calculations of current costs are compared with speculative gains from future space exploitation. America's vision can be synthesized in a few consistent principles.

First, space is military high ground, and as a superpower, the United States must be able to dominate and exploit that territory.

Second, exploring new frontiers defines the American pioneering spirit and confirms American resolve and authority as a world leader.

Third, the United States needs the economic advantages derived from the space program, but the up-front costs should not outweigh the anticipated gains.

Fourth, no matter how much we appreciate the successes of foreign competitors, Americans want to be first.

Without question, America's first ventures into space were rooted in the Cold War, but Americans saw the opportunities of the new frontier, and our goals expanded from meeting a military challenge to include scientific study, technological development, and human exploration.

Even before he became president, Lyndon Johnson was advocating American dominance in space. At a Senate hearing in January 8, 1958, then Senator Johnson warned, "From space, the masters of infinity would have the power to control the earth's weather, to cause drought and flood, to change the tides and raise the levels of the sea, to divert the Gulf Stream and change temperate climates to frigid." Although Johnson's predictions about controlling the weather from space have not yet proved feasible, his insight that control of space could be military high ground dominated the fears of Americans at the time.

Spurred by unchallenged Soviet successes, on May 25, 1961, President John F. Kennedy announced a greatly accelerated space program, but

Kennedy was not content with just beating the Russians to the moon—he wanted to launch a new frontier for American expansion. In his 1962 State of the Union address, President Kennedy gave the broad outline of America's goals in space:

> With the approval of this Congress, we have undertaken in the past year a great new effort in outer space. Our aim is not simply to be first on the moon, any more than Charles Lindbergh's real aim was to be first to Paris. His aim was to develop the techniques and the authority of this country and other countries in the field of the air and the atmosphere, and our objective in making this effort, which we hope will place one of our citizens on the moon, is to develop in a new frontier of science, commerce and cooperation, the position of the United States and the free world. This nation belongs among the first to explore it. And among the first—if not the first—we shall be.

Exploring space is a national adventure, but unlike the settling of the continent, where pioneer families personally experienced the hardships and rewards, exploration of space is uniquely a spectator's adventure. Through television, the experience of space exploration is simultaneously universal yet disconnected from the everyday lives of most Americans.

Every person old enough to remember July 20, 1969, retains the memory of Apollo 11. I was eleven years old, and I watched the spectacle with unsuppressed awe, never wanting to leave the front of the television. But I was at home sitting in my own living room, and between 3:17 in the afternoon when the Lunar Lander touched down on the hostile surface of the moon and 9:56 that evening when a man took those giant steps, the first ever on another world, I had dinner with my family and played with my dog. Despite the momentous occasion, I can also recall one of my uncles complaining about how much the space program cost.

In fact, explaining the strategic benefit of the space program to the fiscally minded American taxpayer has become one of the most daunting challenges of American presidents. Every president finds himself defending the space program and trying to translate the various strategic reasons into language that inspire Americans with a sense of mission and explain the advantages of the space program to a frequently skeptical audience. For example, in a statement announcing the space shuttle program on January 5, 1972, President Richard M. Nixon said, "'We must sail sometimes with the wind and sometimes against it,' said Oliver Wendell Holmes, 'but we must sail, and not drift, nor lie at anchor.' So with man's epic voyage into space—a voyage the United States of America has led and still shall lead."

Consider President Ronald Reagan's "Radio Address to the Nation on the Space Program," January 28, 1984: "Our space goals will chart a path of progress toward creating a better life for all people who seek freedom, prosperity, and security."

President George H. W. Bush on July 20, 1989, stated, "And today, yes, the U.S. is the richest nation on Earth, with the most powerful economy in the world. And our goal is nothing less than to establish the United States as the preeminent space-faring nation."

President William J. Clinton on April 14, 1998, said, "The space program has enormous potential to change life here on earth for the better."

Finally, President George W. Bush on January 14, 2004, declared, "Mankind is drawn to the heavens for the same reason we were once drawn into unknown lands and across the open sea. We choose to explore space because doing so improves our lives, and lifts our national spirit. So let us continue the journey."

Americans have a self-image of themselves as pioneers and explorers, and after half a century of success, Americans are deeply attached to the space program and NASA, the embodiment of those achievements. Nevertheless, the space program must have a mission that Americans both appreciate and feel justifies the expense.

After the Apollo program, NASA coasted from one uninspiring program to the next, never quite engaging the American imagination as have manned missions to other worlds. There were two attempts to develop a manned Mars program, but neither one ever got off the drawing board. The original manned Mars program developed in the 1970s, and then the second one proposed by President George H. W. Bush were both attached to astronomical price tags. In neither case was there a strategic competitor worthy of the American effort.

To coin an analogy, NASA was like a winning NASCAR team with the best car, driver, and crew but no competitors, racing itself around a circular track with a diminishing audience. Then on October 15, 2003, China successfully launched its first manned mission into space. Three months later on January 14, 2004, at NASA headquarters in Washington, President George W. Bush announced "a new plan to explore space and extend a human presence across our solar system." The race was back on, but is America still ready to compete?

THE AMERICAN PLAN

America's renewed venture into space must accomplish the principles of American vision. It must maintain the military edge, contribute to scientific exploration, develop the economy, and satisfy America's competitive character.

There are clear military aspects to the new manned missions. A country that can launch a person into space and return him or her safely to Earth, using the same technology, can also launch a nuclear weapon and accurately hit targets on another continent, but that is old tech for the United States. Technologies that permit targeting and docking (or striking) with an object in space can also be used in missile defense.

The new space race must limit technology access to our military competitors but, more importantly, open up cooperation with our friends and allies to surpass the efforts of China and North Korea. Japan, India, and Korea have sophisticated and advanced space programs and are working with the United States on ballistic missile defense. The new space race will be an opportunity to expand that cooperation. The United States also must continue to press on with missile defense development and encourage the participation of allied countries.

Bush's plan gives NASA a mission that also satisfies the science and pioneering spirit with a reasonable price tag. In 2005, the president committed to $100 billion in spending over twelve years, compared with the estimated $135 billion (2006 dollars) that was spent on the Apollo program.

The leadership at NASA is keenly aware of its fiscal limitations and is planning moon/Mars missions that take into account its future limited budgets and exploits other countries' interest in joining the space age. At a conference entitled "Lunar Exploration Workshop" in April 2006, Shana Dale, NASA's deputy administrator, admitted, "NASA has neither the resources nor the intention to explore alone."[27] To take into account its future budget realities but still realize America's vision, NASA is actively seeking foreign partnerships.

NASA's goal in creating partnerships is sophisticated and takes into account the nationalist element that drives manned space programs. It does not plan to just put Japanese or Indian astronauts on American spacecraft with American crews and then ask their governments to go "dutch" on the costs. Instead, NASA's vision is to create "exploration architecture" that will permit NASA and cooperating countries to build on each others' efforts, without imposing a NASA master plan on foreign or private space programs that have their own interests and priorities.[28]

The NASA plan includes building lunar bases, but the bases will not necessarily be wholly American; ideally, they would be common or shared facilities that would serve as home to American and other lunar explorers. The base concept is to learn to "live off the land" by exploiting lunar resources to produce water, fuel, and other expensive-to-transport commodities. This strategy can accommodate—in fact, encourage—participation of foreign governments and private firms that have their own reasons for studying the moon up close. Sharing these bases with other lunar explorers would increase safety and reduce costs while permitting each country or private firm to engage in its own scientific studies or nationalist flag planting.

The same strategy could create other common infrastructure on the moon, such as lunar communication satellites needed for exploring the backside of the moon. These kinds of items do not have to be American to be useful to lunar explorers, and as the infrastructure expands, then lunar exploring and eventually exploitation become more efficient, safe, and cheaper.

As the United States looks for partners, the most likely countries are from the Asia-Pacific. There were thirteen countries at NASA's April 2006 "Lunar Exploration Workshop," and seven of them were in the Asia-Pacific region: Australia, Canada, China, India, Japan, South Korea, and Russia. Furthermore, as NASA's deputy administrator discussed current lunar exploration, she mentioned five missions; one was American, and three of the four remaining missions were Asian, "Europe's SMART-1 mission now underway and China's Chang'e, Japan's SELENE, India's Chandrayan-1."[29] Furthermore, India's maiden voyage to the moon, Chandrayan-1, which is scheduled to launch in late 2007 or early 2008, will carry two NASA scientific instruments.

International space exploration with a significant Asian component will encourage Asian countries to participate in the negotiation treaties regulating the uses of outer space and thus collaterally accomplish American foreign policy goals of further embedding Asia's giants in rules-based international systems.

Government funding, however, may not be enough to sustain American ambitions in space. Regrettably, Congress and the Bush administration engaged in a historic spending spree that drove the federal deficit to the moon long before any new spending for the Moon/Mars mission hit the federal budget. This profligate spending put at dire political risk any program set in place by a president who will be out of office long before it is realized. Furthermore, for Washington policymakers, NASA is a traditional target during periods of budget tightening, and a cost-cutting era is sure to follow the Bush administration.

Asia's efforts in space do have some lessons for the United States. For example, $20 million of Korea's $26 million astronaut training is being funded by a Korean broadcaster. Russia is also using private sources to generate revenue and has been able to maintain an ambitious launch schedule despite its dilapidated economy. NASA should be permitted and encouraged to use private and corporate sponsors.

Lastly, in his announcement of the renewed space program, Bush said that this new effort was "a journey, not a race," and NASA's deputy administrator Dale quoted a plaque left on the moon by Apollo 17: "May the spirit of peace in which we came be reflected in the lives of all mankind."[30] These sentiments may be appropriate for sympathy cards or bandied about by new age peaceniks, but hippies don't have any money.[31] NASA leadership must stop pandering to academics and one-worlders and instead appeal to the competitive spirit that made America great.

In order to generate support from American taxpayers, policymakers must emphasize the competitive nature of the new space age. NASA needs to send more representatives to NASCAR races and football games to talk about the pioneering and national pride of the space program.

In the end, national pride and international prestige do matter. The United States cannot continue to wear its forty-year-old Apollo laurels as a crown of human achievement. America's leadership and preeminent position as the world's sole superpower will be in serious doubt if Chinese tourists are taking pictures of Neil Armstrong's footsteps on the moon and Koreans are the first on Mars. Policymakers must direct NASA to do more than find increasingly expensive means for Americans to orbit the Earth and fund manned missions to new worlds. It is past time for the United States to restart human exploration of space.

Conclusion: America's Future in Asia

Ocian in view! O! The joy!

—Captain William Clark,
November 7, 1805

Captain Clark, cocommander of the *Corps of Discovery*, was writing of seeing the Pacific Ocean. Reaching it was the goal of the Lewis and Clark expedition, and on that day the United States became a Pacific power. Throughout the next two centuries, the United States was intimately involved in the history of the Asia-Pacific.

At the close of the twentieth century, the United States was the world's undisputed superpower. No other country possessed the combination of economic resources, military strength, political leadership in international institutions, and the moral authority derived from a country ruled by its people. The twentieth century was a long record of American achievement, and the world was shaped by American policies.

During the last one hundred years, the ancient empires of Europe and Asia were dissolved, their demise unmourned and in fact assisted by Americans. New pretenders to the throne of world leadership, such as the communists, were exposed as frauds and disappeared. The American credo of democracy and free market economies spread across the world unchallenged by alternative philosophies. But as Washington policymakers gaze into the future, confident in America's unrivaled position to influence the directions of the world, they see a very competitive field where the United States does not have all the advantages.

To meet the undiscovered challenges of the future, America has two valuable assets: its friends and allies and rules-based international systems that the United States helped create. Both of these assets have strengths and weaknesses.

America's security resides in the strength of its armed forces and the alliance system in Asia. In chapter 3, I explained that the war on terrorism is not a military campaign but is best combated by strengthening the rule of law. Nevertheless, I am not suggesting that there is no role for the American military in defending the United States against military threats from Asia.

Without rival, China is the looming threat to American interests. Even the best-trained police will not stop Chinese missile attacks against Taiwan, prevent the PLA navy from enforcing China's interpretation of its maritime borders in the South China Sea, or deter a Chinese invasion of northern Korea. Only the American military and its allies can accomplish those missions.

The principal tool for strengthening American alliances in the Asia-Pacific region is security cooperation. Security cooperation will not turn dictators into democrats, but it does build military-to-military relationships and ensure compatible military doctrine and institutions.

Training with allies creates personal relationships and contacts among friendly and allied military leaders. It also builds compatibility between armed forces in doctrine and training. When friendly and allied officers train in American military schools, they learn American military doctrine and English, the international language of armed forces in Asia. Weapon sales to American friends and allies create economies of scale that indirectly subsidize United States arms purchases, build a strong American arms industry, and create equipment and logistical compatibility with the American allies. For all these reasons and more, the United States should finance a robust security cooperation program with its Asian friends and allies.

The American alliance system in Asia, on the other hand, is unlike its European counterpart, the North Atlantic Treaty Organization (NATO). NATO is a multilateral alliance of most of the countries of Western Europe that held together throughout the Cold War and is now expanding to encompass most of the countries of the European Union and the former Warsaw Pact.

In Asia, the alliances are all bilateral between the United States and an individual country. Many of the bilateral alliances are not even reciprocal. The United States is obligated to defend Japan in time of war, for example, but Japan is not obligated to assist the United States if America is attacked. There are no formal bilateral alliances between Asian countries and no multilateral security pacts that require the member countries to defend each other as they would defend themselves. The countries of Asia do not stand together but instead are dependent on American benevolence for their independence.

A multilateral alliance would increase Asia's security and decrease its dependence on the United States, but most countries in Asia suffer from political weaknesses that prevent the creation of such an organization.

America's ally with the most economic resources is Japan, but Tokyo is burdened with three heavy millstones that interfere with the creation of a multilateral alliance system: a constitutional restriction on using its military for collective defense, the lingering stigma of its military in the region, and a closed economy. The United States can encourage Tokyo to drop those burdens, but the decision is ultimately and unilaterally a Japanese choice.

Tokyo is taking steps to normalize its military. In 2006, the government introduced legislation to the Diet to create a Ministry of Defense; Japan's armed forces had been only an agency of the government, not a full cabinet position. Also, the Japanese military is assuming increasing responsibilities in its alliance with the United States, including participating in the war on terrorism in the Middle East, conducting counterpiracy patrols in the South China Sea, and developing theater ballistic missile defense. These moves are welcomed in Washington, but this new military activism revives painful memories among Japan's neighbors.

The issue that most symbolizes the fears of Japan's neighbors is the Yasukuni Shrine, a religious memorial that enshrines the spirits of more than two million Japanese who died for Japan in every war since the Meiji Restoration. These people are memorialized in the form of written records that include personal information of the person and how he or she died. The problem is that among the millions of spirits at Yasukuni Shrine are twelve Class A war criminals from World War II. Furthermore, the history written there, at least in English, is substantially different than the history taught to the rest of the world.[1]

As I noted in the first chapter, the Japanese are remarkably unashamed of the behavior of its military in World War II, and Japanese prime ministers occasionally visit the shrine to burnish their nationalist credentials. Every visit by a Japanese government official is accompanied by outrage from its neighbors, including American allies such as Australia, Korea, and the Philippines, who fear that if the Japanese do not acknowledge their history, they are doomed to repeat it. This Japanese myopia and the sensitivity of Asians to this issue are often successfully exploited by China, especially before major international conferences or when Japan is considering increasing its military capability.

For the United States, Japan's inability to face up to its history is a stumbling block to Japan's remilitarization and its acceptance as an ally to America's other friends and allies in the region. As long as Japan continues to ignore the unpleasant aspects of its history, it will be difficult to form multilateral security organizations in the region. Thus, the United States must seek official Japanese contrition about its history and ask countries like Korea to forgive, but not forget, its history with Japan.

Japan, however, is among the few countries in the world that support Taiwan's right to choose it future. The Taiwan Relations Act is the document that binds America to Taiwan's defense, but it is not really an alliance. Furthermore, because of Taiwan's undetermined international status and Washington's equivocation, its military cannot operate with American soldiers. For example, Taiwanese soldiers attend American military schools, but they are not permitted to wear their uniforms. Until there is a definitive determination of its status, U.S. policy prevents a multilateral security relationship with Taiwan.

Although it would be wrong to push Taiwan into independence unless Taiwan is prepared to accept it, Washington can treat Taiwan as a de facto independent country and encourage other countries to do the same. The biggest obstacle to many countries accepting Taiwan's de facto independence is fear of Chinese retaliation, but as we saw in chapter 8, China's bark is bigger than its bite. The United States and countries in Asia should take measures to normalize Taiwan's de facto independent status, such as inviting Taiwan to join international organizations, including ASEAN. As long as the world is unified on treating Taiwan as a discrete political and economic entity, which has not yet determined its future, China can bark, but as a member of the global economy, it cannot afford to bite too hard.

Another valuable American ally is the Republic of Korea. Korea has been an ally for more than fifty years and does not limit itself to defending the Korean peninsula. Korean soldiers fought in Vietnam, and a Korean brigade served in Iraq alongside American soldiers. Korea is also an active participant in United Nations peacekeeping missions. Nevertheless, the reunification of the Korean peninsula could endanger that strong alliance.

When the North Korean regime does finally deteriorate to the point that China can no longer sustain it, the situation will not resemble the collapse of East Germany, where a waning Soviet Union was unable to prevent or even influence reunification. Instead, China is a waxing power seeking to reestablish its ancient perquisites on the Korean peninsula. Beijing will use its leverage in Pyongyang to pressure Seoul to allow China to make key foreign policy decisions for Korea, such as abrogating its alliance with the United States, and thus returning Korea to its former status as a Chinese vassal.

For Koreans, the Cold War was not a titanic global struggle between opposing political philosophies but a painful and personal civil war dividing friends and families—and it is still going on largely due to forces outside the Korean peninsula. Imagine how Americans might react if the American Civil War had dragged on for fifty more years because of interference from outside powers. Most Koreans do not blame the United States. China, after all, is propping up the North Korean regime, but it wants control of the process to reside in Korean hands. Furthermore, southern Koreans are concerned about the health and safety of Koreans in the north as well as the cost and dangers of reunification, and there will be great temptation in Seoul to make concessions to Beijing in order to achieve a peaceful transition to reunification. How to handle these problems is a touchy domestic political issue that is not appreciated enough in Washington.

To preclude Seoul from making unwarranted concessions to Beijing, Washington must lead by following. The Republic of Korea must set the policy in all negotiations concerning the Korean peninsula, and the United States should adopt Korea's position as its own. There can no be disagreements between Washington and Pyongyang; that would only play into China's hands. If the North Korean regime says that it disagrees with the United States, then American policymakers must make it clear that, other than following Seoul's lead, there is no American position to disagree with. Unreserved American support to Korean leadership and policies on the peninsula will guarantee a long and healthy U.S.-Korean alliance.

America's most reliable ally in the region is Australia. Australia fought beside the United States in every war of the last century, and already in this century, Australian soldiers have accompanied American soldiers into both Afghanistan and Iraq. Furthermore, Australia deploys soldiers to many regional hotspots where there are no American troops, such as East Timor, the Solomon Islands, and Bougainville, but where stability is important to American interests. Nevertheless, with only eighteen million people, Australia is too small to be decisive in a confrontation with China.

ASEAN contains formal allies, such as Thailand and the Philippines; close friends such as Singapore, Malaysia, and Indonesia; and unfortunately also one of the world's most reviled governments, the State Peace and Development Council (SPDC), the euphemism for the military junta that rules Burma.

A politically, economically, and militarily strong ASEAN is important to American interests in Southeast Asia, but the SPDC is an obstacle to all those goals. The United States, the European Union, Australia, and practically every civilized nation refuse to sit at the same table as the representatives of the junta. So although there are many ASEAN-plus-other-countries forums, seating Burma or even the presence of an SPDC representative in the room is an awkward issue. Because of Burma's dark presence, ASEAN is regarded as little more than a talk shop, and despite the frequent meetings in the region, few substantive issues are resolved.

From ASEAN's point of view, Burma has been nothing but trouble since it joined the regional grouping in 1997, but ASEAN has changed dramatically, and the junta can no longer count on a political free ride from its neighbors. This is especially true of the democratic countries—Thailand, Philippines, and Indonesia—whose populations now make up a majority of Southeast Asians. There are frequent calls to suspend Burma's membership in the organization, and the United Nations Security Council has placed Burma on its agenda, with little objection from ASEAN.

The ASEAN countries should be encouraged to suspend Burma's membership and replace it with other countries in the region such as Australia, New Zealand, and Taiwan. Geographically, these countries are firmly placed inside Southeast Asia, and their dynamic and open economies would make an enormous and immediate contribution to the ASEAN Free Trade Area. Once relieved of the burden of Burma and enlivened with the presence of developed economies and mature democratic political systems, ASEAN's six hundred million people could step onto the world stage as an actor rather than a venue for superpower competition.

The largest American friend in Asia is India. After fifty years under the Soviet wing, India is finally seeking to take its place in the globe. This new emergence of India affords many opportunities for the United States' security policy. New Delhi's views of regional security are almost identical with Washington's, and India's potential strength augers great things for an alliance. Nevertheless, India's economic reform is slow. Recent rapid economic growth is derived mostly from past reforms, and current reforms are not keeping pace with the changes in India's economy. Without substantial and far-reaching economic growth, India's military will not have the resources to realize India's ambitions.

Unlike Cold War Europe, the common threat in Asia, China, is not viewed the same in all countries. In fact, it is not a foregone conclusion that China will be a security problem even in Washington. China's views on how to achieve its ambitions are evolving, and no matter the circumstances, choosing a confrontation with the United States is fraught with dangers that Beijing may not want to risk. Nevertheless, no China watcher doubts that China's military is preparing to become a regional power and will assert Beijing's views of its national interests.

For the United States' security policy, forming a multilateral alliance has many benefits, but in Asia's context, patience will be a virtue. The United States must wait for the Chinese threat to develop—if it does—and in the meantime seek to reduce the inter-Asian obstacles to forming an alliance. Washington's measures should be largely political, such as reducing tensions between Japan and its neighbors, isolating the SPDC until Burma's government finally changes for the better, promoting Australia and Taiwan as security partners to other countries in Asia, and engaging India's military in regional exercises and security forums. Unlike NATO's objective of confronting Soviet expansion at the gates of the Iron Curtain, the goal of a regional alliance in the Asia-Pacific context will not be to confront China but instead to defend the independence, sovereignty, and territorial integrity of each of its member countries.

American security, however, cannot be measured only in military terms. The power of America's economy is the source of American military strength. The security and efficacy of America's economy and the rules-based global trading system that innervates it are critical American interests. Furthermore, there are a number of international institutions, most prominently the United Nations that the United States helped create, to which all the countries of Asia belong. Asia's great powers are already members of this system, the U.S. policy goal is to get them to comply with and—even more importantly—enforce international rules.

At the end of World War II, the United States and victorious powers created the international systems that exist today, such as the United Nations, the IMF, and the World Bank. These organizations in turn created additional organizations such as the General Agreement on Trade and Tariffs (GATT), which evolved into the WTO in 1995. The international community also created the Treaty on the Non-Proliferation of Nuclear Weapons, which continues to create new treaties and agreements today as the challenge of controlling nuclear proliferation evolves. Although the United States has yet to ratify the United Nations Convention on the Law of the Sea, it, too, is part of the evolution of rules-based international systems. Former deputy secretary of state Robert Zoellick has called these new creations "a system of systems."

Despite the importance of today's international institutions and Asia's political and economic strength, none of the great Asian powers were present at the founding of the world's international system. Japan was a defeated country and not invited; China's current government was a guerrilla army at the time; Korea was only just emerging from 250 years as an Asian colony; India, Indonesia, and most of the rest of Asia were still European or American colonies. The only Asian government present at the founding of the United Nations was the Republic of China, and in 1971, the UN withdrew its recognition of that government.

The result of the absence of Asian representation is twofold; first, a Euro-centric or Atlantic preeminence in the important institutions, such as the United Nations Security Council; and, second, Asia's palpable lack of ownership of the rules of international systems.

Indicators of this lack of ownership are the frequent violations of the rules by Asian countries. China, Pakistan, and North Korea are by far the worst violators of the NPT regimes. All five of the de facto nuclear powers—India, Pakistan, North Korea, Iran, and Israel—are on the Asian continent. When Europhile analysts are asked why Russia remains on the UNSC, they often site Russia's thousands of nuclear weapons. That argument reinforces the position of NPT violators that believe the only way to get respect from the United States and Europe is to build a large stockpile of nuclear weapons.

In trade, in the IMF, Europe is overrepresented, and Asia is underrepresented. Voting power for IMF members is supposed to be consistent with its participation in the global economy, but like most international systems, Europe retains a larger vote block than the size of its economy justifies. Consequently, Asian countries fail to enforce the rules they had little hand in creating. For example, Asian countries are the worst violators of Intellectual Property Rights (IPR). USTR estimates that the United States loses between $200 to $250 billion a year to IPR counterfeiting. Another example of lack of ownership, India, under the guise of a least developed country, led the opposition to the Doha Round that killed a trade agreement intended to assist the world's developing countries.

The pinnacle of the international system is the United Nations Security Council (UNSC). The Euro-centric element of the current international system is most prominently displayed in the UNSC where three of the five permanent seats with veto power are occupied by European countries—the United Kingdom, France, and Russia—even though the empires that put them there are long vanished. Furthermore, because the European Union is represented in most UN forums, European countries get two votes, one as their own individual countries and a second vote from the European Union.

Russia continues to retain its seat and veto power despite the implosion of the Soviet Empire. In fact, Russia's strength continues to erode; its population is only slightly larger than Japan's, 144 million to 125 million; and Russians are suffering from a demographic crisis derived from a combination of a low birthrate and a high death rate. Russia's population has already dropped by five million over the last ten years and may drop to half its current population by midcentury.[2] Furthermore, Russia's economy is only one-sixteenth the size of Japan's economy, $5.1 trillion compared with $307 billion, and the bulk of Russia's economic growth comes from selling commodities such as oil and not from increases in its industrial or service sectors.

India has the world's second-largest population, and by the end of the century, it will possess the largest population. Indonesia is the world's fourth-largest population and third-largest democracy. Japan's economy is larger than every country that sits on the UNSC except the United States. South Korea has a larger economy than Russia. So Asians cannot be faulted for wondering why rules of the international system apply less equally to them.

Starting at the top of the international system, the United Nations must be substantially reformed in order to give ownership of international institutions to its most prominent members. It is outside the scope of this book to delve into the arcane minutia of United Nations reform, but there are four principles that should guide the effort. Any reform should protect, not erode, sovereign national rights. Democracy matters; democratic countries should get more proportionate representation than authoritarian countries. Economics matter; the United Nations economic institutions should give proportionate representation to countries by the size of their participation in the global economy. Lastly, there should be no permanent grants of perquisites to any country.

It is a peculiarity of American foreign policy that most people in the world know more about America than Americans know about them. Most people in Indonesia know who the president of the United States is, while many Americans cannot name the prime minister of neighboring Canada. This problem is not solely the fault of America's education system but rather an indicator of America's place in the world. In their book *The Right Nation*, John Micklethwait and Adrian Woolridge explain this phenomenon:

> Today every man has two countries—his own and America. American culture is so omnipresent that everybody has, as it were, a virtual American buried inside his brain. American power is so overwhelming that people

> everywhere watch American politicians just as closely as they watch their own. . . . People around the world feel that they are citizens of the United States in the sense that they are participants in its culture and politics . . . [but American politicians] . . . are plainly not accountable to these non-Americans.[3]

This issue of accountability and ownership is the heart of the problem of American leadership in the world. The impetus of the American Revolution was lack of representation in London. The same problem now exists in Asia, and the United States is viewed as part of the system that locks out Asian participation. Former deputy secretary of state Zoellick often encouraged China to be a stakeholder in international systems, and no doubt China is a beneficiary of that system, but the countries of Asia will not be better stakeholders until Asia has more votes in those systems. To protect American interests in the international systems, the United States must use its leadership to redress the imbalances and give Asia its voice in these institutions.

Lastly, the United States must use its education system to develop the suite of skills necessary to compete in a global economy. One area that could dramatically transform America's competitiveness is language education.

In the United States, the language most frequently taught in school is Spanish, and considering America's history, population, and geographic location, that is a good choice, but after Spanish, the languages of choice are French and German. The high school my children attended in northern Virginia even taught Latin, but no Asian languages.

In 2006, the Bush administration launched the National Security Foreign Language Initiative (NSLI) to promote the teaching of so-called critical languages, including some Asian ones such as Mandarin Chinese, but still retaining Russian. The program, however, is a reaction to the war on terrorism and focuses on Middle East and South Asian languages such as Bangla, Farsi, Turkish, Urdu, and Arabic as critical languages. Although there is much to like about the program, the NSLI is not a comprehensive review of America's future language needs.

State and local schools should not wait for the federal cavalry to save the education of their children. State governments need to take the lead and start teaching East Asian languages and not just Mandarin. Korean and Japanese are important languages, and the number of teachers available is only limited by the imagination of the school boards.

Another language completely overlooked is Indonesian. More than three hundred million people are estimated to speak Indonesian. Indonesian and Malaysian are mutually intelligible and are essentially the same language. Three countries speak Indo-Malay as their first language—Indonesia, Malaysia, and Brunei; Singapore has Malaysian as one of its four official languages; and Indo-Malay is also spoken in southern Thailand. Indonesian-related languages are spoken from the Malay Peninsula all the way to the Polynesian languages of Hawaii, encompassing the Philippines and most of the Pacific islands, but have you ever seen Indonesian offered in any American public schools?

Language training would change the way Americans think about Asia, but more important, it would give American businesspeople, diplomats, and soldiers the tools they need to successfully compete in Asia. As mentioned in chapter 1, thousands of languages are spoken in Asia, so English is Asia's international language. For Asian countries, foreign language training often means English language training. When Japanese visit Indonesia, for example, their conversation, more often than not, will be in English. The same is true of a Korean in Thailand or Chinese in the Philippines. Americans already can speak English and can get along in most international environments, but already speaking English means the United States can spend the time and resources training Americans in a host of Asian languages and gain a competitive advantage.

A FINAL NOTE

Throughout this book, I have explained the advantages of international rules-based systems and the urgent need to embed Asia in those systems. The United States must also encourage Europe and Russia, which represent vested interests in the existing international system, to make room for Asia. Without full participation from Asian countries the system cannot properly function to protect American or global interests.

Notes

CHAPTER 1: RISING ASIA

1. *Foreign Affairs* 27 (1948–1949): 540.

2. One respected expert said recently, "You look back on those [intelligence] studies, and it's only been a decade, China has exceeded—in every area of military modernization—that which even the far-off estimates of the mid-1990s predicted." See comments by former deputy assistant secretary of defense Kurt Campbell in Mike Shuster, "Growing Chinese Military Strength Stirs Debate," *Morning Edition*, National Public Radio, October 17, 2005, http://www.npr.org/templates/story/story.php?storyId=4961290. See also www.apec.org, FAQ_#9.

3. Language information obtained from *Ethnoloque: Languages of the World*, www.ethnoloque.com.

4. Shuster, "Growing Chinese Military Strength Stirs Debate," 12.

5. Neil King Jr., "Rice Wants U.S. to Help China Be Positive Force," *Wall Street Journal*, June 29, 2005, A13, http://online.wsj.com/article/0,,SB112001578322872628,00.html.

6. See Robert Zoellick, "Zoellick Remarks at U.S. Embassy Beijing," August 2, 2005, http://www.state.gov/s/d/rem/50498.htm.

7. Robert B. Zoellick, "Whither China—From Membership to Responsibility? Deputy Secretary of State's Remarks to National Committee on U.S.-China Relations," New York City, September 21, 2005, issued by the Office of Public Affairs, http://www.state.gov/s/d/rem/53682.htm.

8. John W. Garver, *Protracted Contest: Sino-Indian Rivalry in the Twentieth Century* (Seattle: University of Washington Press, 2001), 35.

9. Ted C. Fishman, *China Inc.: How The Rise of the Next Superpower Challenges America and the World* (New York: Scribner, 2005), 49.

10. Henry Kissinger describes the policy process of the 1969 opening to China. One view, he said, opposed the opening because it "would make Soviet-American cooperation impossible," while another view held that relations with the USSR "should not be a major factor in shaping our China policy." A third view, which he called "a kind of 'Realpolitik' approach," argued that the Soviets "would be more conciliatory if they feared that we would otherwise seek a rapprochement with Peking." He concludes, "Not surprisingly, I was on the side of the Realpolitikers." See *White House Years* (Boston: Little, Brown, 1979), 182.

11. In 2003, during the early days of the American campaign in Iraq, I was asked by a Japanese television station to appear on one of their news programs to help explain the military aspects of the campaign in Iraq. During the interview, the Japanese correspondent asked me about accidental deaths of Iraqi civilians caused by American military operations. I admitted that there was a significant risk of accidental civilian deaths in any military campaign, but then to my shock the correspondent tried to draw a comparison between the American operations in Iraq and the Japanese army's systematic massacres in Nanjing. I vehemently tried to disabuse him of that comparison, but he was insistent that the Nanjing massacre was the result of the normal behavior of soldiers in war.

12. Edward J. Lincoln, *Arthritic Japan: The Slow Pace of Economic Reform* (Washington, D.C.: Brookings Institution Press, 2001), 17–18.

13. Stephen P. Cohen, *India: Emerging Power* (Washington, D.C.: Brookings Institution Press, 2001), 9–10.

14. Borrah Ranjan, "Subhas Chandran Bose, the Indian National Army, and the War of India's Liberation," *Journal of Historical Review* 20, no. 1 (2001).

15. Stephen P. Cohen, *The Idea of Pakistan* (Washington, D.C.: Brookings Institution Press, 2004), 26.

16. Garver, *Protracted Contest*, 54.

17. Discovered on the island of Java, Indonesia, in 1891, the skullcap and teeth are estimated to be seven hundred thousand years old and were once the oldest known human remains.

18. Milton E. Osborne, *Southeast Asia: An Illustrated Introductory History*, 5th ed. (Sydney: Allen & Unwin, 1990), 122.

19. Sukarno, like many Indonesians, had only one name.

20. According to the Heritage Foundation/*Wall Street Journal*'s *Index of Economic Freedom*.

CHAPTER 2: SOUTH CHINA SEA MARITIME TERRITORIAL DISPUTES

1. Energy Information Administration, U.S. Department of Energy.

2. American Meteorological Society, http://ams.allenpress.com/amsonline/?request=get-document&doi=10.1175%2F1520-0485(2000)030%3C2419:SCSISC%3E2.0.CO%3B2.

3. http://community.middlebury.edu/~scs/why.html.
4. http://community.middlebury.edu/~scs/why.html.
5. China Geological Survey, http://www.cgs.gov.cn/Ev/news/20040114/001.htm.
6. China Geological Survey.
7. A *stere* is a metric unit of measure equivalent to one cubic meter or one kiloliter.
8. *People's Daily*, http://english.people.com.cn/english/200011/23/eng20001123_55968.html.
9. Energy Information Administration, U.S. Department of Energy.
10. "The South China Sea Dispute: Prospects for Preventive Diplomacy," a special report of the United States Institute of Peace, August 1996.
11. http://community.middlebury.edu/~scs/miranda/.
12. http://www.prio.no/research/asiasecurity/0.
13. http://www.globalsecurity.org/military/world/war/spratly-ship.htm.
14. http://www.globalsecurity.org/military/world/war/spratly-ship.htm.
15. http://www.globalsecurity.org/military/world/war/spratly-ship.htm.
16. Energy Information Administration, U.S. Department of Energy.
17. Energy Information Administration.
18. http://news.bbc.co.uk/2/hi/asia-pacific/4350881.stm.
19. http://www.bizjournals.com/pacific/stories/2003/04/28/daily83.html.
20. http://news.bbc.co.uk/2/hi/asia-pacific/4350881.stm.
21. http://www.oceansatlas.org/servlet/CDSServlet?status=ND0xODM0MyY2PWVuJjMzPSomMzc9a29z.
22. http://www.zmag.org/content/showarticle.cfm?SectionID=17&ItemID=8445.
23. http://community.middlebury.edu/~scs/why.html.
24. Barry Wain, "The Sea—Asia's Depreciating Asset," *Asian Wall Street Journal*, June 8, 2001.
25. "Survival Space," *National Geographic*, December 1998, http://community.middlebury.edu/~scs/maps/map_big.jpg.
26. United Nations Convention on the Law of the Sea (UNCLOS), *Exclusive Economic Zone*, Part V, 1982, 228.
27. This chapter owes an intellectual debt to Mark J. Valencia for his extensive academic research on this subject. His ADELPHI Paper 298, *China and the South China Sea Disputes* (Oxford University Press, October 1995) was particularly valuable, as were his many other books and articles on the subject.
28. Translated by Chang Yu-Lan, intern at the Heritage Foundation: On the Chinese official website of State Bureau of Surveying and Mapping (SBSM), China established their national standard of publishing or circulating maps. There are many regulations for map designers on how to measure, how to draw, and how government reviews applications for permission to publish or distribute the map. See http://www.sbsm.gov.cn/territory.php?col=393&file=3468. The official website of SBSM presents "the standard territory diagram of China." SBSM provides several examples that illustrate the border lines of China for publishers. See http://www.sbsm.gov.cn/territory.php?col=392&file=3484.

29. Max Herriman, lieutenant commander, Australian Centre for Maritime Studies Incorporated, "China's Territorial Sea Law and International Law of the Sea," *Maritime Studies* 15 (1997): 3. See also discussion of China's claim by Xavier Furtado in "International Law and the Dispute over the Spratly Islands: Whither UNCLOS?" *Contemporary Southeast Asia* 21, no. 3 (December 1, 1999).

30. UNCLOS, China's Declaration.

31. http://www.aseansec.org/13165.htm.

32. Zou Keyuan, "The Sino-Vietnamese Agreement on Maritime Boundary Delimitation in the Gulf of Tonkin," *Ocean Development and International Law* 36 (2005): 15.

33. UNCLOS, article 50.

34. UNCLOS, article 121.

35. Ministry of Foreign Affairs of the People's Republic of China, "Jurisprudential Evidence to Support China's Sovereignty over the Spratly Islands," 2000.

36. See introduction to Edward H. Schafer, *Shore of Pearls* (Berkeley: University of California Press, 1970).

37. Marjorie Ann Browne, "The Law of the Sea Convention and U.S. Policy," Congressional Research Service, updated May 12, 2006, 1–2.

CHAPTER 3: THE WAR ON TERRORISM

1. U.S. Embassy in Manila, "Facts about the U.S.-Philippines Visiting Forces Agreement," January 2006, http://manila.usembassy.gov/wwwhr711.html.

2. U.S. Department of Defense, Defense Security Cooperation Agency (DSCA), *DSCA Facts Book 2005* (Washington, D.C.: Administration and Management Business Opertaions, 2005), www.dsca.mil.

3. Members of the Philippine press did not want to reveal their identity for fear of retribution.

4. http://www.jfcom.mil/about/fact_jiacg.htm.

5. Interview by Dana Dillon, February 2004. The interviewee preferred to remain anonymous.

6. U.S. Department of State, *Country Reports on Terrorism 2005*, 70.

7. U.S. Department of State, *Country Reports on Terrorism 2005*, 79.

8. Raphael Perl, "Trends in Terrorism: 2006," CRS report for Congress, July 21, 2006, 16.

9. Global Research, "Inside Indonesia's War on Terror," October 14, 2005, http://www.globalresearch.ca/PrintArticle.php?articleId=1085, 2.

10. Dennis C. Blair, Council on Foreign Relations, news media attending—on the record, New York City, March 21, 2002, http://131.84.1.218/speeches/sst2002/020321cr.htm.

11. Admiral Thomas B. Fargo, commander, U.S. Pacific Command, before the House International Relations Committee, Subcommittee on Asia and the Pacific, on the U.S. Pacific Command Posture, June 26, 2003, 30.

12. Admiral William J. Fallon, commander, U.S. Pacific Command, before the Senate Armed Services Committee, on the U.S. Pacific Command Posture, March 7, 2006.

13. Fallon, March 7, 2006.

14. The United States armed forces define three levels of military activity: tactical, operational, and strategic. A shorthand explanation could be tactical, "take that hill"; operational, "take that country"; and strategic, utilize all types of national resources to accomplish a national objective. The national security strategy does not require a military solution, but it does require political leadership.

15. James Carafano and Dana Dillon, "Winning the Peace: Principles for Post Conflict Operations," *Heritage Foundation Backgrounder* #1859.

16. Terror Free Tomorrow, "A Dramatic Change of Public Opinion in the Muslim World: Results from a New Poll in Pakistan 2005," 4, http://www.terrorfree tomorrow.org.

CHAPTER 4: NUCLEAR-ARMED ASIA

1. This chapter is adapted from a paper I wrote with Baker Spring. Although the words of this chapter are mine, Baker contributed much to my thoughts and ideas on the subject; particularly, it was Baker's idea to insist on a criteria-based exception for nonweapon states like India.

2. Definition provided by the Heritage Foundation's arms control expert, Baker Spring.

3. From Baker Spring.

4. *Centrifuges* are metal tubes that spin uranium hexafluoride gas in order to separate out the uranium 235, which is needed to make a nuclear reaction.

5. David Albright and Corey Hinderstein, "Unraveling the A. Q. Khan and Future Proliferation Networks," *Washington Quarterly* 28, no. 2: 114.

6. BBC News, February 12, 2004, http://news.bbc.co.uk/2/hi/americas/3481499.stm; and Malaysian Investigation Report, http://www.rmp.gov.my/rmp03/040220scomi_eng.htm.

7. http://www.latimes.com/news/nationworld/world/la-adfg-network28nov28,0,5729684,full.story.

8. Albright and Hinderstein, "Unraveling," 120.

9. Albright and Hinderstein, "Unraveling."

10. Albright and Hinderstein, "Unraveling," 115.

11. Albright and Hinderstein, "Unraveling."

12. "Press Release by Inspector General of Police in Relation to Investigation on the Alleged Production of Components for Libya's Uranium Enrichment Programme," February 20, 2004, http://www.rmp.gov.my/rmp03/040220scomi_eng.htm.

13. Albright and Hinderstein, "Unraveling," 120.

14. "A. Q. Khan and Iran," http://www.globalsecurity.org/wmd/world/iran/khan-iran.htm.

15. Michael Laufer, "A. Q. Khan Nuclear Chronology," *Proliferation Brief* 8, no. 8, http://12.150.189.35/npp/publications/index.cfm?fa=view&id=17420.

16. "A. Q. Khan and Iran."

17. Albright and Hinderstein, "Unraveling," 115.

18. "A. Q. Khan and Iran."

19. Albright and Hinderstein, "Unraveling," 113.

20. Albright and Hinderstein, "Unraveling," 114.

21. Albright and Hinderstein, "Unraveling," 116.

22. Albright and Hinderstein, "Unraveling," 114.

23. Laufer, "A. Q. Khan Nuclear Chronology."

24. Laufer, "A. Q. Khan Nuclear Chronology."

25. http://news.bbc.co.uk/2/hi/south_asia/4180286.stm.

26. http://www.cnn.com/2004/WORLD/asiapcf/02/05/pakistan.nuclear/.

27. Thomas Woodrow, "China Opens Pandora's Nuclear Box," *China Brief* (The Jamestown Foundation) 2, no. 24 (December 10, 2002), http://www.jamestown.org/publications_details.php?volume_id=18&&issue_id=664 (April 5, 2006).

28. Center for Nonproliferation Studies, "China's Missile Exports and Assistance to East Asia," *Nuclear Threat Initiative*, http://www.nti.org/db/china/meapos.htm (April 5, 2006).

29. Central Intelligence Agency, "Unclassified Report to Congress on the Acquisition of Technology Relating to Weapons of Mass Destruction and Advanced Conventional Munitions: January–June 2003," November 2003, www.cia.gov/cia/reports/721_reports/jan_jun2003.htm (April 5, 2006).

30. Central Intelligence Agency, "Unclassified Report to Congress."

31. Central Intelligence Agency, "Report to Congress on the Acquisition of Technology Relating to Weapons of Mass Destruction and Advanced Conventional Munitions: July–December 2003," November 2004.

32. David Morgan, "U.S. Not Certain North Korea Has Nuclear Weapons," Reuters, February 28, 2006, www.boston.com/news/world/asia/articles/2006/02/28/us_intelligence_not_certain_nk_has_nuclear_arms/ (March 27, 2006).

33. Larry A. Niksch, "North Korea's Nuclear Weapons Program," Congressional Research Service, Library of Congress, March 25, 2005.

34. Federation of American Scientists, "Nuclear Weapons Program—North Korea," www.fas.org/nuke/guide/dprk/nuke/index.html (March 24, 2006).

35. Niksch, "North Korea's Nuclear Weapons Program."

36. Niksch, "North Korea's Nuclear Weapons Program."

37. Center for Nonproliferation Studies, "Nuclear Overview: North Korea," Nuclear Threat Initiative, February 2006, www.nti.org/e_research/profiles/NK/Nuclear/print/index_157.prt (March 24, 2006).
38. Center for Nonproliferation Studies, "Nuclear Overview: North Korea."
39. U.S. Department of State, "Joint Statement of the Fourth Round of the Six-Party Talks," September 19, 2005, www.state.gov/r/pa/prs/ps/2005/53490.htm (March 24, 2006).
40. U.S. Department of State, "Joint Statement."
41. Michael Richardson, "The Proliferation Security Initiative (PSI): An Assessment of Its Strengths and Weaknesses, with Some Proposals for Shaping Its Future," *Trends in Southeast Asia Series* 3 (2006): 11, Institute of Southeast Asia Studies, Singapore.
42. George Perkovich, *India's Nuclear Bomb: The Impact on Global Proliferation* (Berkeley: University of California Press, 1999), 30.
43. Percovich, *India's Nuclear Bomb*, 30.
44. Percovich, *India's Nuclear Bomb.*
45. Percovich, *India's Nuclear Bomb.*
46. http://nuclearweaponarchive.org/India/IndiaOrigin.html.
47. From Arms Control Association.
48. Richardson, "The Proliferation Security Initiative (PSI)," 22–24.

CHAPTER 5: PIRATES OF THE SOUTH CHINA SEA

Parts of this chapter are based on an article I wrote for *SAIS Review*, vol. 25, winter-spring 2005, pp. 155–165, "Maritime Piracy: Defining the Problem."

1. Martin N. Murphy, "Slow Alarm: The Response of the Marine Insurance Industry to the Threat of Piracy and Maritime Terrorism," *Maritime Studies* 148 (May–June 2006), Australian Association of Maritime Affairs.
2. As with any crime, it is unrealistic to expect to totally eliminate piracy, but reducing it to negligible levels is well within the power of government.
3. *Utusan Online*, "New Definition Sought for Acts of Piracy, Isolated from Terrorism," Kuala Lumpur, October 8, 2004, 1.
4. 1982 United Nations Convention on the Law of the Sea (UNCLOS) (article 101).
5. International Chamber of Commerce, International Maritime Bureau, "Piracy and Armed Robbery against Ships," Annual Report, January 1–December 31, 2003, 3.
6. UN International Maritime Organization, MSC.4/Circ.53, June 1, 2004, 1.
7. *Utusan Online*, "New Definition."
8. Interview conducted on March 2, 2004, in Kuala Lumpur, Malaysia.

9. Kog Yue-Choong, "Environmental Management and Conflict in Southeast Asia—Land Reclamation and Its Political Impact," Institute of Defense and Strategic Studies, Singapore, January 2006, 3.

10. UN International Maritime Organization, "Port State Control: An Update on IMO's Work in 2003," 3.

11. UN International Maritime Organization, "Port State Control."

12. UN International Maritime Organization, "Port State Control."

13. International Chamber of Commerce, "Piracy," 28.

14. International Chamber of Commerce, "Piracy," 29.

15. UN International Maritime Organization, MSC.4/Circ.50, "Reports on Acts of Piracy and Armed Robbery against Ships," April 27, 2004; annex 2, "Regional Analysis of Reports on Piracy and Armed Robbery against Ships Which Were Reported to Have Been Allegedly Committed or Attempted during 2003," 1–2.

16. International Chamber of Commerce, "Piracy," 31.

17. International Chamber of Commerce, "Piracy," 38.

18. On October 12, 2000, terrorists attacked the USS *Cole*, using a suicide bomb on a supply raft, while the *Cole* was anchored in the port of Aden, Yemen, killing seventeen American sailors.

19. On October 6, 2002, terrorists, in a small dinghy loaded with explosives, attacked the *Limburg* while off the port of Aden, Yemen, killing one crewman and spilling ninety thousand barrels of oil.

20. International Chamber of Commerce, "Piracy," 3.

21. International Chamber of Commerce, "Piracy," 41.

22. International Chamber of Commerce, "Piracy," 48.

23. International Chamber of Commerce, "Piracy."

24. Murphy, "Slow Alarm," 10.

25. Murphy, "Slow Alarm," 5–11.

26. Murphy, "Slow Alarm," 12.

27. International Maritime Organization, "Report on Acts of Piracy and Armed Robbery against Ships: Annual Report—2005," March 22, 2006, 1.

28. International Maritime Organization, "Report."

29. International Maritime Organization, "Report."

30. Ed Holt, "Indonensia Accepts $1m 'Bail' for Mirna," *Lloyd's List*, September 19, 2005.

CHAPTER 6: TRADE AND AMERICAN FOREIGN POLICY IN ASIA

1. Aaron Schavey, "Manufacturing Bogus Claims," http://www.heritage.org/Press/Commentary/ed081602.cfm.

2. Spencer Jack, "The Military Industrial Base in an Age of Globalization," Heritage Foundation, 25.

3. Office of the United States Trade Representative, Trade Facts, April 14, 2005, 1, http://www.ustr.gov.

4. Office of the United States Trade Representative, "Summary of U.S. Bilateral Investment Treaty (BIT) Program," February 24, 2006, http://www.ustr.gov.

5. World Trade Organization, "WTO in Brief," April 2005, www.wto.org.

6. United States Trade Representative, "Administration Requests Extension of Trade Promotion Authority," press release, March 30, 2005.

7. Robert B. Zoellick, "Whither China: From Membership to Responsibility?" remarks to National Committee on U.S.-China Relations, New York City, September 21, 2005.

8. Robert Zoellick has coined the term "responsible stakeholder" to address this phenomenon with China.

9. *Hong Kong Standard Weekly*, "Big Red Hiding Wood," April 8, 2006.

10. Ismail Awang, "Future of the World Timber Market," keynote speech, Malaysian Timber Council, September 17, 2002.

11. Office of the United States Trade Representative, "U.S. Trade Relations: Entering a New Phase of Greater Accountability and Enforcement, Top-to-Bottom Review," February 2006, 14.

12. Office of the United States Trade Representative, "U.S. Trade Relations," 15.

13. Office of the United States Trade Representative, "U.S. Trade Relations," 24–27.

14. Morgan Stanley Economists, "India: The Next Trillion-Dollar Economy," January 28, 2003.

15. Department of State, Bureau of Economic and Business Affairs, "U.S. Bilateral Investment Treaty Program," January 10, 2006.

16. Office of the United States Trade Representative, Trade Facts, "NAFTA: A Strong Success Story," March 2006, 1, http://www.ustr.gov.

17. Office of the United States Trade Representative, "Enterprise for ASEAN Initiative," http://www.ustr.gov.

18. Office of the United States Trade Representative, "Enterprise for ASEAN Initiative."

19. U.S. Census Bureau, Foreign Trade Division, Data Dissemination Branch, http://www.un.int/vietnam/dev_bus/Foreign%20direct%20investment%20in%20Vietnam.htm.

20. One is highest level of economic freedom; five is the lowest level.

21. John C. Hulsman, Gerald P. O'Driscoll, and Denise H. Froning, "The Free Trade Association: A Trade Agenda for the New Global Economy," *The Index of Economic Freedom 2001* (Washington, D.C.: Heritage Foundation, 2001), 33.

22. A very similar idea was proposed by Gerald P. O'Driscoll Jr. in "The Terms of Trade: A Coalition of the Willing?" *Wall Street Journal*, December 19, 2005.

CHAPTER 7: UNIFICATION OF THE KOREAN PENINSULA

1. I must begin this chapter with a disclaimer: Of all the countries I am writing about in this book, Korea is the only one I have never visited. Furthermore, since the death of North Korea's leader, Kim Il Sung, in July 1994, I have been predicting the demise of the North Korean government in the next six months. So I cannot claim any special predictive powers on the "when" or "how" of Korean unification.

2. There is also a fourth alternative of North Korea "muddling through somehow," but since that scenario precludes unification, it will not be considered in this chapter.

3. http://www.cia.gov/cia/publications/factbook/geos/kn.html.

4. http://www.cia.gov/cia/publications/factbook/geos/ks.html.

5. Mark Hartley, "Hyundai's North Korean Nightmare," *Daimnation*, October 26, 2005.

6. "Country Profile 2006: North Korea," *The Economist Intelligence Unit Limited 2006*, 16.

7. U.S. State Department, "Country Reports on Human Rights Practices—2004: North Korea."

8. Antony Barnett, "Revealed: The Gas Chamber Horror of North Korea's Gulag," *The Observer*, February 1, 2004.

9. World Food Programme, "WFP DPR Korea EMOP 10141.2 Emergency Food Assistance to Vulnerable Groups," 3.

10. Scott Snyder, "North Korea's Challenge of Regime Survival," *Pacific Affairs* 73, no. 4 (Winter 2000–2001): 521.

11. "Country Profile 2006: North Korea," 16.

12. Jonathon D. Pollack and Chung Min Lee, "Preparing for Korean Unification: Scenarios and Implications," http://www.rand.org/pubs/monograph_reports/MR1040/index.html.

13. Thomas Woodrow, "China Opens Pandora's Nuclear Box," *China Brief* (The Jamestown Foundation) 2, no. 24 (December 10, 2002), http://www.jamestown.org/publications_details.php?volume_id=18&&issue_id=664 (April 5, 2006).

14. Center for Nonproliferation Studies, "China's Missile Exports and Assistance to East Asia," *Nuclear Threat Initiative*, http://www.nti.org/db/china/meapos.htm (April 5, 2006).

15. Central Intelligence Agency, "Unclassified Report to Congress on the Acquisition of Technology Relating to Weapons of Mass Destruction and Advanced Conventional Munitions: January–June 2003," November 2003, http://www.cia.gov/cia/reports/721_reports/jan_jun2003.htm (April 5, 2006).

16. Sang-Ho Choe, "China, Korea Dispute Ancient Kingdom," *boston.com*, January 31, 2004.

CHAPTER 8: ONE CHINA, TWO CHINAS, ONE TAIWAN?

1. Huang Fu-san, *A Brief History of Taiwan: A Sparrow Transformed into a Phoenix*, Government Information Office, Taipei, http://www.gio.tw/taiwan-website/5-gp/history/index.htm, quoted in J. Bruce Jacobs, "Understanding Taiwan's History," part of the Democratizing Taiwan project funded by a Discovery Grant from the Australian Research Council.. See introduction: 2 and chap. 1: 1. Noted anthropologist Inez de Beauclair identifies Taiwan's Yami people as "proto-Polynesian" in her *Ethnographic Studies* (Taipei: Southern Materials Center, 1986), 13–14. There is also considerable archeological and linguistic evidence that the Polynesian populations of the Pacific originated in Taiwan. See David Frazier, "Taiwan, the Homeland," *Far Eastern Economic Review*, January 22, 2004, http://www.feer.com/articles/2004/0401_22/p054current.html.

2. For a review of the linguistic evidence, see Jared Diamond, "Taiwan's Gift to the World," *Nature*, February 17, 2000, 709–10, http://www.nature.com/nature/journal/v403/n6771/full/403709a0.html.

3. Huang Fu-san, *A Brief History of Taiwan*, chap. 2: 3.

4. Huang Fu-san, *A Brief History of Taiwan*, chap. 4: 1.

5. Xue Huayuan, Dai Baocun, and Zhou Meili, *Taiwan, bushi Zhongguo de: Taiwan guomin de lishi* [Taiwan Is Not Chinese: A History of the Taiwanese People] (Danshui: Quncehui, 2005), 59; an English translation is Hsueh Hua-yuan, Tai Pao-tsun, and Chow Mei-li, *Is Taiwan Chinese? A History of Taiwanese Nationality* (Tamsui: Taiwan Advocates, 2005), 56.

6. Xue et al., *Taiwan*, 135. Hsueh et. al, *Is Taiwan Chinese?* 132.

7. Jacobs, "Understanding Taiwan's History."

8. S. C. M. Paine, *The Sino-Japanese War of 1894–1895: Perceptions, Power and Primacy* (Cambridge: Cambridge University Press, 2003), 291–92. Paine cites Hayashi Tadasu, *The Secret Memoirs of Count Tadasu Hayashi*, ed. A. M. Pooley (New York: Putnam, 1915), 57.

9. An especially good survey of this period is George H. Kerr, *Formosa, Licensed Revolution and the Home Rule Movement, 1895–1945* (Honolulu: University Press of Hawaii, 1974).

10. George H. Kerr, *Formosa Betrayed* (Boston: Houghton Mifflin, 1965), 199–201.

11. Dispatch No. 311 from the ambassador in China (Stuart) to the secretary of state, dated Nanking December 4, 1946. Reprinted in *FRUS* 10 (1946): 590.

12. Kerr, *Formosa Betrayed*, 240.

13. Representatives from Mainland China constituencies elected in 1947 were allowed to retain their seats indefinitely, and as they died off, losing candidates for those seats (who managed to escape to Taiwan) were appointed in place of the dead. Legislative Yuan and National Assembly members were virtually members for life and faced no electoral challenge until constitutional revisions in 1992.

14. U.S. ambassador John Leighton Stuart's memorial to Chiang Kai-shek of April 18, 1947. See China White Paper, 925.

15. Dean Acheson, *Present at the Creation: My Years at the State Department* (New York: Norton, Inc., 1969), 355–58.

16. Hong Xuezhi, 44. Earlier U.S. estimates put the Chinese force at about 180,000. See Alan S. Whiting, *China Crosses the Yalu*, RAND Corporation Research Study R-356 (New York: Macmillan, 1960), 118. By November 24, there were "a total of 450,000 Chinese troops in Korea, including 380,000 combat fighters."

17. Hong Xuezhi says there were "twelve infantry divisions, three artillery divisions," with an additional twenty-four divisions concentrating on the border. Hong, 44. Also see Billy C. Mossman, *U.S. Army in the Korean War: Ebb and Flow November 1950–July 1951* (Washington, D.C.: Center for Military History, United States Army, 1990), 55.

18. Edmund Morris, *Dutch: A Memoir of Ronald Reagan* (New York: Random House, 1999), 377–78.

19. *Report No. 96-7, Taiwan Enabling Act; Report of the Committee on Foreign Relations, United States Senate, Together with Additional Views on S.245*, March 2, 1979 (Washington, D.C.: U.S. Government Printing Office, 1979), 7.

20. Section 4(b)(b)(1), Taiwan Relations Act, PL 96-8, April 10, 1979.

21. The Taiwan Relations Act, PL96-8, section 2(b)(6), reads, "It is the Policy of the United States to maintain the capacity of the United States to resist any resort to force or other forms of coercion that would jeopardize the security, or the social or economic system, of the people of Taiwan." In section 3(c), the TRA directs that "the President and the Congress shall determine, in accordance with constitutional processes, appropriate action by the United States in response to any such danger."

22. *Mutual Defense Treaty between the United States of America and the Republic of China*, signed at Washington, December 2, 1954. See Treaties and Other International Acts Series TIAS 3178. Article II of the MDT says, "The Parties separately and jointly . . . will maintain and develop their individual and collective capacity to resist armed attack and communist subversive activity directed from without against their territorial integrity and political stability." Article V states that each party will "act to meet the common danger in accordance with its constitutional processes."

23. This is a fundamental tenet of international law; see Lassa Oppenheim, *International Law: Peace*, 8th ed., ed. H. Lauterpacht (1955), 452, cited in Y. Frank Ching, "One China Policy and Taiwan," *Fordham International Law Journal* 28, no. 1 (December 2004): 6–8.

24. *Defense Science Board Task Force on High Performance Microchip Supply*, U.S. Department of Defense, February 2005.

25. This is at least the public position whenever anyone can actually squeeze a position out of an executive branch spokesperson. In a letter from the State Department to Senator John East (R-N.C.), the department answered the direct and simple question "What is the United States' position on the matter of sovereignty over Taiwan?" with the answer "The United States take no position on the question

of Taiwan's sovereignty. We view this as a matter the Chinese themselves must resolve." See Committee on the Judiciary, Subcommittee on the Separation of Powers, *The Taiwan Communiqué and the Separation of Powers*, United States Senate, 97th Congress, 2nd Session, Transcript of Hearing, September 17 and 27, 1982, 140. In July 1982, President Reagan gave personal assurances to Taiwan's president Chiang Ching-kuo that, among other things, "the United States has not changed its long-standing position on the matter of Taiwan's sovereignty." For a longer discussion of President Reagan's "six assurances," see Assistant Secretary of State for East Asia and Pacific Affairs John H. Holdridge's testimony in "China-Taiwan: United States Policy," Committee on Foreign Affairs, U.S. House of Representatives, August 18, 1982, 15–16. Holdridge also describes the six assurances in his memoir, *Crossing the Divide: An Insider's Account of Normalization of U.S.-China Relations* (Lanham, Md.: Rowman & Littlefield, 1997), 232.

26. Public Law 96-8 (United States Code, title 22, chapter 48, sections 3301–3316), enacted April 10, 1979.

27. Emphasis added. In a prepared statement for testimony before the House International Relations Committee on April 21, 2004, Assistant Secretary of State James Kelly declared that "The U.S. does not support independence for Taiwan or unilateral moves that would change the status quo as we define it" and that this was a "core principle of administration China policy." See "House International Relations Committee Hearing on Taiwan; Statement of Assistant Secretary of State James Kelly," April 21, 2004, http://wwwa.house.gov/international_relations/108/Kel042104.htm.

28. "House International Relations Committee Hearing on Taiwan Statement of Assistant Secretary of State James Kelly," April 21, 2004, http://wwwa.house.gov/international_relations/108/Kel042104.htm; emphasis added.

29. Emphasis added. For a transcript of the hearing, see "The Taiwan Relations Act: The Next Twenty-Five Years," testimony before the Committee on International Relations, U.S. House of Representatives, April 21, 2004, 40, at http://commdocs.house.gov/committees/intlrel/hfa93229.000/hfa93229_0f.htm.

30. On February 27, 2006, for example, State Department spokesman Adam Ereli was asked, "Do you think Chen Shui-bian's move is a change of the status quo, and what is the U.S. definition of . . . the status quo?" Ereli tried to turn the question around: "President Chen has said that he is committed to the status quo and that he is committed to the pledges in his inaugural speech." But the questions persisted: "I just want to get this right. So you don't consider this as a change of status quo?" To which the cornered Ereli could only admit, "You know, I'm not going to define it further than I already have." Needless to say, he hadn't described it at all. A transcript of the February 27 briefing is at http://www.state.gov/r/pa/prs/dpb/2006/62221.htm.

31. "Statement of Assistant Secretary of State James Kelly," April 21, 2004.

32. The U.S. government never formally issued the "six assurances" that were conveyed by President Reagan to Taiwan's president, Chiang Ching-kuo, on July 14, 1982. But Reagan did authorize President Chiang to release the text of the assurances on the

day of the announcement of the August 17, 1982, communiqué with China. That same day, then–Assistant Secretary of State John H. Holdridge repeated these assurances to the Senate Foreign Relations Committee, and later, Holdridge's successor, Paul Wolfowitz repeated the substance of the six assurances to the Senate Committee on the Judiciary: see Taiwan Communiqué and Separation of Powers, Hearing before the Senate Committee on the Judiciary, March 10, 1983. Wolfowitz said, "It is important to bear in mind some things that we did not agree to in the communiqué. We have not agreed to consult in advance with the PRC on arms sales to Taiwan, nor shall we do so. We have not changed our position that the Taiwan question is a matter for the Chinese on both sides of the strait to resolve, and we will not interfere in this matter or pressure Taiwan to enter into negotiations. *We have not changed our longstanding position on the issue of sovereignty over Taiwan.* We do not seek any of these changes nor should we seek to change the protection of the Taiwan Relations Act itself." Emphasis added.

In his memoirs, Holdridge claims that Taipei was alerted to the August communiqué negotiations and suggested the six points as "guidelines in conducting [U.S.] relations with Taiwan." My own memory is that the six assurances were drafted by Dr. Gaston Sigur, then at the National Security Council. Holdridge also claims that the fifth point regarding the U.S. position on sovereignty was that the U.S. "would continue to regard Taiwan as part of China, the question of reunification would be left to the Chinese themselves." See Holdridge, *Crossing the Divide*, 231–32. In fact, the fifth point read, "We have not agreed to take any position regarding sovereignty over Taiwan," when presented to President Chiang on July 14, 1982, a position that was modified for public consumption later to read, "The U.S. has not altered its position regarding sovereignty over Taiwan."

These six assurances have been embraced by all subsequent U.S. administrations as part of the canon of U.S. policy toward Taiwan. Secretary of State Colin Powell reiterated this during testimony before the Senate Foreign Relations Committee on March 8, 2001. He confirmed that the assurances "remain the usual and official policy of the United States." See "Hearing of the Senate Foreign Relations Committee for the Fiscal Year 2002 Foreign Operations Budget," transcribed by Federal News Service, March 8, 2001.

33. See "Marshal Ye Jianying's Nine-Point Proposal," Beijing, Xinhua News Agency, September 30, 1981.

34. "The Taiwan Question and the Reunification of China," issued by the Taiwan Affairs Office and the Information Office under the State Council of the People's Republic of China, August 31, 1993.

35. "The One-China Principle and the Taiwan Issue," issued by the Taiwan Affairs Office and the Information Office of the State Council of the People's Republic of China, February 21, 2000.

36. "The One-China Principle and the Taiwan Issue."

37. Paul Eckert, "China PM Warns Taiwan Voters on Chen," Reuters, March 15, 2000.

38. "Putting a Check on 'Taiwan Independence' a Pressing Task," *China Daily* (Beijing), May 17, 2004, 1, http://www.chinadaily.com.cn/english/doc/2004-05/17/content_331143.htm.

39. White House Press Secretary Scott McClellan, White House Daily Briefing, May 19, 2004, http://www.whitehouse.gov/news/releases/2004/05/20040519-8.html.

40. This was described to me, firsthand, by a correspondent who was in the meeting. But for other reporting, see Danny Gittings, "General Zhu Goes Ballistic," *Wall Street Journal*, July 18, 2005, A13, http://online.wsj.com/article/0,,SB112165176626988025,00.html; Jason Dean, "Chinese General Lays Nuclear Card on U.S.'s Table," *Wall Street Journal*, July 15, 2005, http://online.wsj.com/article/0,,SB112135825292585833,00.html. See also Alexandra Harney, "China 'Ready to Use' N-Weapons against US," *Financial Times*, July 14, 2005, http://news.ft.com/cms/s/28cfe55a-f4a7-11d9-9dd1-00000e2511c8,ft_acl=,s01=1.html; Joe McDonald, "Chinese General Threatens U.S. over Taiwan; Response Might Be with Nuclear Weapons, Reporters Told," Associated Press, July 15, 2005; Joseph Kahn, "Chinese General Threatens Use of A-Bombs If U.S. Intrudes," *New York Times*, July 15, 2005, http://www.nytimes.com/2005/07/15/international/asia/15china.html.

41. See "Military Power of the People's Republic of China 2006," Office of Secretary of Defense, issued May 23, 2006, p. 20, at http://www.defenselink.mil.

42. Supposedly, General Zhu was "punished" for his indiscretion before a gaggle of foreign reporters with tape recorders humming, but, as one unidentified Chinese source put it, "the punishment could not be too harsh or we would be seen as too weak toward the United States"; see "China Punished General for Talk Of Strike At U.S.," Reuters, December 22, 2005.

43. This is the literal translation of "*Fan Fenlie Guojia Fa*," more commonly known in English as the "Anti-Secession Law." For a full text, see http://news.xinhuanet.com/english/2005-03/14/content_2694180.htm.

44. See, for example, Ted Galen Carpenter, *America's Coming War with China: A Collision Course over Taiwan* (New York: Palgrave Macmillan, 2005).

45. For a short review of "war avoidance" theory, see Steven Geoffrey Gieseler, "Debate on the 'Democratic Peace': A Review," *American Diplomacy*, University of North Carolina at Chapel Hill, January 3, 2004, http://www.unc.edu/depts/diplomat/archives_roll/2004_01-03/gieseler_debate/gieseler_debate.html.

46. Stephen Richards Graubard makes this point in *Kissinger: Portrait of a Mind* (New York: Norton, 1973), 17. Kissinger's book, *A World Restored: Metternich, Castlereagh and the Problems of Peace 1812–1822*, was republished in paperback by Weidenfeld & Nicholson, London, on October 19, 2000.

47. State and NSC policy-level spokespersons rarely, if ever, describe America's interest in the survival of a democratic Taiwan. Instead, they couch U.S. support in terms of "obligations under the TRA." For example, when asked by the Chinese language press about U.S. arms sales to Taiwan, Secretary of State Colin Powell only said the U.S. "completely understands Chinese concern about the arms-sales issue" but

that the U.S. "also has responsibilities under the Taiwan Relations Act. When selling arms to Taiwan, the US considers all factors." See "Interview with Phoenix TV," Secretary Colin L. Powell, Washington, D.C., February 19, 2003, http://www.state.gov/secretary/former/powell/remarks/2003/17806.htm. Condoleezza Rice told reporters that "the U.S. is very clear on our policies about Taiwan, one China policy. We are basing our policy on the three communiqués. And we, of course, always remind people that we also have obligations under the Taiwan Relations Act to help China—to help Taiwan defend itself." See "Dr. Rice Previews President's Trip to Asia and Australia: Press Briefing by National Security Advisor, Dr. Condoleezza Rice," October 14, 2003, http://www.whitehouse.gov/news/releases/2003/10/20031014-4.html.

48. Chen Fengxing, "Jiang Bingkun: Liangan shi liangge zhuquan guojia; Qiangdiao woguo zhengce wei 'yi yige zhongguo wei zhixiangde jieduanxingde liangge Zhongguo zhengce'" [PK Chiang: There are two sovereign nations on either side of the Strait; stresses that Taiwan's policy is "an interim two China's policy with One China as its conceptual guide"], *United Daily News* (Taipei), November 22, 1993, 1.

49. Meng Ronghua, "Li Zongtong: Liangan dingwei teshu guo yu guo guanxi" [President Lee: The two sides of the Strait are defined as special state-to-state relations], *Central Daily News* (Taipei), July 10, 1999, 1, http://www.cdn.com.tw/daily/1999/07/10/text/880710a1.htm.

50. See Presidential Office Press Release, 2005-08-02, "President Chen Receives the Youth Friendship Ambassadors of the Formosa Foundation in the United States." See also "Taiwan People Want to Be Their Own Masters: President," Central News Agency, Taipei, August 13, 2005.

51. Taiwan's "Green" camp comprises President Chen Shui-bian's left-of-center, labor/environment-oriented Democratic Progressive Party (DPP) and the solidly proindependence Taiwan Solidarity Union (TSU). The "Blue" camp is dominated by the right-of-center, probusiness Kuomintang (Nationalist) party (KMT) and includes the smaller pro-China People First Party (PFP).

52. For an authoritative statement of the KMT's position on Taiwan, see KMT Chairman Ma Ying-jeou's speech at the London School of Economics, "Bridging the Divide: A Vision for Peace in Asia," February 13, 2006. Ma noted that "insofar as the political question is concerned, should the Kuomintang regain power in 2008, we will try to resume the disrupted cross-Strait talks under the so-called 'Consensus of 1992.' This is a tacit consensus reached by the two sides in 1992 in Hong Kong accepting the 'one-China principle' but allowing different interpretations by each side, in order to find the common ground and cement mutual trust in the first place. For us, the 'China' is Republic of China; for them, it is the People's Republic of China." He added, "But as the ROC Constitution is a one-China constitution, it does not rule out the option of eventual reunification between Taiwan and Mainland China if the overall conditions across the Taiwan Strait are ripe, that is to say, when the developments in Mainland China reach a stage when its political democracy, economic prosperity and social well-being become congruent with those of Taiwan."

53. "Zongtong yu Tainan Xiangqin Huanzhong Xinnian Tuanyuan Canxu" [President's Dinner Remarks to Tainan Kinsmen New Year Gathering], Taipei Central News Agency, January 29, 2006. President Chen announced the "cessation" (*zhongzhi*) of the council on February 27, 2006.

54. Chen was clear that his speech would "satisfy" the Americans. See Zheng Renwen and Huang Qianyu, "Bian ti Jiuzhi Yanshuo San Yuanze" [Chen Shui-bian raises three principles for inauguration speech], *Taipei Central Daily News*, May 4, 2000, 1. Those three principles were (1) the U.S. will be satisfied (*zuo dao rang Meiguo manyi*), (2) it will be accepted by the international community (*rang guoji shehui kending*), and (3) the Chinese communists will find no excuse to say Taiwan is provocative (*Zhonggong zhaobudao jiekou lai shuo Taiwan tiaochi*). On May 15, 2000, the State Department spokesman Richard Boucher was asked, "Let me come back to Taiwan. The same *Post* article indicated that Raymond Burghardt, the AIT director in Taiwan, has tried to exert influence in the writing of President-elect Chen's inaugural speech. Would you confirm or deny that, or . . . ?" Boucher replied, "No, I'm not going to talk about that. We have meetings with a lot of people a lot of times. We don't get into every single one and try to talk about it." When pressed on whether the U.S. representative in Taipei had "been given any talking points on his speech," Boucher demurred. "I'm not going to try to characterize it one way or the other." The so-called five no's were in a part of the speech that read, "Therefore, as long as the CCP regime has no intention to use military force against Taiwan, I pledge that during my term in office, I will not declare independence, I will not change the national title, I will not push forth the inclusion of the so-called 'state-to-state' description in the Constitution, and I will not promote a referendum to change the status quo in regards to the question of independence or unification. Furthermore, the abolition of the National Unification Council or the National Unification Guidelines will not be an issue." See President Chen Shui-bian's inauguration speech, "Taiwan Stands Up," Office of the President, Republic of China, May 20, 2000.

55. For a discussion of the "*yibian yiguo*" controversy, see John J. Tkacik Jr., "Taiwan Hornet's Nest," *Asian Wall Street Journal*, August 5, 2005, A12, http://online.wsj.com/article/SB1028499722513917040.html.

56. See Richard Boucher, spokesman, Department of State Daily Press Briefing, Washington, D.C., March 14, 2005, http://www.state.gov/r/pa/prs/dpb/2005/43404.htm: "Mr. Boucher: The decision by the Chinese leaders to have the National People's Congress adopt an anti-secession law today is—it's unfortunate. It really does not serve the cause of peace and stability on the Taiwan Strait and for that reason we believe it to be unhelpful." Assistant Secretary of State-designate for East Asian and Pacific Affairs Christopher Hill told senators during his confirmation hearings, "We don't believe there is any justification for making these unhelpful statements that suggest that there are other options out there that the Chinese can use beside peaceful dialogue," and added, "It is unthinkable to resort to military means to solve [cross-strait issues]. So clearly any Anti-Secession Law that alludes

to the legality of military means is simply not helpful." See Charles Snyder, "Rice to Tell Beijing US Upset over Law," *Taipei Times*, March 17, 2005, 1, http://www.taipeitimes.com/News/front/archives/2005/03/17/2003246563.

57. George W. Bush, "President Discusses Freedom and Democracy in Kyoto, Japan, Kyoto Kaikan, Kyoto, Japan," White House Press Release, November 16, 2005, http://www.whitehouse.gov/news/releases/2005/11/20051116-6.html; see also Jennifer Loven, "Bush Hails Taiwan as Model of Freedom," Associated Press, November 16, 2005.

58. For a longer discussion of this, see John J. Tkacik Jr., "Revenge of the Panda Hugger: The Bush Administration's China Policy Is Hardening," *The Weekly Standard* 11, no. 23 (February 27, 2006), http://www.weeklystandard.com/Content/Public/Articles/000/000/006/784vnqpk.asp.

59. For the State Department's official position on Taiwan's sovereignty as of July 13, 1971, see a memorandum from the Office of the Legal Advisor entitled "The Legal Status of Taiwan," a copy of which appears in John J. Tkacik Jr., ed., *Rethinking "One China"* (Washington, D.C: Heritage Foundation, 2004), 180–91. For an extended discussion of the Taiwan "sovereignty" issue, see Chiang, *One-China Policy and Taiwan*.

CHAPTER 9: THE ASIAN SPACE RACE AND THE MASTERS OF INFINITY

1. "China Plans Three-Men Space Launch after 2008 Olympics," Kyodo News Agency, April 27, 2006.

2. James Oberg, "International Space Exploration Program," Testimony before the Senate Commerce, Science, and Transportation Committee, April 27, 2004, www.commerce.senate.gov/hearings/testimony.cfm?id=1165&wit_id=3336 (May 9, 2006).

3. Oberg, "International Space Exploration Program."

4. "China Plans 3-Men Space Launch After 2008 Olympics."

5. Guy Gugliotta, "China Keeps Reaching for the Stars; Second Manned Flight Keeps Country in Elite Group of Space-faring Nations," *Washington Post*, October 15, 2005, www.washingtonpost.com/wp-dyn/content/article/2005/10/14/AR2005101402213.html (May 11, 2006).

6. "China to Embark on Unmanned Mission to the Moon Soon," *People's Daily* (China), March 3, 2003, http://english.people.com.cn/200303/02/eng20030302_112549.shtml (May 11, 2006).

7. James Oberg, "International Space Exploration Program."

8. John Johnson Jr., "Shooting for the Moon, Once Again," *Los Angeles Times*, February 12, 2006, at http://www.latimes.com/news/science/la-sci-moon12feb12,0,3841305.story?page=1&coll=la-home-headlines (May 12, 2006).

9. "No Room for India on Shuttle Flights," *The Times of India*, May 10, 2006, http://timesofindia.indiatimes.com/articleshow/1523235.cms (May 12, 2006).

10. Ramnath Shenoy, "India Expresses Interest in Mars Mission," Press Trust of India, January 17, 2006.

11. Bruce K. Gagnon, "Japan Joins U.S. in Dangerous Space Race," ZNet Japan, July 7, 2005, www.zmag.org/content/print_article.cfm?itemID=8246&sectionID=17 (May 10, 2006).

12. A. J. S. Rayl, "Hayabusa: Japan's Asteroid Mission Prepares to Drop Lander and Rehearse for Two Soft Landings," November 2, 2005, http://www.planetary.org/news/2005/1102_Hayabusa_Japans_Asteroid_Mission.html (May 12, 2006).

13. Eric Talmadge, "Japanese Rocket Lifts Off with Satellite," Associated Press, January 24, 2006, http://www.cbsnews.com/stories/2006/01/24/ap/tech/mainD8FAOO0O0.shtml (May 12, 2006).

14. W. Wayt Gibbs, "Plan B for Energy," *Scientific American*, September 2006, p. 108.

15. Japan Aerospace Exploration Agency, "JAXA Vision 2025," March 31, 2005, http://www.jaxa.jp/about/vision_missions/long_term/jaxa_vision_e.pdf (May 12, 2006).

16. Si-young Hwang, "Korea Pushes for Self-Reliant Space Program," March 13, 2006, http://news.nate.com/Service/natenews/ShellView.asp?LinkID=4&ArticleID=20060313001142701 18 (May 10, 2006).

17. "Space Project Needs to be Cost-effective," *Korea Times*, August 23, 2005, http://search.hankooki.com/times/times_view.php?term=space+project+needs+to+be+cost-effective++&path=hankooki3/times/lpage/tech/200508/kt2005082218031512350.htm&media=kt (May 10, 2006).

18. Korea Aerospace Research Institute, "Space Center Development Program," http://www.kari.re.kr/english/pro/pro_02_05.asp?show=31 (May 11, 2006).

19. Tae-Gyu Kim, "Korea Bets on Satellites in Space Race," *Korea Times*, August 8, 2005, at http://www.times.hankooki.com/lpage/tech/200508/kt2005080820040311790.htm (May 10, 2006).

20. Tong-hyung Kim, "Korea Seeks to Bolster Aerospace Technology," *Korea Now*, April 16, 2005, http://koreanow.koreaherald.co.kr/SITE/data/html_dir/2005/04/16/200504160007.asp (May 12, 2006).

21. Si-young Hwang, "Korea Pushes for Self-reliant Space Program."

22. Bruce S. Middleton, "Thriving in the Asia Pacific Region," *Space News: Business Report*, January 14, 2003, 3.

23. Middleton, "Thriving," 3.

24. Middleton, "Thriving," 2.

25. Associated Press, "Malaysia Signs Astronaut Deal with Russia," May 19, 2006.

26. Gibbs, "Plan B for Energy," 104.

27. Shana Dale, "Remarks at NASA Lunar Exploration Workshop," April 25, 2006.

28. Dale, "Remarks," 3.

29. Dale, "Remarks," 4.

30. Dale, "Remarks."

31. With the notable exception of Ben Cohen and Jerry Greenfield, cofounders of Ben & Jerry's ice cream.

CONCLUSION: AMERICA'S FUTURE IN ASIA

1. Chris Nelson, "US-China-Russia on Iran, Japan History, Bush Trade," *The Nelson Report*, July 27, Samuelsinternational.com.

2. Fred Weir, "Russia's Population Decline Spells Trouble," *Christian Science Monitor*, April 18, 2002.

3. John Micklethwait and Adrian Woolridge, *The Right Nation: Conservative Power in America* (New York: Penguin, 2004), 294–95.

Index

About the Author

Dana R. Dillon is senior strategic analyst at BCP International. He served twenty years in the U.S. Army, the last six years at the Pentagon, where he specialized in intelligence and foreign policy. He is a frequent commentator on Fox News, CNN, and MSNBC. He lives in Fairfax, Virginia.